Doreen Kartinyeri

Doreen Kartinyeri
My Ngarrindjeri Calling

Doreen Kartinyeri and Sue Anderson

First published in 2008
by Aboriginal Studies Press

© Doreen Kartinyeri and Sue Anderson 2008

All rights reserved. No part of this book may be reproduced or transmitted in any form or by any means, electronic or mechanical, including photocopying, recording or by any information storage and retrieval system, without prior permission in writing from the publisher. The Australian *Copyright Act 1968* (the Act) allows a maximum of one chapter or 10 per cent of this book, whichever is the greater, to be photocopied by any educational institution for its education purposes provided that the educational institution (or body that administers it) has given a remuneration notice to Copyright Agency Limited (CAL) under the Act.

Aboriginal Studies Press
is the publishing arm of the
Australian Institute of Aboriginal
and Torres Strait Islander Studies
GPO Box 553, Canberra, ACT 2601
Phone: (61 2) 6246 1183
Fax: (61 2) 6261 4288
Email: asp@aiatsis.gov.au
Web: www.aiatsis.gov.au/aboriginal_studies_press

National Library of Australia
Cataloguing-In-Publication data:

> Kartinyeri, Doreen, 1935–2007
> Doreen Kartinyeri: My Ngarrindjeri Calling
>
> Includes index.
> Bibliography.
> 9780855756598 (pbk.)
>
> 1. Women, Aboriginal Australian — Biography. 2. Stolen generations (Australia). 3. Narrinyeri (Australian people) — Legal status, laws, etc.
> 4. Sacred sites (Aboriginal Australian) — South Australia — Hindmarsh Island. 5. Hindmarsh Island (S. Aust.)
>
> 920.00929915

Index compiled by Michael Harrington
Printed in Australia by Ligare Pty Ltd

Aboriginal and Torres Strait Islander people are respectfully advised that this publication contains names and images of deceased persons, and culturally sensitive material. AIATSIS apologises for any distress this may cause.

Cover image: *The People* by Sandra Saunders, oil on canvas, 2000. Courtesy, private collection.
A *mi:mini* is gathering rushes for weaving. Her coat is woven from the rushes. The *kornies* are netting fish in Lake Alexandrina.

Contents

Acknowledgments	vi
Illustrations	viii
Note on Language	x
Family tree	xii
Map	xiii
1 Raukkan	1
2 A Family Torn Apart	26
3 Suffer the Little Children	43
4 Unexpected Kindness	66
5 A Hollywood Life	87
6 From Madwoman to Historian	114
7 Putting Black History on White Paper	146
8 The Royal Witch-Hunt	174
9 Epilogue	200
Afterword	205
Notes	208
Index	212

Acknowledgments

There are many people who have helped with the compilation of this book. Sandra Saunders was by Doreen's side from the tabling of the envelopes, and then stood alongside both Doreen and me to help get her story right. Sandy also became a friend of mine, and I am grateful for her valuable commentary on early and later drafts of this book. Her input was invaluable and her friendship immeasurable.

Doreen's sister Doris recommended me to Doreen in the first instance, and remains a dear friend since I interviewed her for the Bringing Them Home Oral History Project in 2000. Doreen's family, particularly Lydia and Willie, put up with my many intrusions into their space, and Klynton read and commented on the draft manuscript and helped make some changes.

Dr Mary-Anne Gale provided advice on Ngarrindjeri language words, and Ribnga Green and Jared Thomas, in their roles with Tandanya National Cultural Institute and Arts SA respectively, gave their support and encouragement. Carolyn Blanks conducted some last-minute archival retrieval at short notice, and Kate Battersby transcribed about half the recordings with great promptness and efficiency. My friend and colleague Dr Suzi Hutchings commented on the draft manuscript and helped me reduce the word length as requested by our publishers. Joanna Richardson and Claire O'Connor kindly read the draft manuscript and provided vital legal advice. My PhD supervisor, Dr Christine Nicholls, also provided much moral support and some editorial advice. Doreen's friend and colleague Jackie Huggins introduced us to Aboriginal Studies Press, and Rhonda Black, its Director, was considerate in dealing with the appraisal of the manuscript. Many others lent their support, advice and research materials, including Dr Rod Lucas, Dr Deane Fergie, Steve Hemming, Professor Diane Bell, Neva Wilson, Dr Joy Wundersitz and Margaret Wallace.

We could not have conducted our work without some financial help, as Doreen lived at Point Pearce on the Yorke Peninsula and I live in Adelaide, some two and a half to three hours away by car. I am therefore extremely grateful for the grant funding we received from the Australian Institute of Aboriginal and Torres Strait Islander Studies, Arts SA and The Hon. Stephanie Key MP, then South Australian Minister for Social Justice and for the Status of Women.

Illustrations

Between pages 50–51

A Raukkan school photo, c. 1943.
Outside the Raukkan Post Office waiting for the Mail.
Doris Kartinyeri at Colebrook Home, c. 1948.
United Aborigines' Mission letter for Colebrook Home, 1946.
Salvation Army Fullarton Girls' Home, 1940.
Doreen on the balcony at the Fullarton Girls' Home, 2005
Letter from Doreen Kartinyeri to the Aboriginal Protection Board, c. 1950s.
Letter from the Secretary, Aborigines' Protection Board, c. 1950s.
Thelma Kartinyeri and her children.
Doreen's father, Oscar Kartinyeri.
Aunty Rosie and Uncle Nat Kropinyeri, c. 1940.
Doreen with Reg Graham, 1953.
Doreen and Sid Chamberlain, 1979.
Terry Wanganeen and Doreen Kartinyeri's children and grandchildren, 1985.
Launch of the Rigney genealogy, 1983.

Between pages 130–131

Doreen demonstrating how to commence weaving.

Small mat woven by Doreen in the Ngarrindjeri style.

Feather flowers made by Doreen for the launch of the Rigney genealogies.

Doreen and one of her early genealogies.

Doreen and her sister Doris Kartinyeri displaying historic photographs c. 1980.

Doreen and Sue Anderson at Doreen's house in Point Pearce, 2004.

Doreen after receiving her honorary doctorate, 1995.

Doreen burning letters.

Raising the Ngarrindjeri flag on Hindmarsh Island, 1995.

Ngarrindjeri demonstration against the Royal Commission, Adelaide 1995.

Sandra Saunders' painting representing the legal system.

Doreen being supported by her son Klynton after the von Doussa judgment, 2001.

Doreen Kartinyeri.

Note on Language

Ngarrindjeri words are often used alongside English ones, and these have been retained in the text. Where a word only occurs once or twice, an English translation has been added in square brackets. Some Ngarrindjeri words, however, are used throughout.

Family relationships are often referred to in Ngarrindjeri terms. *Mainu* is grandfather, *Mutha* is grandmother, and *Pike* is great-uncle. The word *Kabbarli*, which refers to an older female relative, came from a language of the west coast of South Australia, and is a specific kin term.

The English words Aunty and Uncle are used both to refer to relatives and as respectful titles for older community members. Grannies are grandchildren, not grandparents.

Mi:mini is the word for woman. *Puthari* is the Ngarrindjeri word for a traditional midwife.

Kunamara is the generic term for a deceased person, sometimes followed by their surname; it is traditionally forbidden to mention the name or show the picture of a deceased person.

Nunga is the generic word for Aboriginal people from southern South Australia, while *Anangu* refers to Aboriginal people from northern South Australia. *Boandik* is an Aboriginal group from the south-east of South Australia.

Gunya is the word for white people. *Krinkri*, which means ghost, also refers to the Ngarrindjeri people's first sighting of white men, who looked to them like ghosts because of the colour of their skin.

Aboriginal place names are frequently used. Kurangk is the Coorong. Kumarangk is Hindmarsh Island. Raukkan is Point McLeay Aboriginal Mission, established in 1959 alongside Lake Alexandrina.

Point Pearce is an Aboriginal mission on Yorke Peninsula, established 1867. Three Miles is a name given to an Aboriginal fringe camp three miles out of town. Both Tailem Bend and Murray Bridge had Three Miles camps.

A *wurley* is a windbreak or tent-like structure for living in. The word comes from *wodli*, in the Kaurna language of the people of the Adelaide plains, and is now widely used across Australia. *Waddy* is now an English term for a fighting/hunting club. The Ngarrindjeri word is *plonggi*.

Family tree

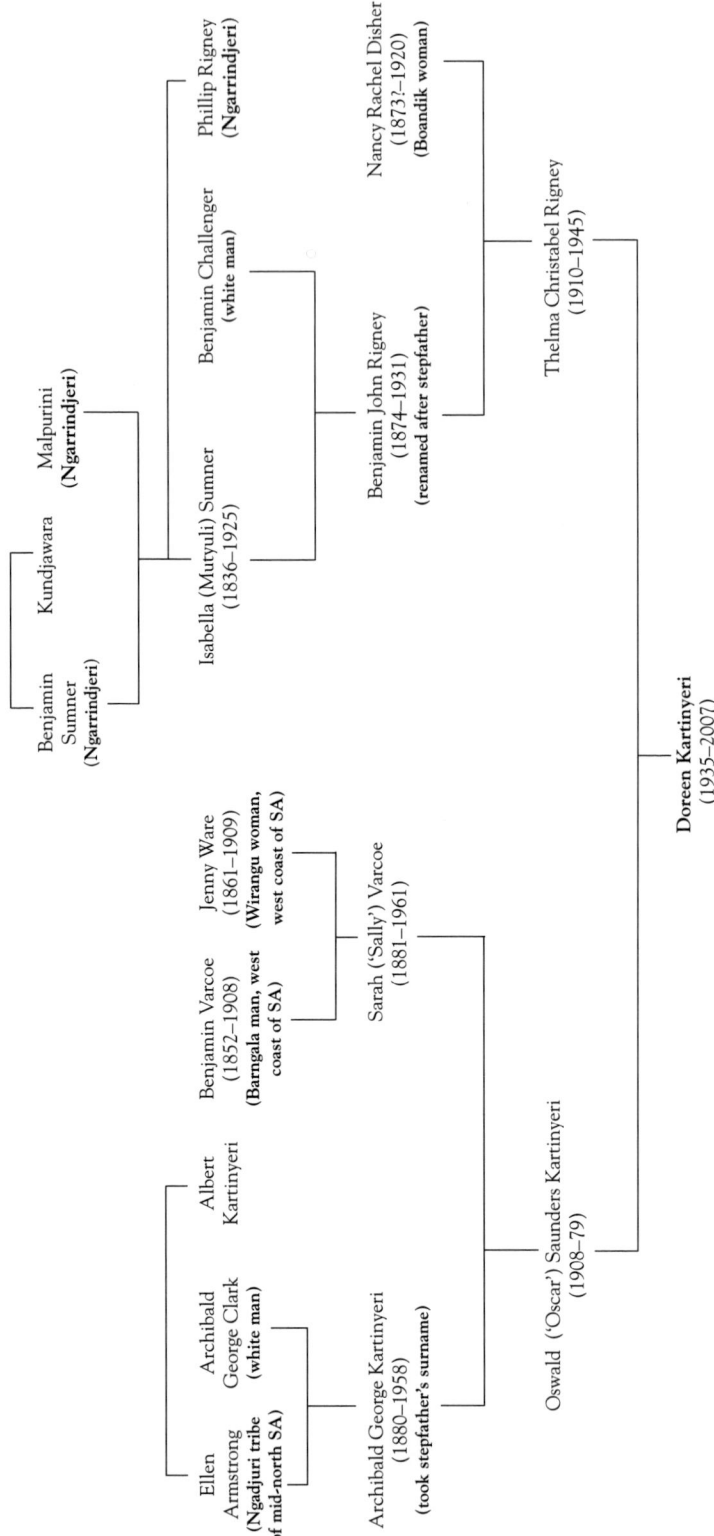

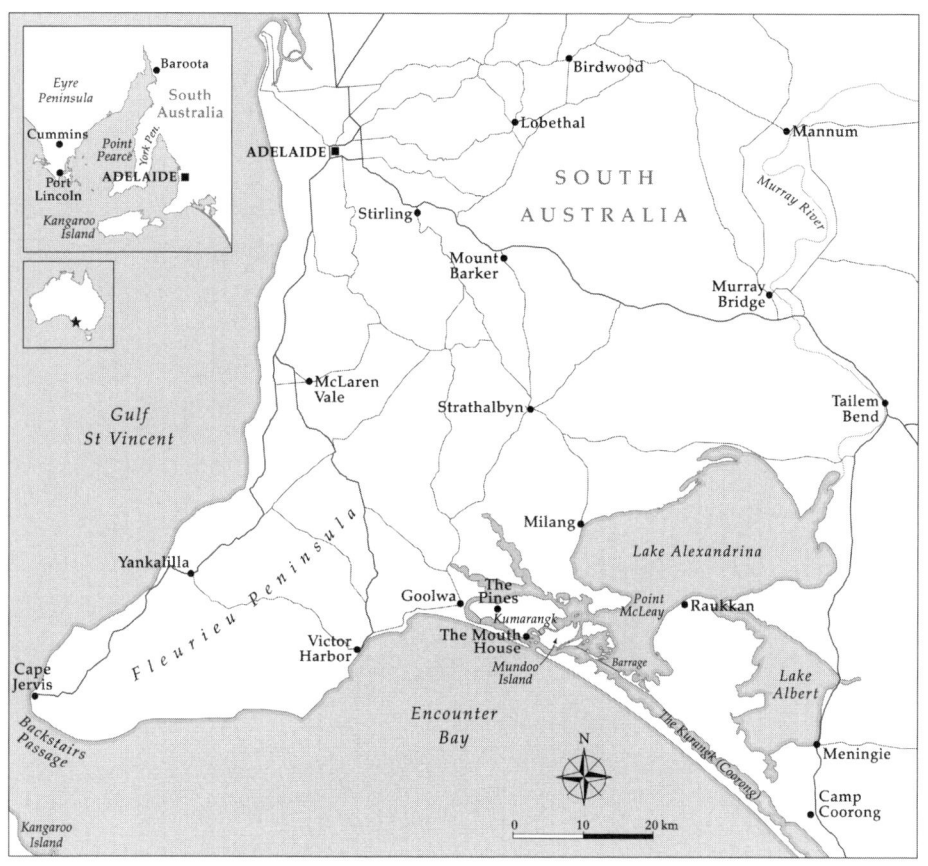

Ngarrindjeri, Narungga and Kaurna country

1

Raukkan

Monday, 6 March 1995: the envelopes

It was late afternoon and I was exhausted from all the work. I had my full-time job in the South Australian Museum and now the extra work of trying to protect the heritage of my Ngarrindjeri people. I had been running all around town, talking to lawyers, anthropologists and others who were keeping me informed of what was happening, and I was busting my brain trying to take it all in and thinking of what to do next. I didn't know anything about the legal system or how it worked, so I had been talking to lawyer Tim Woolley at the Aboriginal Legal Rights Movement in King William Street to try and understand what was happening, and now I was keen to get home. I headed downstairs to reception and was just making my way out the front door when Sandra Saunders, the Director of Aboriginal Legal Rights, called out to me. 'Doreen,' she yelled, 'wait a minute!'

Sandra was on the phone to Sue Kee from Robert Tickner's office [Federal Minister for Aboriginal Affairs]. She said she had some terrible news for me. She took me upstairs to her office and told me that the shadow minister for the environment, Ian McLachlan, had one of his staff members open the secret envelopes and he had tabled them in Federal Parliament.

I felt like someone had punched me hard in the stomach, had kicked me with full force in the guts. I went numb. I screamed, 'Oh no,' and fell to the floor. I clutched my stomach tight as I rocked back and forth on the floor of Sandra's office. I closed my eyes and started to cry and then I could visualise all the pakanus [grandparents] and ngatjus [aunts] and muthar [grandmothers], all the old ladies looking down at me. They were looking at me wild way, anger in their faces. Where was Aunty Rosie? I needed to see her now. As I looked at the faces of my ancestors one by one I apologised to each of them. 'Sorry, sorry, sorry. You told me never to tell a man and now I have. I know now I've done the wrong thing'. I sang out for their forgiveness, all the time wailing and crying. Although it wasn't my fault that McLachlan had done such a terrible thing, if I had not written the information down in the first place, he couldn't have done it. One thing the old people used to say, 'Never put black history on white paper'. And this is what I'd done. Goodness knows, if anyone was well aware of how treacherous some whitefellas could be, it was me, but somehow I still believed the system would protect us. Aunty Rosie's words came into my mind: 'Never tell whitefellas what you know about your culture; they'll pick your brains and bleed you dry'. I had lived by that as a young woman, but this time I was in an impossible situation. If I didn't tell the whitefellas at least some of what I knew, they wouldn't protect Kumarangk [Hindmarsh Island]. Now that I had, McLachlan had threatened to tell the world and betray my people. I knew I would pay for this error of judgment. Finally Aunty Rosie's face came into view and I felt a little better. She didn't look at me as wild as the others. She was there with me. How could this have happened?

Then I started to get fuckin' angry.

Beginnings

I am Doreen Maude Kartinyeri, second child of Thelma and Oswald (but always called Oscar) Kartinyeri. Nicknames are a big thing with my people, and mine is Dodo, and I got that because my older brother Oscar stuttered. I am a Ngarrindjeri *mi:mini* [woman], but like many Aboriginal people today I have different ancestral roots.

1 ~ Raukkan

I am Ngarrindjeri, but I am also descended from the Wirangu, Nauo, Barkandji, Boandik and Ngadjuri Aboriginal peoples of South Australia. My children have strong connections with Narrunga through their father and they were brought up in the Narrunga community at Point Pearce on the Yorke Peninsula. On both my parents' sides I have an English great-grandfather. I know all my family genealogy. I learnt a lot about kinship from my parents and grandparents when I was just young and it's been important all my life. As a young married woman I learnt more from my Aunty Rosie [Kropinyeri] and other old people about many different families. According to my *Mainu* [grandfather], the name Kartinyeri means 'We came, we stayed and we belong'. My culture is my life.

The greatest thing that ever happened in my life was giving birth to my nine children — seven sons and two daughters. That was a magnificent achievement. Not just because I'm so proud of them all, but also because family is so important. I learned that from my Mum and Dad growing up on Raukkan [Point McLeay Aboriginal Mission] with my brothers and sisters, grandmother and grandfather, all my aunties and uncles and lots of cousins. We were a big loving family and the children respected the old people.

The most traumatic thing? Well there were two. Losing my Mum when I was ten, just a little girl, and then losing my first child at seven months. It's a terrible thing to have a baby die in your arms.

Apart from my own children, over the years I've raised twenty-three foster children; so here I am, a mother of nine, with twenty-seven grandchildren and nine great-grannies [grandchildren].

Looking back on my years at Raukkan I feel two very strong emotions — happiness and sadness. When I was a young teenager I had to get special permission from the Protector of Aborigines to go back there, and I went along to the office in Kintore Avenue in Adelaide and got permission, because this is what the rules and regulations were for Aboriginal people then. I took a chance they would say no, I can't go back. I was on edge waiting for that permission to come through. But when they said yes, it was great, because I was going home to see my loved ones.

Now that I don't need a permit to go back onto Raukkan, usually I'm only going back for funerals, to bury a family member. I am now the oldest living person in the Kartinyeri family from my grandparents Archie and Sally Kartinyeri.

The trip in to Raukkan has always been a very rough ride. The road has never ever been surfaced. On the left you pass Poltalloch, a great big mansion with only a few white people living there. Not like Raukkan where lots of big families lived in little two roomed houses. Uncle Ted and Aunty Sarah Karpany used to live in a little shack there on the shore front, Granny Tokey Butcher used to work in the big house, and a couple of other young girls a bit older than myself used to go out there and do domestic work. They had some beautiful horses there, lovely stables. The owners of that house were pretty well off.

Then you come past Glenora — the dairy that belongs to the mission — and over a cattle pit into Raukkan. When you come up the hill into Raukkan you'll see some of the cottages, and then as you go through the first little lane of cottages on your left-hand side you can look up the road and you'll see the church. I've got photographs of Raukkan taken in 1861, in the 1880s, and right up to the present time, and you can see the different stages of development.

My Mum, Thelma (née Rigney), lived all her life on Raukkan. My Dad was born and brought up there too. I was born there in a little tin place in 1935. Although there was a little hospital on the mission then, not always was the white sister there and she hardly ever delivered babies, so the Aboriginal *putharis* [midwives] would have to go to the homes to deliver the babies in the tribal way. Some of the *putharis* I remember were Aunty Martha Rankine (my father's sister), my Aunty Laura Kartinyeri (my father's aunt), and old Beattie Gollan, who was excellent. Before that there was Ivy Karpany, who would sit with the women from the time they sent for her. Ivy and her husband Bill Karpany eventually moved to Point Pearce [Aboriginal Mission on Yorke Peninsula], and she passed all her knowledge on to the women at Point Pearce. Midwifery is a very important part of Ngarrindjeri culture and so is weaving, which brings people together.

1 ~ Raukkan

The house where our family lived was just two rooms made of flattened kerosene tins, and the only stone part was a little chimney, but I was lucky I could live with my parents, because when my Mum and Dad were young, the kids had to live in dormitories. My earliest memories of the mission was when I was about six, I suppose, when we lived down near the lake. There were about eight little brick houses along the lake and one right on the end near Mungarawa. They were built by the Aboriginal men when the mission was set up. We were only living in a two-room cottage, my Mum and my Dad, my elder brother Oscar and my two younger sisters, Nancy and Doris Alma (called Alma by my parents). Alma was just a baby when she died of diphtheria and I hardly remember her. Then my mother had Ron and we moved up to the mission into my Aunty Martha's house in about 1942. I loved Aunty Martha and got on very well with her, even though she wasn't very popular with a lot of our other relations. She was a bit stern, but she had a big family and quite a lot of responsibility. Her husband, Uncle Reggie, was a returned soldier from the First World War and he needed to get treatment at the Repatriation Hospital, so we moved into their house when they moved to Adelaide. My father's parents, Archie and Sally Kartinyeri, moved in with us, and that's where my sister Connie was born, so then there was my Mum and Dad, Oscar, me, Nancy, Ron and Connie. One more sister, Doris Eileen, was to be born later.

I never knew my mother's parents, Rachel (née Disher) and Ben Rigney, because they died before I was born, but I learnt from Aunty Rosie that her mother was *Boandik*. Grandmother Rachel and her brother Richard Disher were from Mypolonga. There was a massacre up the river and they were put in a bark canoe and they floated down the river to Renmark, from where they were sent in to Raukkan. Aunty Rosie said that her mother used to talk about that massacre.

Mum had a lot of photos of the family stuck on the wall. There was a lovely one of her grandmother, Mutyuli, and old James Rankine, who used to work together at Poltalloch in the late 1800s. James was the chauffeur in a horse and buggy, and Mutyuli (or Isabella as she was also known) used to do the cooking.

Point McLeay (Raukkan) Mission

The mission had a hospital, school, church and there was a big square of lawn. There was the superintendent's house, the headmaster's house, the store, the dispensary and there were tennis courts. Up the top of the hill is a row of houses we call the Top Row.

There was no electricity on Raukkan in those days. We had candles, kerosene lamps or lanterns. Some people had big long silver torches, which took about six to eight batteries that had to come from Tailem Bend, but mostly people used candles. We'd use an empty camp pie tin with the top rolled back to act as candle holders. We had a little pelmet on the wall and we'd hook it up on that. It was beautiful. Each of us kids had our own piece of candle to see our way to bed. There were four or five of us to a double bed and the last one to bed would have to blow out the last candle.

In the adjoining house lived Bertha Wilson and her parents and brothers and sisters. My bedroom wall was the wall of their kitchen. Bertha was fifteen years older than me, and not long afterwards she had her first child. I could hear Bertha talking in the kitchen next door and I was fascinated to listen to what she was talking about. Connie shared my room and when we were going to sleep I would tell Connie to shush so I could listen to Bertha. Bertha was a big gossip and would talk about all the people on Raukkan, and who was going with who. Some of this stuff was a shock to a young girl like me, so sometimes I put my hands over my ears. But my interest in kinship made it intriguing. For the same reason I also used to listen to people yarning while they sat on the lawn waiting for the mail.

But her gossiping turned me off Bertha. And I could never work out how she knew all the details of everything that went on, because she wasn't one to be going from house to house. I wondered how she felt she had the right to talk about others like that.

There'd be one tap between about three houses and you'd have to cart buckets of water on a yoke over your shoulders. All the houses had wood ovens and meat was kept in a meat safe. This was a metal box with sieve wire right around it. They used to hang it in the doorway to let the breeze blow through it and this would keep the meat cool.

There was no sewerage or septic tanks, so the toilets were buckets emptied by the men into a big pit.

Camping at the Kurangk

When trees were cut down, the people would plead with the superintendent not to burn the limbs so they could use them to build their *wurlies* [windbreaks, tent-like structures]. We used to pick the sheoak apples and bring them home in sugarbags and boil them in a saucepan with sugar and they were beautiful. The people didn't want to cut the trees down because so much had been cleared and so much had been destroyed, but they had to do that work or they wouldn't get paid or they'd get their rations cut. What the men used to do was smooth down the branches with pieces of broken bottles — because they never used to have tools in their homes that a lot of people have today — and then before they'd really dry out they'd lay them in the waters of the little creeks running off the Kurangk [Coorong] and the Lake. This is to keep them pliable, so that when you bend them they don't snap. They would bend them over in a dome shape. In the old days they'd use the sinews of the kangaroo and wallaby legs to tie them together and cover them with brush or seaweed. We used string and flour bags cut open and pegged together with little thin sharpened sticks, woven in and out. Then they'd throw the bags over the sticks, leaving a flap for a door.

Sometimes we'd just have a windbreak. They were different. People would collect up branches with lots of leaves on them. They'd have one big piece of wire and they'd hook the branches onto the wire. These sorts of branches would also be used as a broom for sweeping the ground.

I didn't know what the men used to go out the Kurangk for, camping, and we never asked questions. We were told only when we were supposed to be told. At Raukkan we would be able to go and play and run around anywhere, but down there we couldn't. There were certain places we were allowed to go, and certain places we weren't allowed to go and we were told that we were not to touch anything we found, but to go and tell the old people. We went in a horse and cart and we never took wood with us, or water. Even though we were on the edge of the sea my grandfather knew exactly where to find fresh water, and he'd dig wells and he'd tell us about other things the old people used to do down the Coorong.

My grandfather used to tell us about a lot of things, but my grandmother would want to stop him. *Mainu* used to cut all the kids' hair at Raukkan, and he made each child pick up their own hair and get rid of it themselves. When I asked him why he did this, he told me that no woman is allowed to touch the hair of a man's body, chest, head, anywhere, and we could be *milin* [killed by sorcery] if we did. In the old days the men used to think their hair was the main part of their manhood. They used to rub their loose hair like wool, stick it together with clay and make hair hats out of it. There's a film in the South Australian Museum of Clarence Long (Milerum) making hair hats.

My grandmother used to say to *Mainu*, 'Don't go filling those kids' heads with those silly stories, Archie'. I was only small and I didn't think much about why she wanted to stop him, but later I started to understand that people were bitter about how white people used our information, often against us. I can remember her plain as anything telling us. 'When the white people want to ask you questions, don't go telling them anything.'

Down at the Coorong we slept on beds of dried seaweed covered with old grey government blankets with a nice fire going. A couple of the men played mouth organs and guitar and we'd sit around the fire and sing Christmas carols. It was wonderful. We'd have Christmas dinner there. Cape Barren geese and swans would be boiled in a kerosene tin to tenderise them and then they'd be wrapped up in seaweed and put in the ashes to cook. Lovely, beautiful.

For school holidays during the year we'd go up to Tailem Bend to stop with Aunty Connie [née Varcoe, her mother's maiden name] and Uncle Roly [Kartinyeri] who lived at the Three Miles [camp, three miles out of Tailem Bend]. My sister Connie was named after her, my Mum's elder sister, and she worked in the hotel and the Tailem Bend Hospital. She used to get a ride into town each day and we kids would run amok. Aunty Laura was there a lot and Knocky and Gertie lived in the shack next door. Uncle Roly used to pull up the dead willow roots from the banks of the river with a horse and rope and he'd leave them on the cliff to dry out for firewood.

The store

What they had in the store was what the government felt was necessary for the people on the mission, like sugar, tea and flour. When they opened the store at nine o'clock in the morning, there would already be a line-up outside the store. If they ran out of things, the ones at the end of the line would miss out and that would cause a lot of conflict.

The store also sold clothes and they weren't what you'd call expensive, but I think they were things that the government got as contributions for Aboriginal people. The churches and the Aborigines' Friends Association also used to come in and have sales of hand-me-down clothing from white families, but mostly clothes were made from second-hand items by the women on the mission.

An abundance of wild food

Whatever was provided by the government wasn't enough, so thank goodness we always knew how to fish and hunt. We lived on fish, ducks, kangaroo and rabbits.

If a swan was left for a couple of hours after it was shot it would be very difficult to pluck, so they would put the swan in the boiling hot water, give it a few minutes to cool and the feathers would just come out easily. Then you'd have a beautiful plucked bird. We used to pull out the *waltjeris* and *bamberis* [the innards] and squeeze them clean. We used to love the giblets, and we got quite nice sized ones from swans, little ones from ducks and chooks too. We would wrap them up in rushes and put them in the coals, and while they were cooking they smelled lovely.

We were allowed to shoot swans and ducks in those days. They were all plentiful. The men would go out swan-egging in the season. You can feed about four kids on one swan egg. Nice big ones, very much like the size of emu eggs. It was part of our tradition, hunting on land and in water. At Raukkan anybody who wanted to go and throw a line out would be allowed to do it any time. As soon as white people came out and there were boats on Lake Alexandrina, that's when the restrictions started to come in. The 1917 *Fisheries Act* allowed 'full-blood' Aboriginal people to catch what they needed for consumption as long as they didn't use explosives or noxious matter. That was one way the old people used to catch fish. They would mix up special bush weeds and throw it into the water and the fish would get stunned and drift in to the shore and people would knock them out with a *waddy* [club].

Over at Raukkan the *thukeris* [boney bream], would get washed up on the shore at certain times of the year and you'd only have to go and pick them up. *Thukeri* is good. My grandmother Sally would put them on the coals and cook them in the ashes. She'd open them straight up the middle and when she'd finished eating all you could see left was the skeleton of bones.

Apart from rabbit and water-rat skins, Aboriginal people didn't have a market for wild game then, whereas today people can make a living out of it. My brother Oscar used to go out with *waddies* for rabbits. After he cleaned the skins, he'd get a piece of wire about a couple of metres long (or a bit smaller for rat skins) and he'd bend it in a 'U' shape. Then he'd turn the rabbit skin inside out and pull it over the wire like a jumper, stick the wire in the ground and let the skin dry out. We all used to help to do that. There'd be lots of skins standing up in the sand drying off. He used to make traps to catch water rats and he'd sell them and the rabbit skins to a buyer who came into the mission. I could cope with the rabbits because we could get a big feed after, but I hated the water rats. They smelt strong.

Unfortunately the only place the men could get their wire for this was from the fences. The police came to Aunty Laura's at Three Miles [camp outside Murray Bridge] sometimes, looking for stolen fence wire, but they used to put the rabbits where the police couldn't find them so they didn't get caught.

The old ladies loved fishing. That was their only enjoyment except for church. They put a packed lunch of damper and a bottle of water stopped up with a cork into a blanket and they'd throw that over their back and tie it with a big knot at the front. Us girls would carry their bags and sit with them for an hour or so, and then we used to go looking for them when the sun was going down to carry their things back for them. A lot of the shovels would go missing from the shed. When the superintendent went around looking for them he found shovels all right, but they were all little short-handled ones because they cut the handles off to make it easier to sit down on the sand and dig for worms for bait. Sometimes they'd fish with two lines, one attached to each foot. Today they've got restrictions on how big your catch can be, but Aboriginal people did that anyway because they knew there'd be none there the next year when you came back.

Until whitefellas started to clear the land, *mantharis* or wild tomatoes were all over the place and *katharis* — a little bush with tiny red berries — as well as *wa:tjis,* which are weeds that grow in the rushes. I'd dig in the ground with a digging stick for *thalgis* or sweet roots; they're very crispy like celery. I'd wash the mud off and eat them with salt and pepper. There's quite a lot of salt pans down at Kumarangk, and when the salt was dry we'd scoop it out and rub it into whatever we'd want to preserve and it would keep for months without going off.

Cultivated food and mission life

During the 1940s they decided to turn some of the property into a big vegetable garden that the men looked after. Occasionally we pinched figs and mulberries from the garden at night. In church we would have sermons about God's fruits and I wondered if they were the same kinds of fruits I'd been pinching, but that is all I could say I ever stole in my life.

Oh, except for honeycombs. Uncle Seth Dodd used to keep bees and I loved that honey, so I used to help myself from time to time. Until I got stung! My chin swelled up and my throat was so puffed up it was hanging down. I never pinched honey again after that.

Once a day the Mail came into Raukkan. We called the truck that because it used to bring the mail, but it was also the main means of transport for people coming in and out of the mission.

A doctor came out from Tailem Bend every Wednesday morning, and he'd stay there until about three o'clock that afternoon to see anyone that needed him. Now if you got sick on Wednesday night after the doctor had gone, you'd have to see the superintendent, and if he thought you were all right you'd have to wait a week to see the doctor. When my Nanna got pleurisy Dad got the superintendent and he came down to see Nanna and said we should take her to hospital. If the superintendent hadn't approved her to go to hospital, who knows how she would have been by the following Wednesday? Those were the government policies and they kept to all those bloody rules.

It was worse with the dentist. If you got a toothache the night after he'd been you'd have to wait another month to get it fixed.

The little dispensary only had the bare necessary things like bandages, milk emulsion, cod liver oil, epsom salts, and malt for delicate kids. For any major cuts or haemorrhaging the old people knew how to stop the bleeding tribal way. Once I was pinching apricots out of the fruit tree and I couldn't reach them. Oscar told me to put my foot on a little limb and of course it broke and down I came, gashing my leg on the way. My mother washed my wound with kerosene and told Oscar to go and get cobwebs and she packed it up with that.

When I was young the superintendent was Mr Clarrie Bartlett. He was the storekeeper when he first came to Raukkan, then he became superintendent and eventually he became Secretary of the Aborigines' Protection Board [in 1953].[1] I remember my father telling me Mr and Mrs Bartlett came to Raukkan as a young married couple, then they had three children — Joan, Lyle and Rhonda. They were older than I was, and Lyle was a bit older than my brother. Well those three children made a lot of friends on Raukkan and their parents did not stop them from being friends with the Aboriginal kids. Mrs Bartlett's brother was Mr Bill Goodhand, who took over the position of storekeeper from Mr Bartlett when he became superintendent. Eventually Mr Goodhand became superintendent.

The Protector of Aborigines, Mr Penhall, would visit Raukkan for special occasions and sometimes to discuss issues with the older Aboriginal people on the mission. I was born fearing the word 'Protector'. In fact we feared any whitefella who came to the mission.

I grew up hating the words, '*Krinkri* [ghost] coming, *gunya* [white person] coming'. We all used to run and hide for fear of being taken away.

School

Mr W.T. Lawrie — Wilfred Theodore his name was, but we used to call him 'W.T.' — was the schoolteacher on Raukkan for thirty-seven years [1913–51]. Mrs Lawrie took cooking, cleaning and sewing lessons once or twice a week, and there were other teachers come and go during that time. W.T. was accepted by the Aboriginal people on the mission because they had no choice, but there was something about Mrs Lawrie I don't know how to explain. She was good to the people there. I think I remember this so strongly because we weren't used to getting much good treatment from other whitefellas.

It was only Aboriginal children who went to the school. Obviously our school wasn't good enough for the white staff's kids, because they used to catch the Mail in the mornings to attend school in Narrung and it was only about one and a half miles away. Sometimes Uncle Hendle Rankine took them in the horse and cart and he brought them home in the afternoon. I didn't know anything about discrimination in them days, and we never thought anything of it because that's just how life was for us then, but I see now that was racism in action.

Nearly everybody spoke Ngarrindjeri language, playing in the schoolyard or in our own homes, even though you weren't allowed to speak it in school or in church. I couldn't understand why they were stopping us because some of the older men couldn't always understand English. Even though Nanna came from Poonindie and spoke her own language, she learned the Raukkan language really well. She had two brothers who never married — *Pike* [great-uncle] Jerry and *Pike* Dennis — and they used to speak Ngarrindjeri well too. I remember a lot of the Raukkan language and I still talk it sometimes.

W.T.

They say W.T. must have been a good teacher to stay there all that time. He taught three generations: my Aunty Martha (my Dad's sister), her two eldest daughters, Sarah and Ellen (Topsy), and then he taught two of Sarah's sons. But he was strict. I didn't like him very much. If we were having singing classes and you didn't open your mouth wide enough, he'd stick a ruler in there and sometimes he'd cut your lip. I never could fathom the whitefellas' way of educating kids. It wasn't about learning like our old people taught us; it was about learning by repeating everything over and over parrot fashion and about how to sit up straight.

He was such a big, tall man and he'd talk very, very slow. He'd walk around with a book or paper in his hand and he'd ask you questions. One day he asked me something and I didn't know the answer, so I didn't say anything. This was unusual for me, because outside of school I was always a good talker. My grandfather always used to say to me, 'There she goes, she's been eating *muldari* (magpie) eggs again!' That meant I was a chatterbox.

W.T. said, 'Don't you have anything up here?' (tapping me on the head) and I said, 'Yeah, I've got hair'. He said, 'What did you say?' and I said, '*Thu:wi*,' because that's our word for hair. This was a very devil-may-care thing to say. W.T. got so angry I had to stand in the corner. We were all trying not to laugh. I have to say I never learned a thing that day.

At Raukkan we had to do our schooling in stages — one year each of Lower Grade 1, Upper Grade 1, Lower Grade 2, Upper Grade 2 and so on. For those that were smart he made sure they got little awards, like picture [movie] tickets for free. A bloke from Narrung used to come in and run the pictures in the hall. There'd be Tarzan and cowboys and Indians, Roy Rogers, Gene Autrey, Gary Cooper and Veronica Lake and all them. Saturday nights we'd have dances and sometimes we'd have singsongs and concerts.

The Lawries had two children, Enid and Mac. Mac was short for McLeay and he was named after the Point McLeay mission. We were allowed to go down to play in their backyard in Enid's playhouse, and some of the older women went down for Enid's and Mac's little parties. But not many of the white staff on Raukkan would go into the Aboriginal homes. I remember old W.T. used to go to find out what's wrong with the kids if we were away from school, but I never remember Mrs Lawrie or Enid or Mac going to any of the homes to play.

W.T. finished up on Raukkan in 1951. That last day we had a big farewell for him and his family and I remember it really, really well. I was only a young teenage girl. We had a beautiful turnout and there was a lot of tears being shed by the old ladies and old men. I remember the speech that he gave. Uncle Roland and Aunty Fidy Carter gave speeches and they presented W.T. with all these lovely gifts that we all threw in a few shillings for. They presented him with those gifts and Mrs Lawrie cried and cried. It was very emotional.

We waved Mrs Lawrie and Mac and Enid off in the car, and then we all walked up to the Monument and saw Mr Lawrie and two of the Ngarrindjeri boys, Vernon and Proughton Carter, getting on the boat and taking off to go across to Goolwa. And then that night we heard that old W.T. had died. He got sick on the boat, but it was actually in Goolwa, just after the boat was tied up, where his heart gave out. I remember Mrs Lawrie saying how wonderful those boys were to him and how they helped him.

The community was all in shock. Dad asked me to stay with Nanna that day because she was pretty upset. No matter what anyone thought about old W.T., deaths and funerals are an important part of Ngarrindjeri culture and by then my Nanna had had more than her fair share of these.

They buried W.T. out at Payneham in Adelaide. They say it was the biggest funeral.

Church

Religion played a big part in our lives. Christianity had been put into the Aboriginal people's lives in the early days of Raukkan, and quite a lot of the older generations were very devout Christians. My grandmother was born into a religious environment at Poonindie mission on the Eyre Peninsula, and she had religion all day just about. I can remember sitting down and listening to my grandmother read the bible. Nanna was religious and Cissy Gollan, *Mutha* [grandmother] Bessie, Tokey Butcher, and the ones a bit younger than them like

Aunty Dugidi, Aunty Kumi, Aunty Lorna and my Mum, as well as the next generation like Aunty Fidy. They were all hard working, clean living — didn't drink, didn't swear. They didn't necessarily give up their Aboriginal cultural traditions, but church was a big part in their lives and we had really good services.

Mainu David Unaipon, whose picture is on the $50 note because he was a great inventor, was the first Ngarrindjeri preacher.

In church the blackfellas would sing like you'd never heard singing before, and some of the women played the organ and the piano. The boys were more into guitars. We loved singing hymns, which we learnt from listening to the old people who sang in beautiful harmony. We were never naughty in Sunday School. We were like little black angels. In 1925 a window was erected in the church in memory of all the Raukkan soldiers that got killed in the First World War, and that was a thing that was sacred to us. I grew up with strong Christian values. We always had to tell the truth, and somehow the older people always knew when we were lying, and if we lied we would be punished.

Traditional life

Raukkan fellas, whatever they got they shared with everybody. If we saw certain things we were not allowed to touch them and we never asked questions because if the old people told us something we'd definitely have to listen.

The women all used to make feather flowers. I remember Aunty Fofon, Henry Rankine's mother, was an expert at making feather flowers. She had a lot of patience because she could work with the most delicate feathers and make them look like any flower you could see. I remember a beautiful fan she made with big long feathers from under the wing of the pelican, which she dyed different colours. Her crafts were in demand by tourists passing through Tailem Bend. My Aunty Martha used to send her feather flowers up there too and some of her woven baskets.

They were also sold to tourists who used to come on the old steamer from Goolwa. The Protector let white people come in and see the way Aboriginal people lived. Buses would go from Adelaide to Goolwa for the ferry tours regularly through the summer, and forty or fifty people would come in to Raukkan on the boat. The visitors took a lot of photographs, and sometimes they would send a copy back to Raukkan school. The steamer had been coming into Raukkan from back in the late 1800s, and I've got photographs showing all the little girls wearing white aprons over their school clothes. I remember my Aunty Rosie saying she got sick of having to dress up in a little white pinnie every time the steamer came in. I don't know whether those people thought that's what people on the mission wore all the time.

I remember diving off the top of the steamer for pennies that were thrown into the water. The boys were better divers than us girls who never came up with much. But it was something the Raukkan fellas used to look forward to, because the white people would bring boiled lollies over for the children. The Aboriginal women would sell feather flowers and their weaving to help bring in a little extra money, which was badly needed. Sometimes the tourists would come up to the school and we'd sing for them and they would look at our work. Some of the kids were really outstanding students.

I remember one white girl saying, 'I didn't realise they were so black'. Aunty Fofon Rankine turned round to that child and said, 'Are you colour blind?' The mother answered her and said, 'No, she's not'. Aunty Fofon said, 'She must be, because there's a difference between the colour of my shoes and my skin'.

Making feather flowers and weaving mats and baskets was a really good industry and it was something the women liked to do. Even though we weren't actually doing the weaving ourselves, we'd be listening to all the old women yarning. I'd be there taking it all in.

I never learned weaving or making feather flowers from my mother, because she died when I was young, but I do remember sitting down pulling feathers out of a pelican skin and helping Mummy dye them different colours. On a nice day we'd put them out on a piece of old paper or hessian. I used to love doing that. In the evening after we'd bring them in I'd sit down by his rocking chair and listen to my grandfather's yarns. In later years I learnt how to weave and make feather flowers from my Aunty Rosie.

We used to go down to the lake to pick rushes for Mum's weaving and Mum used to tell me, 'Just pick the rushes up one at a time'. You mustn't pull the roots out because you'll stop their growth. You leave them to get to a certain height and that's when you pick them. If you're going to one place one year you've got to avoid that place the next year, because they may not be big enough to pick, the right length.

My Aunty Rosie told me that when she and her father, my grandfather Ben, used to go looking for *mantharis* over on Kumarangk, he wouldn't let her stray from the dirt paths, so her crutch wouldn't pierce the ground. Aunty Rosie passed the stories on to me about the significance of Kumarangk, and I didn't realise what a big part they would play in my life later on.

They never had many roads on Kumarangk, just mostly little horse and cart tracks. Not very many big vehicles went there when I was young. It would be only in the last thirty or forty years that the place started to develop, and in the last ten years it's changed a lot.

The women

Sewing classes were given on Raukkan from the earliest times. I remember a Mrs Thornber and Mrs Reid, wife of the Minister there. The Red Cross used to send big boxes of old rags and clothes from Murray Bridge. Mum made up some pillowslips out of some old rags she got from the Red Cross, and that was the first pillowslip I ever had. She used to unpick all the clothes, wash them out, cut them out and make up little articles of clothing for all the children with a little hand machine, and then later she got a treadle. She used to sit up late in the night running up little dresses. I think she worked a little bit too hard, because I can remember my Dad saying, 'Oh you want to blow that candle out now, Thelma'. She was sitting there sewing by candlelight, two candles. She wasn't allowed to have three because three lights in one room was bad luck.

Mum became a member of the Red Cross and she used to cook up pasties and other food and send it to all the other kids around the mission who didn't have much. Mum was also raising my cousins Lila, Elsie and Thelma (named after her), after their mother, Aunty Eva

Rigney (née Sumner), died. Just before winter set in, the Mail used to bring in big heaps of heavy grey government blankets. Mum cut them in half and sewed them together as a quilt cover. Then she'd fill them with left-over material scraps.

Knitting was another thing the women were encouraged to do. A lot of them learnt to knit and crochet at the Church Home League, where white women would come in from the district and have little afternoons with the women.

There was a milking team and they sold the milk and cream that they'd separated in big machines. All Aboriginal people received free milk. My mother was working after school in the dairy as a milkmaid at the age of thirteen. I know that, because my grandfather wrote a letter after his son was killed in the First World War, and he said so in his letter. The old ladies used to do the milking in the mornings and the young girls in the afternoons.

The men

The men on Raukkan didn't always have well-paid jobs, and they were mostly doing ordinary labouring jobs. My Dad was a labourer on the mission when I was little. I remember sitting on the big old horse-drawn plough when he was ploughing sometimes. The men would look after the cows and sheep. Back in the 1800s wool was a big industry at Raukkan. They used to have wool brought in by boat from around the district and they'd wash it down on the shore of Lake Alexandrina. There was a carpentry shed out the back of the church and the men learnt that trade really well.

To get better-paid jobs, the men had to go off the mission and work round the districts stump picking, shearing, working on the railways and highways. While they were away their families would go on rations until the men got paid. Those rations weren't very much, just flour, sugar, tea, a plug of tobacco, rice, half a pound of butter, sago and maize if you were sick, and a tin of either plum or apricot jam or golden syrup.

They'd kill sheep twice a week. The best cuts of meat were allocated to the white officers' families first and then each Aboriginal family got a portion of meat according to the size of their family. Apart from being a baker and a barber, my grandfather Archie was a butcher for many, many years. He used to often bring home a sheep's head and put that in a big pot of water with an onion and a parsnip to flavour it and then set it in an old pie dish to cool. It would end up like potted meat and us kids really liked it. Lambs tails were also a favourite with us, cooked in the ashes.

The Aboriginal men would go down to the meat shop early and cut the meat up ready to be served out. Then you would have to line up for your family's portion, first come, first served. That went totally against our cultural practice of sharing everything equally and caused divisions amongst our people that weren't there before. It caused fights between the people if somebody missed out.

Apart from using pieces of glass of different shapes for different uses, the men would nail a bit of tin onto a piece of wood to act as a knife. The most important tools for the men were a tomahawk, a rasp and a spade. I remember when the men used to do the carpentry work they'd keep the handle of the hammer only to fashion carving tools. The kids would copy the men to make their own cricket stumps, but no-one was allowed to touch Grandfather's special wood for making *waddies*.

They'd use fine white lake sand to smooth wooden objects like *waddies* right down finely with their hands. Sometimes of an evening you could hear the sound of the men chip, chipping away with their tin knives to make *waddies*. The men could turn their hand to anything. They were all thinkers, not just *Mainu* David Unaipon. When *Mainu* David invented the comb shears — before that the shearers were just using blades to cut the wool — he did it to make life easier for his people, and that was a big lift for them.

Child Endowment and the colour of your skin

Mum and Dad were able to get Child Endowment payments for us children, but this allowance and other benefits worked on a very strange system to my way of thinking. My father was classed as a 'full-blood' and my mother was classed as a 'quarter-caste'. 'Full-bloods' weren't entitled to Child Endowment, but 'half-castes' and those of lighter skin colour were. This meant that sisters and brothers often received different benefits. For example Aunty Opie and her sister Aunty Joycey (née Wanganeen), when they started to have children one was entitled to Child Endowment and the other wasn't. Same mother and father; same features, but different entitlements because one was lighter skinned than the other.

The anthropologists used to classify people as 'full-blood', 'half-caste', 'quadroon' and 'octoroon', but whitefellas don't classify themselves as 'full-blood English' or 'half-caste Scottish' or whatever. I could never figure out what difference it made.

I'm not what you'd call dark, I'm a cacky colour really, where my sisters Connie and Doris have nice brown complexions. I've always been ashamed of my colour. I would have loved to have been real dark like my Dad. Mum was more fair than me. Her brothers and sisters were different shades of black and so were her parents and aunties and uncles. When I was a child a lot of the parents had white grandfathers, so where the logic of the government policy is, I really don't know. It was very hurtful to be classed as different from your brothers and sisters because of the colour of your skin. It wasn't until I was married in the 1950s, when my father-in-law Bob Wanganeen from Point Pearce and Uncle Percy Rigney from Raukkan went to Canberra to lobby for 'full-blood' women to get Maternity Allowance, and Child Endowment that this issue came to a head.

Somehow it was seen in the wider community that the more white-skinned you were, the more like white people you were, but we still weren't treated the same as white people. I remember a white woman applied to Raukkan for a 'half-caste' domestic help. That meant my cousin, who was the next on the list to get a job, wasn't able to go because she was of darker appearance. She was really upset. Then some of my cousins who are fairer skinned would get called 'black bitches' straight out by people driving past them.

Clearing the land

But going back to them early days, one of the main jobs the Aboriginal men were given was clearing the land — stump picking. All the farmers in the district were clearing the land, and the superintendent on Raukkan sent the men to clear the little farms belonging to Raukkan called Block K, Yalkarie and Teringie. The people knew that if they refused to go on that sort of job then their rations wouldn't be supplied. But Aboriginal people don't like to see the land cleared and they don't like building fences and being fenced in. They feel as if they're suffocating.

I remember I used to sleep sound, but one night I got up — I must have heard Grandfather come in — and I wondered where he had been. At that time they were clearing and putting up fences on the other side of Teringie. Grandfather had a bit of a cut on his hand and I said, '*Mainu*, what you doing?' 'Oh I'm washing this blood off my fingers, my girl'. I thought, how come he's bleeding from the hand this time of the night?

So I went back to bed. We'd get up in the morning and he'd have toast and porridge and everything made for us, fire made. So I did ask him next day, 'Is your hand still bleeding, *Mainu*?' 'No, my girl. I fixed it up last night. It's right.' I said, 'How you done that?' 'Oh, on a piece of wire.'

That day Aunty Martha's daughter Flo and I were doing our chores — carting water and washing clothes — and all us girls around the same age, Edie [Rigney], Hester [Rigney], Wanda, Julie and me, were talking. Hester's father was my Mum's uncle, and we used to call him Grandfather Gordon. He used to do little odd jobs round the office and he used to always be called into the *ma:thuwis* [the bosses] and listen to them talk. He heard that some of the fellas went down to Teringie and pulled all the fences down. I thought, 'Oh that's what *Mainu* must have been doing'. So I asked him. I said, '*Mainu*, what they talking about down the office about all these men pulling the fences down?' And I saw the look on his face! Well, after the police left it became common knowledge that it was Raukkan men that pulled the fences down.

Tragedy

Even though my early years on Raukkan were ruled by the white administration and government regulations and we didn't have much, it was a happy family life. I don't ever remember my parents arguing. I don't remember my father drinking. Very few men drank on Raukkan at that time. Some of them that went away shearing and working used to have the odd drink off the mission, but very few of them ever drank on the mission. It was a good life.

But like many of my people, my family was struck by tragedy. My sister Doris Alma had already died young of diphtheria. Then one day in 1943 when I was eight, five of us kids — me, Ruby Wilson, Hester Rigney, another girl and my little sister Nancy, who was only seven — were booked in to have our tonsils removed at the Raukkan Hospital. The doctors were just pulling tonsils out left, right and centre. We all had our tonsils removed except Nancy because the doctor ran out of time, so he booked Nancy in as first one on the list for a month later. The following month Nancy was taken down to the hospital by my Dad.

I was in school when Mr Lawrie told my cousin Flo Rankine to take me and Oscar home. First thing that came to my mind was that I'd done something wrong, because I was always getting punished, standing in the corner or picking up stones in the yard for the stone heap. But no, so off we went, and I remember thinking that this was the first time we had been let out of school early and that we could do all sorts of nice things in this spare time, because Oscar and I were very close.

When we got to the house we saw the police from Meningie there. I never thought about Nancy. I thought it must have been my Nanna or *Mainu*. Dad was trying to calm my mother down. I just couldn't imagine what was going on. My mind went absolutely blank. Nancy had died on the operating table in Raukkan hospital. A healthier kid you could never imagine.

Apparently Mum ran down to the hospital and went berserk. She belted hell out of the sister and Dr Turner and she cut his eye. It was the shock of my sister's sudden death.

The only other time I can remember my mother getting vicious like that was before Nancy's death, when my sister Connie was a baby. The sister on the mission at that time was Sister Pearl McKenzie, who was to play a major role in my life, as well as the lives of many other Raukkan people. Connie was born on 18 May, and she was only two days old when Sister McKenzie put her in the crib on top of a hot water bag. The hot water bag was put in the crib to warm it, but was meant to be removed before the baby was placed in it. Sister McKenzie was sitting in her room having a cup of coffee. Well Mum got Connie in her arms and just lifted Sister McKenzie right off her chair and straight through the window. They reckoned she had the punch of a sledgehammer.

I'll never forget Nancy's funeral. She wasn't much younger than me and only a tiny bit shorter and we almost took the same sized clothes and shoes. Mum made things the same for Nancy and me and we had little beret caps and a little brooch each. I got myself dressed that day and then I heard my grandmother saying, 'Is that Nancy's skirt she's got on?' I looked down and saw it was short and my bony legs were showing and I realised it was Nancy's skirt I was wearing by mistake. I was so upset.

The old church was beautifully decorated. I can remember the hymns they were singing. The Minister, Mr Reid, conducted a beautiful service, and then we had to walk behind the ute taking my sister in a little white coffin. It was something I always remember, because on her coffin she had a beautiful bouquet of little tiny red roses. Granny Glanville Harris, Veronica Brodie's grandmother, had a nice big creeper of these little red roses on her verandah and she made a big wreath of them for my sister's coffin. Up at the Top Row all the school children formed a big archway that they drove through as we walked behind. Aunty Martha was there *lamun* [carrying] her baby on her back.

That day is one of my saddest but most constant dreams. It keeps coming back into my mind all the time.

After that I just lost interest in everything. I wasn't doing the usual things. I didn't want to go out and play. I remember Nanna asking me, 'You going to go to Sunday school today?' and I would say, 'Nope'.

Lila and Thelma were taken away from Mum by the Protector of Aborigines and placed in the Fullarton Girls' Home after Nancy's death, and when my mother was pregnant with my sister Doris the following year, Elsie was also taken to the Home. That was hard because I felt like I had lost three more sisters, rather than cousins.

After Nancy died Mum and Dad decided to take us all for a holiday over to Point Pearce to visit Mum's eldest sister, Aunty Rosie Kropinyeri and her husband Uncle Nat. We caught the Mail to Tailem Bend and the train to Adelaide. I had been to Adelaide only once before when I was too little to remember. My father told me I was sick and spent a few days in the Mareeba Hospital at Woodville. This time we stayed overnight with Aunty Muriel Williams in her house just off Carrington Street, and it was like my first time in a city. Then after we had been back from Point Pearce for a short time, Mum announced she was pregnant.

On 9 September 1945 my baby sister Doris Eileen was born at Raukkan hospital. My brothers Oscar and Ron and my sister Connie and I saw her the day after she was born and we were so happy. But then complications set in and they told Dad that they were taking Mum and the baby to Murray Bridge Hospital. Dad at that stage was doing a bit of work on the railways just out from Tailem Bend, but he had come in to Raukkan when he knew Mum was due to have the baby. He could do this because they would put the men on for a few months and then off again so they could share the work out amongst them.

So Dad was there when Doris was born and when they took Mum to Murray Bridge. They didn't have an ambulance or anything, so they took Mum in the old ute. Sick as she was, she had to ride in this bumpy old car seat for over one hour's trip. She was in the hospital there for about two weeks with Dad by her side when Grandfather Gordon Rigney took Oscar and me up to Murray Bridge. We walked from the station to the hospital and we were happy to see Mum and the baby for the second time.

It was 8 October, barely a month after Doris's birth, that Grandfather Gordon came up to the house again to see Nanna and Grandfather. I woke up to hear my grandmother sobbing in her little room. I went into the kitchen and *Mainu* was sitting by the old fireplace crying. Mummy had died.

2

A Family Torn Apart

...1995

I was very, very angry that Ian McLachlan could have done this thing. When I had recovered enough, Sandra and I got on the phone again to Sue Kee in Robert Tickner's office in Canberra to find out more about what had happened. We were asking lots of questions, but Sue Kee couldn't answer everything in detail. So we decided to find out from the horse's mouth and ring McLachlan's office and then Chris Gallus' office direct [Shadow Minister for the Environment and Aboriginal and Torres Strait Islander Affairs]. But first Sandra went and got the Aboriginal Legal Rights lawyers — Tim Woolley and Chris Charles — to come and sit in on the calls.

We had the phone on speaker, and we asked Ian McLachlan if they had taken photocopies of the contents of the secret envelopes, and he said yes. I asked him how many copies (thinking he'd made one for himself and one for Chris Gallus), but he said 'many'. *Many!* Of course later he denied that, but we had the lawyers present and they heard what he said, even though McLachlan didn't know he was on speaker phone and he didn't know the lawyers were there. Next day Sandra did an affidavit to say exactly what he'd said.

That's when I just lost it, after he admitted that. I demanded he give the paperwork back. McLachlan said he'd already handed all the papers to Chris Gallus, so we called her. I told Chris Gallus to give it all back to Robert Tickner through Sue Kee, but she said she wanted to return it to me personally. I said, 'Pig's arse you will', at which she threatened to ring Sarah (Milera) and the other Ngarrindjeri women and return it to them. Well, that's when I really went off. I screamed no to her and hung up. Then we rang Tickner's office again and asked Sue Kee to go round to Chris Gallus's office and demand the papers back. That worked and the papers were finally handed back to Sue Kee. The next day Deane Fergie[1] flew to Canberra to bring them back. But the damage had been done. McLachlan's office had photocopied the secret envelopes and sent them to the media. I couldn't have imagined how they could go so low — to me that seemed lower than a snake's arse.

But that affidavit of Sandra's came in handy. It was read out in Parliament and McLachlan lost his position on the shadow front bench. And he had been predicted to be the next Prime Minister of Australia.

But instead of being thrown out in disgrace for such a despicable act of violence against Ngarrindjeri people, it was only for lying to the Parliament!

1945

Mum's death was the most devastating thing. Us kids were still grieving for our sister Nancy. Every Sunday afternoon we used to pick flowers out of the garden, where Mum had dahlias and daisies and a few other little things growing, and go up to the cemetery and sit down by Nancy's gravesite. Now we had lost our mother.

Grandfather Gordon took Oscar and me up to Tailem Bend to meet our father. It was Eight Hours Day [Labour Day], a public holiday on a Monday, and the Raukkan football team was playing against the Tailem Bend side. Grandfather Gordon took us to the football to keep us occupied until the train came in from Murray Bridge with Dad on it. When it was time he walked us up to the railway station to meet our father. I don't know how Grandfather Gordon managed all this because he loved my Mummy like she was his own daughter. He was a very kind-hearted, loving man and he would put himself out for almost anybody, like he did for me and Oscar that day.

The train pulled in and we saw Dad come to the gate. He was crying. We knew Mum had died, but being kids we didn't fully understand what was going on. Dad knelt down and took Oscar and me in his arms and we all cried and cried.

After a while Dad let go and got up. He knew we had to get back to the football game so we could all get a lift back to Raukkan with the footballers. So he hooked his little sausage bag over his shoulder and we went back to the football.

The next morning he went down to the office and made arrangements for my mother's funeral for that Friday. While we waited those four days for the funeral we were having lots of visitors, and my Nanna and Dad and all of us were crying and crying.

I remember my sister Nancy's funeral vividly but I can only just vaguely remember my Mum's. Her death happened so sudden. She had survived the birth of six other children, so I didn't see any reason why she would die like that. I don't think I could accept it, and I was in a daze. I remember going into the church and sitting down at the front, and then having to walk up to the cemetery behind the ute that carried my mother's coffin. No hearse or nothing. We took her up to the cemetery on that Friday in an old ute and we buried her.

Next morning being Saturday, Uncle Frank Lovegrove came up to the house early to take Aunty Martha and Dad into Murray Bridge to pick up the baby. Dad rolled up some of the baby clothes that Mum had ready for Doris and took them with him. When they got in to Murray Bridge Hospital, Doris wasn't there. The baby was gone.

I believe Aunty Martha went to see the matron in the Maternity Ward where Mum had been and was told Doris was no longer there. She pushed past the nurses and insisted on having a look for herself. They used to keep the Aboriginal babies in a separate room from the white babies, and Aunty Martha went into both rooms to be sure, but found no black babies there. The sister told Dad that someone from the Protector's office, a sister, came out and took her. We knew what that meant. Plenty of Raukkan kids had been taken away by the government authorities. Thelma, Lila and Elsie were in Fullarton Girls' Home. We also had other relatives taken to Mount Barker and Kent Town and Colebrook Home. Dad thought that's where Doris must have gone.

There were an unusual number of deaths related to childbirth at Raukkan around that time, and all the women who died already had children. Adeline Wilson passed away leaving five or six children, Minnie Wilson left eight, Louisa Wassa had five or six kids, and my mum had already had six. Later on Aunty Rosie told me she put it down to white interference in the traditional birthing ways. She said if the *putharis* were left to birth the kids, this wouldn't have happened. I'd still like to get to the bottom of it.

My father's grief, my pain

Dad was beside himself. He had just lost his beloved wife and now his new baby was gone. He didn't know what to do. Dad was so disturbed he wasn't able to answer any of our questions, and Aunty Martha had to tell us everything that happened. I remember running down to my Aunty Phyllis's place [Phyllis Kartinyeri, née Rigney] screaming that Daddy was home but no baby; I was in a state of shock. I went back to the house, and Bill Robinson [the farm overseer at the mission] came down to deliver the message that Sister McKenzie had taken Doris into Adelaide to organise someone to look after her, because Nanna was too old to look after any more children. This was the excuse that the government gave, and it was a weak excuse because there were so many of our aunties and uncles and older cousins who would have been able to help Dad look after his children. I remember many, many relatives coming in to find out what had happened, and Aunty Martha had to tell them all that Sister McKenzie had taken Doris away.

Sister McKenzie was now the 'Welfare Officer' for the Protector and it was her job to take the children away. Like the Protector, she too came to be feared and loathed because she would often do it by deception. I remember one of my aunties and her husband were fighting. Sister McKenzie told her she would take the children until they sorted their problems out. Those kids were never returned to the mother and father. The way I saw it was that there were rules and regulations and if you break them, you'd get punished. And the way they punished you was by taking your kids away.

At that time Raukkan was a very closed community. We had a few white people coming in from time to time from round the districts, but we didn't have regular contact with the outside world. We knew the superintendent and the mission staff and we knew the Protector of Aborigines, Mr. Penhall [Chief Protector of Aborigines 1938–9; Secretary of Aborigines Protection Board 1940–53] by name and by sight because he made a lot of visits to the mission. But we knew nothing about the running of things or what the Protector's office did. We knew the government had all sorts of rules and regulations for us which we didn't like but couldn't do anything about, but we didn't know what their policies were or how they operated. We weren't even told, let alone asked our opinion. We might be told that the Protector was coming to talk to us, but not about anything like policy. If the government wanted to do something, the government did it. They took our new-born baby sister without even telling Dad.

It seems to me they had a funny way of 'protecting' Aboriginal people. I think that 'Protector of Aborigines' was the worst name they ever gave anyone. As far as I was concerned a protector was someone who'd look after you. Well they didn't look after my family and they didn't look after a lot of others. I told the Protector that many times later. I said, 'You call yourself fucking Protector of Aborigines. You weren't that to me'.

Mr Robinson made arrangements for Dad to go down to Adelaide to see Mr Penhall, and Mr Penhall told him that Doris was taken just until they sorted things out, and that we'd be able to get Doris back. But he would not tell Dad where Doris was.

Dad was in a terrible state. He stayed in Adelaide wondering what to do and where Doris might be. He sat outside on the square where the War Memorial is and he'd watch everybody coming and going from the Protector's Office. Any baby girls, he'd run up and have a look at them and see if they were Doris. Then he'd go down to the railway station and walk backwards and forwards looking at any blackfellas and he'd run up to every little black baby to see if it was Doris. He must have been half out of his wits, poor Dad.

Then he would go up to Whitmore Square for a feed from the Salvation Army and back to Light Square and sleep there on the grass. He didn't have any money for accommodation or any relatives to stay with in Adelaide, or if he did he didn't know where to find them.

He would have been in danger of being picked up by the police, because in those days the police would harass Aboriginal people for 'loitering' and having 'insufficient means of support'. If you had no money on you they could arrest you. I remember Oscar telling me how he was once part of a group approached by the police and asked to show their 'means of support'. Kaurno Walker pulled out two shillings and showed the police. They had good sign language between them and talked to one another with nods and looks that the police didn't see. So he quickly passed the two bob on to the next one and so on and the policeman didn't catch on that it was the same two bob going round. I think it was a matter of survival. Blackfellas had this instinct and often got a laugh out of it too!

The whole time Dad was away Nanna was crying — crying for Mum, crying for Doris, and now crying for Dad too. It started to become unbearable for me, because I was grieving too. I didn't go back to school for the rest of the year, and W.T. seemed to understand that I had to look after Nanna. I would make sure there was a bottle of water by her bed and she'd have little sips of it all the time to calm her nerves. I told her she'd be having to *karnji* [urinate] all day, but she wanted me to fill it up from the rainwater tank all the time. She just needed me to fuss over her.

Dad came back to Raukkan early in the new year really dirty and exhausted. His eyes were all sunken in. I remember that in just a couple of months his hair turned from black to completely white. So Nanna made him stay home. She said, 'Give it up now Oscar. You can't find her'. 'I've got to find her, Mum', he used to say and he'd make us kids cry.

At night when I said my prayers I would ask, 'Oh God, why did you take my Mummy from me?' Oscar would talk to me in Ngarrindjeri and keep me going, but Dad would say, 'You have to come to grips. Mummy died for God's will'. He asked me, 'If you went into a garden, what flower would you pick?' I said, 'The best'. Dad said, 'That's what God took'.

Nanna couldn't keep him long. He just had to keep trying, so we scraped up all our pennies and halfpennies for him and he went back again looking for Doris. He went to plead with Mr Penhall again. Mr Penhall told Dad that Doris had been fostered out, although he wouldn't tell him where, and got him to sign a document. Dad thought he was signing a paper to get her Child Endowment paid to the Protector for Doris's upkeep until she came back to us. That's what Dad said they told him he was signing it for. In fact the letter signed Doris over as a Ward of the State until the age of eighteen.

When I saw that letter about ten years ago, I broke down because I recognised his signature on it. It didn't have all the detail on it, but if it did he wouldn't have read it, because with blackfellas they used to say, 'Sign your name here' and you would have to sign it. You could be signing your own death warrant and you wouldn't have known. Dad knew there was nothing else he could do. That was the procedure.

Dad came back to Raukkan again, and this time Aunty Martha joined forces with Nanna, and they would not let him leave again because they were worried about his health. They didn't need to bother. He was so exhausted he could hardly walk. Dad suffered off and on from asthma and this, combined with his worry and living rough in Adelaide, had taken its toll on him. I couldn't bear to see my Dad suffer like this.

Dad was so devastated that he sort of pushed everybody away and wouldn't have much to do with us kids for a little while. He started to become angry and to really hate white people for breaking up his family. All his life I remember him saying, 'Such is life with a lovely wife and a bastard of a one without her'. He began to get into trouble on Raukkan, but everybody seemed to understand. The police would be called up from Meningie and they'd say, 'Come on, Ozzie, cut it out now. There's nothing you can do. The baby girl is in the right place'.

Mr Bartlett was very concerned about my Dad, and Dad later told me that Mr and Mrs Bartlett wanted to adopt Doris. That was before Mr Bartlett became the Secretary of the Aborigines' Protection Board, and they were very fond of my mother, but apparently because of his work with Aboriginal people, adoption was not possible, and my Dad could not have agreed to that anyway.

Nanna

Nanna was also suffering. Not only had she lost her daughter-in-law, but she didn't know where her new grand-daughter was, her son was distraught, and she and Grandfather had three grand-children to look after. In their time, Nanna Sally and *Mainu* Archie had eight children, forty-nine grandchildren and 138 great-grandchildren. By this time my brother Oscar was out at Yalkarie stump-picking, even though he was only thirteen and the stumps were really big. They used to put a chain around the stump and get a horse to pull it out. How a young teenage boy managed with that work I don't know. Nanna was so mournful; she used to be crying all day and all night and calling to God for help. She kept her little bible with her all the time.

My cousins Flo and Sarah and I would get together with Nanna and get her in a really good mood, and then it could just be a little minor thing that would trigger Nanna off again and we'd have to go through all that thing of calming her down again. It really depressed me. I can still hear her crying even today, after all those years.

Nanna became obsessed with her religion. She'd say, 'Doreen what are you doing?' and I'd say, 'Nothing Nan, what for?' 'Oh come and listen to me. I want to read this psalm from the bible.' I only went in there to please her. I didn't want to hear this psalm I'd heard a million times before. So I'd go and sit on Nanna's bed and wait till she'd finished, and then I'd say, 'Thanks Nanna' and kiss her on the forehead and off I'd go. I only did that for peace.

The minute she put it down she couldn't find it, so Nanna would walk around with her bible and she'd keep it by her bed at night. Grandfather would make us sit down and listen to her read it sometimes, not because he was over-religious, but because he was a very, very good living man. Everybody loved Nanna and *Mainu* on Raukkan.

Grandfather Archie

You could walk right round this world and you'd never find another fella like my grandfather. Not one of us grandchildren would ever disobey him. He was my idol. I loved him. He had lovely ways, kind voice, never seen him get into an argument, and there used to be a lot of arguments and fights on Raukkan amongst families then because of the way people had to live. He was everything a little girl who'd just lost her mother could ever want. He used to sit me down and say to me, 'Well, Doreen, things are not as bad as they really seem to you. What you've got is what your mother and father gave you, and no-one can take that away from you. Even though God's taken your Mum and they've now taken your little sister, they can't take away who you are'. He made me feel that I was something. He was the only one in the house who could comfort us children. He never stopped to worry about himself; he'd be there if any of his children or grandchildren needed him, and it was my grandfather Archie that kept me strong and kept me going.

Thank goodness for *Mainu* because everyone was really upset. Connie was only three and she was crying every night for Mummy. I used to make her little things, little toys out of sticks and cotton to give her to quiet her down. In the night Connie would jump into bed with me and I would cuddle her until she went to sleep.

Ron (we called him Squashy) was only about five years old and he had a different reaction. He withdrew from everybody. Oscar and I would try and get him to have a cry for Mum but he never could. Grandfather would try to help by getting Squashy to sit and whittle with him. He gave him a pocket-knife and sticks to whittle, but Ron would just keep with the movement, not really looking at what he was doing, like he was in a trance. After a while he began to get fidgetty in school. He got made to stand up in the corner because he wouldn't sit still in his seat. You'd think the schoolteacher would have understood

2 ~ A Family Torn Apart

what Squashy was going through, because the teacher lived on Point McLeay and knew what had happened. Eventually Squashy started to get a nervous twitch. It got worse and worse until he was about eight years old, when Aunty Martha took him to see the doctor, where they diagnosed him as having St. Vitus Dance and he was sent down to Escort House, a hospital in Semaphore.

Because of the little ones I did my crying in private after Connie went to sleep, but it seems like I cried myself to sleep every night for a long time.

Flo moved into the house to help, and Aunty Martha and Aunty Phyllis were there for us, and so were all my uncles and my other cousins. There were relatives living off the mission who wanted to come back to help look after us too, but they were exempted, so the government wouldn't let them back into Raukkan.

Exemptions

Being exempted[2] meant that the colour of your skin didn't change; the way the rest of the community treated you didn't change; you were still discriminated against, but your entitlements changed. It meant that you could live and work off the missions, but you couldn't go back to the missions to visit your family or friends. You could get Child Endowment, but you couldn't get rations, so you had to work, although Aboriginal people didn't get paid the same as white people for the same work.

To prove you were exempted you had to wear a tag on a chain around your neck, which we called 'dog tags'. That seemed an appropriate title because we were still treated like dogs. This was so the police could know who was exempted and who wasn't. That was useful for the police because under the same legislation it was a punishable offence to 'consort' with an Aboriginal person.[3] That meant that no white people or exempted people were allowed to have any sort of relationship with an Aboriginal person, and most Aboriginal families suffered greatly because of that.

A limited exemption was for three years. During that time you could back out of it or it could be revoked by the Board for some reason or other. Lots of people decided not to go on with it; after all, it meant denying your whole identity, and yet still suffering for it. Once it became unconditional, the Board couldn't revoke it and that was it for life. That's how it was for my Aunty Rosie and she suffered badly for being exempted.

In the 1940s the government was offering jobs off the missions to Aboriginal people to encourage them to become exempted. Once they had become exempted the State didn't have to pay for their upkeep, so it wasn't the welfare of Aboriginal people in their mind, but saving money. At Raukkan the Protector would let the superintendent know of any jobs available — usually with the railways or the highways — and the superintendent would post up notices for people to apply for the jobs.

The government placed all the children who had been raised in Homes into menial jobs as soon as they turned fourteen. The boys generally went onto farms and the girls into domestic work. These children usually worked for their board only and perhaps a small allowance, but no proper pay. They were often placed out into jobs that they didn't like and many were abused by their employers. It was all about funding. The Board would use the person's allowance or Child Endowment to partly fund the employment, so the employer got cheap labour and the Board got a cheap solution to funding Aboriginal people. My Mum and Dad never got exempted.

The pain continues

One day we were all playing outside the house when I fell over and skinned my arm. I went to go in the back way, past Bertha Gollan's place, to get it looked at and as I walked to the back door I heard my Nanna and four of my aunties talking in the kitchen. I heard my name being mentioned and I stopped dead. I hid behind the water tank to listen. I could hear my Nanna saying, 'No I don't want her to go'. Go! My name was being mentioned and that I had to go! I was shocked. I didn't understand what was going on, so I listened more. I heard Aunty Martha say, 'Well, I can't take her because I have to go down to Adelaide to the rehabilitation centre with Reg all the time'. Then

Aunty Phyllis said, 'Well, I can't take her because I've got too many kids of my own'. Aunty Dorrie [Kartinyeri] didn't say much. Aunty Ruth, who didn't have any kids, said, 'Well I can't take her. I couldn't handle her, she's too much for me'. I was a bit shocked when I heard that, because I thought I was a good sweet little girl. I didn't look on myself as being a bad kid. You can imagine how I felt, like no-one wanted me.

Lastly I heard Nanna say, 'They won't let me keep her. I can only keep two and I have to keep Connie and Ronnie because they're the two youngest'. I couldn't believe my ears. I just couldn't believe it, after all that had happened to me. I just sat down there and cried.

I think it must have been Aunty Martha who made the final decision. I knew she would have taken me if she could. I was very close to her four daughters, Flo, Ellen, Sarah and Mary. Eventually I heard her say to Nanna, 'You must let her go because you can't look after her and none of us can do it'.

Nanna fought against it, but she had to give in. I think what Sister McKenzie and Mr Bartlett did was work on my aunties to persuade Nanna to let me go. Whether they were threatened in any way I don't know, but knowing the way the Protector and Sister McKenzie worked in those days, I would say they would have had a lot of influence on them. Dad was very annoyed, and I know he and Aunty Martha had a very bad falling out about it, and they never spoke to each other for a long time.

So with that, after I saw them leaving, I wiped my eyes and I was sitting down there for quite a while wondering what to do. I thought, 'Shall I go inside or what? Might as well face the music', because that's how I'd been brought up. If I done anything wrong, I'd expect to get the punishment and I'd go and face it. So I walked in and saw Nanna sitting there feeling very sorry for herself, reading her bible. I pretended I never heard.

Nanna petted me up for a few weeks. I think she was trying to find the courage to tell me what the decision was. It was getting on towards Christmas when she finally said to me, 'Sister McKenzie will be coming out soon and she's going to take you down to the Home. You're going to be with your sisters down there, Elsie and Doris'. Lila and Thelma had already reached fourteen and were out at work. I said, 'But I don't want to go, I want to stay with you and Dad and Connie and Ronnie'. 'Don't you want to go and see your little sister?' I said, 'Yeah, but —' So there I was, torn between wanting to stay and yet wanting to go and see Doris, my baby sister.

But I really didn't want to leave Nanna and *Mainu*. I thought I'd be able to help in the house, because I was very good at that. I'd do my work and whatever I was told to do. I was desperate to stay with my family after all my trauma. I decided to take things into my own hands.

A ten-year-old's resistance movement

My cousin Mavis, who was my Aunty Laura Kartinyeri and my Uncle Rangi's daughter, used to go with this white bloke who now drove the Mail, called Keith Humphries. His nickname was Woppy. I saw him over at the post office one day and I got an idea. Here I am, ten-year-old kid, scheming. I said to Woppy, 'If Sister McKenzie's on the Mail, when you get to the cattle pit, will you blow the horn?' He said, 'What for?' I said, 'Because she's going to take me away and put me in the Home'. He understood and was sympathetic but he said, 'What are you going to do when she comes?' I told him I was going to hide. Woppy agreed to blow the horn.

So when I did hear that horn blow one day I just ran into the house, grabbed a little bunny-rug, a box of matches and a potato and onion and I went down the back of the mission into the prickly pears and I stayed down there. I figured no-one would look for me there. After it got dark I dug a little hole and made myself a little fire and cooked my potato and onion and ate them. I didn't go home that night, I slept down there.

Next morning I waited until after eight o'clock when the Mail had gone and then I went back home. As soon as I walked in, Nanna asked me where I slept that night. I told her I'd slept at Aunty Phyllis's place.

It wasn't unusual for us kids to spend the night at an aunty's place. 'No you didn't', she said, 'We sent Oscar and Coco (my cousin) looking for you and you weren't down there'. I said, 'I mean I slept at Aunty Martha's'. I wasn't a very good liar. She just said firmly, 'Where did you sleep, my girl?' I gave in. I said, 'I slept down the prickly pears because Sister McKenzie was on the bus'. She said, 'How did you know?' and I had to tell her how I got Woppy to blow the horn. Of course I got into trouble for not telling them where I was.

With tricks like this I managed to avoid Sister McKenzie for about two months until towards the end of January 1946. The school year was about to start and they'd all been putting pressure on me to agree to go to the Home. Nanna said to me, 'Stop running away, my girl. It's causing trouble. You're making your father very upset and we are all upset. Why don't you go down to the Home so you can be with your sister?' I was coming to realise that I would have to go, so I consoled myself with the thought that I would at least be with Doris, and with my big 'sister' Elsie, so I finally gave in and agreed. The super-intendent sent for Sister McKenzie to come and get me.

Nanna didn't even want to see me walk over to the Mail the morning I left. She asked Aunty Martha and Flo to take me over and just went into her bedroom and cried, and I walked over to the Mail crying. I didn't like Sister McKenzie hanging on to me all the time and I kept pushing her away. I was proud. If I was going to do it, I would do it on my own. She didn't like me. She kept telling me I was very disobedient. I didn't know what the word meant because I always did what my Mum or my aunties told me.

Pat and Una Rigney and Viola and Ruby Wilson and some other girls were returning to the Home after spending the Christmas holidays at Raukkan. But Sister McKenzie wouldn't let me sit with the other Aboriginal girls on the train. I had to sit with her so she could lecture me all the way to Adelaide. But I said, 'No way, I'm not sitting with you'. She made a grab at me, so I pulled her hairnet off and threw it out the train window. Then she pulled me into her compartment and I didn't get to sit with the other girls.

Military rule

When we got to Adelaide, Sister McKenzie took me to the Salvation Army Girls' Home at Fullarton. She took me into Matron Watson's office so Matron could take all my particulars. I remember Sister McKenzie saying, 'You'll have to watch this one; she's a bit of a spitfire'. Matron Watson said, 'Don't worry, I know how to handle girls like her. We've tamed all the other Aboriginal girls down and they're lovely girls now'. This made me angry. I was thinking, 'Yeah, you're in for something. I'm not like the other girls'. If they wanted to make me more rebellious, they couldn't have gone about it a better way.

I was the only new girl that day and I didn't know what to expect, but the girls who used to come home to Raukkan from Fullarton in the holidays told yarns about the fun they had going to gymnasium classes and learning ballet and so on, so I thought it wouldn't be too bad. As we walked through the building to the back I could see all these little black faces of my relations and some of the white kids peeping round corners to look at me. There were sixty or seventy children in Fullarton then, from babies up to teenagers, and I knew most of the thirty or so Aboriginal children. I thought I would be going to meet them all now and I was looking forward to that.

The Home was an old two-storey mansion, with offices, dining room, kitchen, bathroom and laundry on the ground floor and bedrooms and dormitories upstairs. It had large grounds and a school room. It was named Booth House after General William Booth, the founder of the Salvation Army, and all the staff had officers' rankings like Lieutenant, Captain and Major, and they wore uniforms with medals and the Salvation Army insignia on their collars, cuffs and bonnets. The lower ranks wore fawn-coloured uniforms and the upper ranks navy blue, and the Home was run in military style.

This was all confusing to me because what I knew of the army was associated with war and loss and sorrow. On Raukkan Mum would never let us kids watch war movies because she lost two brothers and Dad had lost one in the First World War. My grandmother's cousin had also been killed, and they were all buried in France or Germany. When I saw the medals the Salvation Army officers were wearing,

2 ~ A Family Torn Apart

I remembered Nanna showing me a medal she kept in a little tobacco box cushioned by cotton wool. She told me the King of England sent it when my uncle was killed. So naturally I connected the Salvation Army to the War that killed my uncles, and it was strange to me because they didn't look like the sort of people to go round with guns shooting people.

Then a woman named Captain Hepper said to me, 'You can come along with me now, dear. We will give you a scrub down.' I thought, 'What's a scrub down?' So she took me to this big bathroom with lots of cubicles and a big row of hand-basins. She told me to put a towel around my neck. I still didn't know what was going on. It was all so strange to me and she moved so quick I didn't have a chance to ask. Next minute I was getting my hair washed with phenol. It was stinging my head and my eyes and I was screaming. Where were the other kids? Why was I being singled out for this torture?

After my hair was washed I was put in the bath, dried off and given the uniform clothes of the Home to put on. They had about three rows of children's clothing in this one big cupboard, all different coloured frocks and some skirts and tops, and the Captain would rig you out with breeches, singlets, a dress and brown leather sandals. I had never seen such big baggy breeches. I was still looking at the clothes when I suddenly saw Captain Hepper had been joined by Captain Goodwin and Lieutenant Jones to hold me down while they cut my beautiful hair. I tried hard, but I couldn't get away from those three white women, I couldn't. I had beautiful long finger curls my Mum curled round her finger, which were my pride and joy. There were no harsh words or anything. It was 'Dear' this and 'Dear' that and 'Please don't make it harder for yourself, Doreen'. But when I saw my hair fall, I said, 'You fucking bastards'. I believe that was the first time God ever heard me swear.

So the very first night I was there, I was punished for swearing. I was told I would be going to bed later than the other girls, which meant that I wouldn't get to talk to them till the morning and I had to sit on the landing. The landing was a big place above the stairs leading into the different dormitories, and that's where I had to sit until all the other girls had quietened down, and then I was taken to my bed. There were about fifteen or so in each dormitory room. All the bigger teenage girls slept on the balcony with canvas awnings for shelter and the younger ones slept in age-groups inside.

I got into bed and after the lights went out Shirley Wilson and Una sneaked up to my bed and gave me a hug and a kiss and we had a cry together. A bit later Ruby Wilson sneaked in — she was in the other dormitory with the older girls — and came to comfort me as well. We sat up talking for a little while. They were telling me what not to do in the Home because I would get punished. They told me I had to go along with the staff, even if I didn't like it. But I didn't take it all in, I was so exhausted.

Next day I was still teary, but I was so glad to see Elsie. As soon as I saw her I said, 'Where's Doris? I want to see my baby sister'. She said, 'Oh sister girl, she's not here'. That completely threw me. They had lied to me. Doris wasn't there at all.

3

Suffer the Little Children

The Adelaide Advertiser, 7 July 1994

A row over the building of the Hindmarsh Island bridge has erupted between the Premier, Mr [Dean] Brown, and the woman he named Aboriginal of the Year this week.

Ms Doreen Kartinyeri said Mr Brown's warning against federal intervention in the bridge issue on Tuesday was a 'kick in the guts' for those who were trying to protect important traditional areas near the proposed bridge site.

On Monday, the Premier praised and rewarded the work of Ms Kartinyeri, a South Australian Museum historian, who was the main contributor to a report on the significance of the site compiled for the federal Aboriginal Affairs Minister, Mr Tickner… The following day [Mr Brown] told Mr Tickner to 'stay out of South Australia' and allow the bridge to go ahead. Last month, Mr Tickner extended a 30-day emergency ban on the construction of the $1.5 million bridge, saying the building site could be land with great Aboriginal heritage.

Mr Brown said the Aboriginal heritage issues surrounding the bridge had already been addressed under the State's *Aboriginal Heritage Act*.

> However, Ms Kartinyeri said the issue had been 'far from adequately addressed' and that Mr Brown had dismissed the Aboriginal heritage values of the area.
>
> Ms Kartinyeri, who has ancestoral [sic] links with the area, said construction of the bridge at its proposed location would destroy a sacred women's site of great importance to the Ngarrindjeri people.
>
> 'The Government is looking at dollar signs. I am looking at what we've got left to offer future generations,' she said.
>
> Ms Kartinyeri said she hoped Mr Tickner would put an end to the bridge. 'If he has any decency and respect for the Aboriginal people of Australia he will not take any notice of what Dean Brown has to say,' she said.

I was furious.

Kundjawara [great-great-grandfather Benjamin Sumner's first wife] and Malpurini [great-great-grandmother, Benjamin Sumner's second wife] are buried down on Kumarangk. That is my people's home and that was something that the old people loved. My ancestors are buried there. How would whitefellas like it if Aboriginal people dug up their great-grandmothers? My teaching since I was a little girl has always been about my people from Kumarangk and Raukkan. From oral histories passed down I heard about how in the old days the whitefellas had raped our women and then they had raped our land. And now in the 1990s they were going to do it again. How can they put a fucking great big bridge into that earth, when my Aunty Rosie wasn't even allowed to disturb it with her walking stick? Those waters and that island are sacred to us and it's my responsibility to take care of them. It always has been and I can never let go of that, no matter what a big burden that can be.

As usual, the authorities and the Aboriginal Heritage Act were not going to help. As soon as I heard they were planning to build a bridge from Goolwa to Hindmarsh Island, I went to Parliament House to talk to the South Australian Minister for the Status of Women, Barbara Weise. Swearing her to secrecy, I shared some of the women's knowledge. I even demonstrated some women's body positions to try and help her understand how important it was. I just wanted her to state in Parliament that she had seen me and been told about the women's knowledge and that she believed I was telling the truth, but no, she wouldn't do anything to help stop the bridge.

I had already been to see David Rathman [Chief Executive of the Department of State Aboriginal Affairs], but he said he couldn't do anything either. Later I found out that Sarah Milera, another Ngarrindjeri woman with knowledge, had also been to see David and had got the same response. All he would do was quote Section 23 of the South Australian *Aboriginal Heritage Act 1988* to me, that the Minister for Aboriginal Affairs had the final say. The Minister was, of course, a whitefella and the government was standing to lose a lot of money if it didn't go ahead with its agreement to build the bridge, so yet again Aboriginal heritage was going to suffer.

I would have thought that since both Sarah and I raised the issue with David, that would have been enough for them to have an investigation into what we were saying. They could have done that quite easily. We could have called Auntie May Wilson, Veronica Brodie, Aunty Gracie Sumner, Aunty Sheila Goldsmith and Aunty Connie Roberts. Some of the older ones were still alive then.

I sat at my desk in my office at the South Australian Museum and stared at the blank piece of paper in front of me. I've always had a good sense of what to do next. If they weren't going to protect this area under South Australian laws, I would just have to go further up. I would have to write a letter to the Federal Minister for Aboriginal Affairs, Robert Tickner. I had to do my duty for my people and my culture.

I knew what I wanted to say. That's another thing I've always had. Just let anyone try and put words in my mouth. I never got much education in the white way and I won't take anyone using big words around me. I often say to people, 'Don't use them big jawbreakers. I don't know what they mean. Tell me what you're saying in words I can understand.' Same with writing a formal letter. It's hard for me to put it in the right way, so often I will get someone I trust to help me. Steve Hemming would help me. I rang downstairs for Steve. Good, he was there. I went down to see him.

Steve was in the tearoom. The Museum archivist Kate Alport was there, and so was Deanne Hanchant, who was working in repatriation, taking back to their communities the Aboriginal skeletons the Museum had held and used for scientific tests over hundreds of years. The Director's secretary was popping in and out. At the time Philip Clarke was Registrar and Steve was Curator of Anthropology and Project Manager for the Aboriginal Family History Unit I was running. They weren't talking at the time because there was some aggro between them.

I told Steve I was upset about them wanting to build a bridge from Goolwa to Kumarangk because I knew how significant that area was, especially to Ngarrindjeri women. I told him about how Aunty Rosie had passed on her knowledge to me. I also told him about Aunty Laura Kartinyeri yarning to me. That's when Steve found out about what was to become known as the Ngarrindjeri 'women's business'. Because he was a man I never told him any details and he never asked, but Steve understood how important this was for me, so I asked him if he would type up a letter for me to Robert Tickner asking him to stop the bridge, and he agreed. We went upstairs to my office.

I showed Steve the notes I had made about what I wanted to say to Robert Tickner and then I told him to type it up as it was. Steve went to his office and typed the letter up. Then he came back and showed it to me. He had changed one of the sentences a bit, so I gave him a piece of my mind. He said he had just tidied up the grammar, but I didn't like my words being mixed around. I told him to go back and retype it. When he'd done that he left it with the secretary to fax it through to Robert Tickner's office, and told the Museum Director Chris Anderson about the letter straight away.

Before this I never was into Aboriginal politics. All I knew was I had to vote on election day and that was it. I was too busy to think about anything else while I was raising my children and foster children, although I had a lot of admiration for the work Aunty Gladdie Elphick[1] was doing during the Don Dunstan era [Labor Premier 1967, 1970–9]. I had a lot of connections with Aunty Gladdie in the 1960s and saw first-hand the way she was working, but this was all local work, all in South Australia. I had heard about Eddie Mabo,[2] but not much else. In 1992 I saw a newsflash on TV and I said to myself, 'Good luck brother, may you win'. Then when the decision came down, I cried, I was so happy. I never would have guessed at the time that I would be involved in a similar struggle that would work very differently for me. But then I didn't understand the way white politics worked.

I remember the first time I ever got involved in Aboriginal politics was after the Native Title Act had been passed in 1993 and a meeting was held at the Aboriginal Legal Rights Movement. I went along and stood up and said I supported native title and any way of Aboriginal people keeping their land. I didn't understand the legal system or bureaucracy, but at least I'd had my say. But that was it. I never knew anything about Keating's Redfern speech, or the Howard government's Ten Point Plan and its proposed Wik legislation,[3] even though those things came later. In fact I only ever learnt a little tiny bit about those things when I got into writing this book and I still don't understand them properly now.

At the time I was working in the Museum I attended a lot of meetings with anthropologists and people wanting to know about Ngarrindjeri culture. I'd tell them lots of things they wanted to know just to please them. I had worked out by then that the best way to get what I wanted in this world was to give whitefellas what they wanted without letting them know that I wasn't giving them all of it. When there were things I didn't want to say, I used to try and put them off. I had to make them know how important Hindmarsh Island is to my culture, without giving it all away.

Writing the letter to Tickner was the first time I had to think politically about the world and what was happening to blackfellas. It made me stand up and speak my mind, and writing that one letter made a significant change in my life. But because I did that I was labelled an 'activist' by the media. I still can't understand how I could be an activist when this was the first time I had ever really stood up for my culture, my own personal precious piece of country.

1945: Fullarton Girls' Home

I was heartbroken. My life was falling to pieces. I was so confused, hurt and angry. I could hear Nanna's voice over and over saying, 'Go in there and be with your sister'. The only sister I had there was Elsie.

Elsie wasn't able to go home to Raukkan for Christmas that year, because Mummy was no longer there, so it was good to see her, but I felt like I was going *wurangi* [mad]. I just couldn't understand what was happening. She took me over to sit down under the mulberry tree in the yard and we were both crying. I said, 'Nanna told me Doris would be here. Nanna lied to me'. Elsie said, 'No, Nanna would never lie to you. That's what they would have told Nanna so that they could get you here,' and she was right. For years I never considered myself part of the Stolen Generations[4] because I had agreed to go into the Home. But I was stolen. They got me there by lying to me and my family.

Elsie was comforting me. I was reflecting on the time when Mum got pregnant and told us she was having another baby. It was so good, we were all so happy. We were looking forward to the baby's birth and the next thing we knew, Sister McKenzie had put Lila, Thelma and then Elsie into the Home, Mummy died and Doris was gone.

Elsie and I cried together for quite a long time and some of the other girls came down and sat with us. Elsie was feeling it too. She had lost two mothers — her own and then mine.

The anger boils

I think that's when I started to really get angry. These bloody white bastards were taking control of everybody. We didn't know what they were doing half the time. It seemed to me like no matter where I turned and who I met in white society, those fellas were aiming guns at me and wanting to bring me down.

I guess I was lucky to know quite a few Aboriginal kids in the Home, like Ruby and Viola Wilson, who'd lost their mother before my mother died, and Shirley Wilson was there, but her mother and father were living, so children weren't just taken because they'd lost their mother. So okay, I had my cousins there, and Ruby Wilson was one of my best friends on Raukkan, and I should have been content, but I wasn't, because I had been so excited at the thought of seeing Doris. She would have been going on five months old, and I can't tell you how devastated I was that she wasn't there.

And so my time in Fullarton was very unhappy. I was there concentrating on not being there and I never made friends with the white girls in that Home. The others all had white friends, but I refused to mix with them. All I had was my Aboriginal family, the only people I could trust. White people were the enemy.

On my second day at the Home I was taken to Matron's office again and I was given a little run-down on what was expected of me. As plain as day I remember Matron Watson saying to me, 'You're not here as a punishment, you're here as a privilege'. You could have fooled me! I didn't understand how the English language worked. The way I understood it if you did something good you got a privilege. I hadn't done anything good or bad, but it sure felt like I was getting punished, not being privileged.

Then I was sent into the schoolroom. Lower primary school was conducted in a building on the grounds and after Grade 4 the girls went to Parkside Primary. All my relations were saying hello and introducing me to their friends, so it wasn't until after about an hour that I realised they had put me back into Grade 2. Sister McKenzie must have given Matron all my background, and knowing I had missed the last term after Mummy died, they must have decided to make me repeat the year. They didn't just put me back to the beginning of Grade 3, but they put me back two whole years. Well that was the last straw. I decided to become what Sister McKenzie said I was, a very naughty girl.

The beginning of rebellion

I deliberately did little things to get into trouble. I wouldn't do my chores, so they'd lock me in the boiler room. I'd while away the time by playing knucklebones with little pieces of coal, sitting on the floor in the dark. After being put in there about ten times they realised that wasn't working, so then they put me into scullery. Every week I was in scullery. I had to wash all the dishes from breakfast, lunch and tea. There were bread and butter plates, soup plates, big plates, knives, forks and spoons for about seventy people to wash. Some of the pots that they cooked in were bigger than me, and I put them on the floor, because I couldn't reach them in the sink, and scrubbed them with a big wire brush. I would only have one other girl to help me, someone else who'd played up. A few times that was a little German girl called Patty Unger. She had been brought down from a migrant camp in Woodside in the Adelaide Hills. She had no brothers or sisters and very few visitors, and some of the bigger white girls used to punch her around. I wonder now whether she got treated badly because of the Second World War.

A visit from Dad

After a few months I had a visit from my father. He was allowed to visit on a weekend, but he had to ask permission first. There was a little room called the Visitors' Room with a little lounge and a table with a lamp. Some of the bigger girls used to bring drinks in for the visitors. It was on this visit that Dad told me he had found out Doris was in Colebrook Home at Eden Hills. He told me I should stop playing up because we now knew where she was and that he and my cousin Nelson had been up there and seen Doris. He also told me that my cousins Flo, and Dennis and Francis, Ellen Rankine's sons, were there too.

There were restrictions on family visits. You were only allowed so many visitors per month, and the children were only allowed to write home once a month.[5] Dad told me that he had wanted to see me the day he saw Doris, but was not allowed to visit me. Perhaps there was some Salvation Army event on, which also meant visitors weren't allowed. It was hard, because he had a long way to travel and he couldn't always afford it.

Dad told me that Doris looked very much like Connie, with short curly hair. That was something Nanna always cried about, whether Doris looked like Connie or like me. I was pleased that at last we knew where Doris was, so I asked Dad when he was taking her home

A Raukkan school photo, c. 1943. (L–R) back: teacher, Shirley Wilson, May Sumner and Elsa Sumner; middle: unknown, Hester Rigney and Doreen Kartinyeri; front: Alice Sumner, unknown and Vida Sumner. Photo courtesy Doreen Kartinyeri Archival Collection, Native title Unit, Aboriginal Legal Rights Movement, Adelaide.

Outside the Raukkan Post Office waiting for the Mail to arrive, c. 1920s. Photo courtesy Doreen Kartinyeri Archival Collection, Native title Unit, Aboriginal Legal Rights Movement, Adelaide.

Doris Kartinyeri (front left) at Colebrook Home, c. 1948.

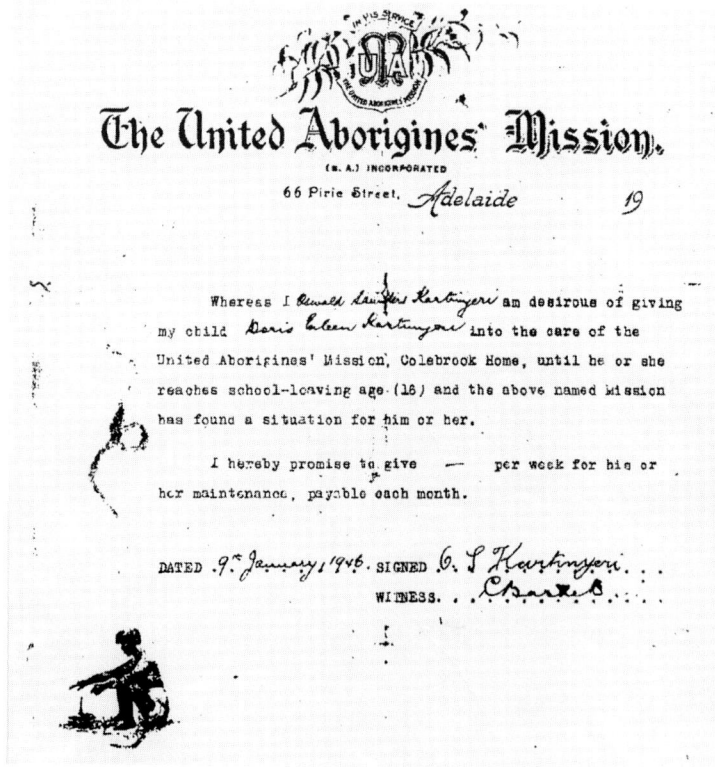

The United Aborigines' Mission letter signed by Oscar Kartinyeri admitting his daughter Doris to the care of Colebrook Home, 9 January 1946. Images courtesy Doris Kartinyeri.

Salvation Army Fullarton Girls' Home, 1940. Photo courtesy Salvation Army.

Doreen on the balcony at the Fullarton Girls' Home, now the Salvation Army Adelaide headquarters, 2005. Photo courtesy Sue Anderson.

> Charleston
> 15.2.58.
>
> Dear Mr. Penhall,
> I have made up my mind about working for Mrs. Motteram, (Mrs. Dunn's mother) at Kings Park, and Mrs. Dunn will let me go when she can get the other girl. I am sure I will like it at Mrs. Motteram place she is very nice, and I would like to work there. I will let you know when I will be going down there.
> I remain yours
> Sincerely
> Doreen Kartinyeri

Letter from Doreen Kartinyeri asking permission to go to Mrs Motteram.

A.D.17/50

W2012/2013

17th Feby.,

Miss Doreen Kartinyeri,
C/o Mrs. G. W. Dunn,
C H A R L E S T O N.

Dear Doreen,

I am quite agreeable for you to work for Mrs. Motteram, as you will then be able to keep in touch with Elsie, and perhaps arrange to have your time off on the same day.

However, I want to advise you not to visit the western end of the City, but when you come to Adelaide keep to the main streets, such as King William and Rundle Streets, etc.

I hope you will be happy in the new job.

Yours faithfully,

WRP
Secretary,
ABORIGINES PROTECTION BOARD.

Reply from the Secretary, Aborigines' Protection Board.

Both letters published courtesy Aboriginal Affairs and Reconciliation Division, Department of the Premier and Cabinet, Government of South Australia.

Thelma Kartinyeri and her children: (L–R) Nancy, Ron, Connie and Doreen. (Doreen had fallen out of the fruit tree, hence her bandaged leg.)

Doreen's father, Oscar Kartinyeri. Photo courtesy Doreen Kartinyeri Archival Collection, Native title Unit, Aboriginal Legal Rights Movement, Adelaide.

Aunty Rosie (Rosetta) and Uncle Nat (Nathaniel) Kropinyeri, c. 1940. Photo courtesy Doreen Kartinyeri Archival Collection, Native title Unit, Aboriginal Legal Rights Movement, Adelaide.

Doreen and Sid Chamberlain at Wingfield, 1979. Photo courtesy Doreen Kartinyeri Archival Collection, Native title Unit, Aboriginal Legal Rights Movement, Adelaide.

Doreen with Reg Graham at Point Pearce, 1953.

Children and grandchildren of Terry Wanganeen and Doreen Kartinyeri at Point Pearce at the time of the Wanganeen book launch, 1985. (L–R) back: Ron, Tahlia, Lynton Snr, Terry, Brenton, Robin, Ricky, Daryl; middle: Christobel, Lydia, Doreen; front: Klynton Jnr, Keven, Terry Jnr and Tina.

Doreen tells her family story

Doreen Kartinyeri hopes that recording the geneology of seven generations of her family, the Rigneys of Point McLeay, may help to preserve her people's sense of identity.

As a young girl in the Point McLeay Aboriginal settlement, Doreen sat at her grandfather's knee to hear stories of how her ancestors had suffered at the hands of the newly arrived white men.

She has drawn on those stories along with recent research to compile a family history and geneology.

The book, *Rigney Family — Point McLeay* was launched yesterday as part of National Aborigines' Week by the Minister of Aboriginal Affairs, Mr. Crafter.

The book covers more than 1000 descendants from her maternal great-grandmother who was born in 1856.

"I hope that the book will help my people to keep their identity at a time when we are in danger of losing our language and our culture," she said.

"There is a tendency for people to drift away, to assimilate. My grandfather used to tell how the English gentleman took advantage of the innocent Aboriginal girl, my great-grandmother. She had two children by him."

Mrs. Kartinyeri says she was a victim of unsympathetic Government policies in which family groups were heartlessly broken up. When she was 11 her mother died. She was put in a welfare home and at 13 sent to work in the country.

A mother of nine, she has maintained close ties with her family.

She hopes the book will be the first of a series of histories and geneologies of SA Aboriginal families.

PAGE 12 — Community 'poorly served.'

Launch of the Rigney genealogy, *The Advertiser*, 1983. (L–R) back: Brenton Wanganeen, Aileen Wilson; front: Roland Love, Doreen, Tania Love, Judy Love and Connie Love with Uncle Ted Rigney. Photo courtesy Advertiser Newspaper Ltd.

and when he was coming back to get me. He pretended he didn't hear me. He said he had to go so he wouldn't miss the train, and got up to leave. I chased him out to the gate. He stepped through the little side gate and headed down the road. June Campbell came after me and wouldn't let me follow him. I stood there peering through the gate. After a while she opened the gate to let me see that he had gone.

I couldn't eat anything that night. I crept upstairs into the dormitory and lay down on the bed. When they called my name for dinner they realised I wasn't there, so they sent a couple of the big girls to look for me. They found me crying on the bed.

I never found out why Dad didn't answer me. I asked him years later and he still didn't tell me. I think he believed it would have all been too much for me to hear that he couldn't take us home because the authorities wouldn't let him, and he was probably right.

The Protector's office

A short time after Dad's visit, it started to come into autumn, and it was time for the Aboriginal children to go into the Protector's office in Kintore Avenue to get fitted for winter clothes. These were clothes for special occasions, as opposed to the everyday clothes that were kept in the Home. I went down there with Rosie Brumby, June Campbell, Pat Rigney, Pearl Wilson and Pansy Wilson, and in the street I bumped into Sister McKenzie. She came up to me and said, 'How are you settling in? You're looking really well', all sweet as pie. But I was furious with her for what Dad suffered looking for Doris, all because they wouldn't tell us where she was. Even though I now knew, I asked her where Doris was. She said she couldn't tell me, that she would look into it but it would take time. I said, 'I just want to know where Doris is. You took her from Murray Bridge and I want to know where she is', but she still wouldn't tell me. I was sick of all the lies.

So I kicked my shoes off and I climbed up the war memorial and I said, 'If you don't tell me where my sister is I'm going to jump'. It was a rash thing to do, but I did things without thinking in those days; I did it out of anger. Looking back on it now, I realise that was a symbolic act, climbing a whitefellas' memorial. But if I'd known my uncles' names were on there I would have been shamed.

Sister McKenzie ran into the office and got June and Rosie to come out and talk me into getting down. I said, 'Not until you tell me where my baby sister is'. June said, 'Sister McKenzie, why don't you tell her? For all she knows that baby might be dead'. I was really frightened because I thought I was going to fall, but I just hung on to the flagpole on top of the statue and I started to cry. Finally June and Rosie managed to talk Sister McKenzie into telling me Doris was in Colebrook Home, but she was getting angry. She said, 'Try and get that girl down from there. The police will be here in a minute'. They had rung the police to arrest an eleven-year-old girl! I said, 'Put me in jail, I don't care'.

So I got down from the War Memorial. Eventually she said she would make arrangements for me to visit Doris in Colebrook. I felt I had won a small victory for a young girl, but it was still some time before I got to see Doris.

Routine in the Home

It took me a long time to work out the routine of the Home because it was so different to life with my family. In the mornings after you washed you'd line up for breakfast and after that we'd have to line up to go into school. I was walking around like a little zombie, just doing what I felt I had to and no more. I never got good grades in school, but if I did try and make an effort they would say I was cheating. Sister McKenzie would be sent out quite often to talk to me about being a cheat, but I never did cheat. Eventually I gave up trying, so then I got punished for not completing things. I ignored all the rules and made my own and I got into trouble for that. I just didn't feel they had the right to tell me how to live my life. You had to ask permission for everything, even to go to the bathroom. If you wanted to go out and sit in the sun in your reading time you had to ask permission for that. Even asking permission had its regulations. You had to put your hand up, your right hand, to be spoken to. If I would call out 'Lieutenant' or 'Captain' they wouldn't answer me. I felt like I had to salute them! And I hated it. So sometimes I'd just sit in the corner of that stuffy little library and read my book rather than bow down to their rules.

I wasn't much for reading then. I got a lot of books off the shelf, but I never read them. But it was a way of sitting down and relaxing and not worrying about chores. What I didn't realise at first was that after about a week they would question you on them. I can remember Captain Hepper (we used to call her Captain Pepper, because she had a bit of a bite to her) saying to me, 'Doreen, what did you think of *Gulliver's Travels?*' I'd had it for about four days but I hadn't read it, so I described the picture on the cover. I really wasn't interested.

Every girl had work to do after school. I never used to finish until about eight o'clock at night sometimes. Fold the clothes, do the laundry, work in the kitchen, in the scullery, make the beds. Every girl over a certain age made her own bed and the bigger ones helped the little ones. Sweeping, mopping and dusting was all done by the girls. None of the staff did it. All they did was give us orders, tell us when they thought we hadn't done something properly, and make us go over it again. I couldn't see how they had us young girls of eleven and twelve doing the work of women. Especially since I learnt later that they were charging the Aborigines' Protection Board a weekly fee for each Aboriginal girl they kept, as well as getting our Child Endowment.[6]

Each change of season we would be lined up to choose what clothes we wanted. One of the things I used to hate was that the white girls would be given their choice first. The white girls would pick out a dress and they'd look at it, turn it over, hang it up against themselves and make their decision. After all the white girls had chosen theirs, it'd be the black kids' turn, so with what was left we'd be lucky to find something to fit. One girl used to be always wanting a flared skirt so that when she'd spin you could see her knickers. She was quite good on her feet and a good dancer, and she looked cute.

Religion was a huge part of daily life. Every breakfast there'd be a prayer said, and then we'd all say grace. Lunchtime, a prayer and grace; evening meal the same. Then after school we had what they'd call Christian Religion. Then we could have a play in the yard before doing our chores. Before bed we'd have a prayer meeting on the landing outside the dormitories, then we'd have to kneel at our beds and pray before we got into bed. At home at Raukkan we used to say grace at the table and a little prayer at night, but not all day like this. In the Home it was always thank the Lord for this and thank the Lord for that. I'd say, 'Thank the Lord for giving me the strength to fight today' and I'd get into trouble for saying that, but I was just trying to get back at everything and everybody.

Matron put in an extra little prayer for unfortunate children. One of the girls fell and hurt herself and she was taken to the Children's Hospital. They said a prayer for her and wished her a speedy recovery and hoped she'd be back here to join her adopted family in this God-given haven. Apparently I was also unfortunate. Matron would pray, 'God give Doreen strength. Suffer the little children to come unto thee'.

We would often have to read passages from the bible, and that was the one I always picked — 'Suffer the little children to come unto me'. Matron asked me one day why I always chose that text, so I told her I just liked it, but I related to that passage, because God knows, I was suffering!

On Sunday we had three services — morning, eleven o'clock and evening. After breakfast we'd all march into the school room for the morning service, then after elevenses — which was a glass of cordial or milk and a piece of fruit and maybe a biscuit – we would line up again. Sometimes in the evening we'd walk down to Parkside and have the evening service with the congregation there. We had a special place in the corner of the church. They'd read texts from the bible, have a sermon and then confession for those who wanted to confess their sins and that would take the best part of the service. Later on we would go to Sunday services in the Salvation Army building in Carrington Street in the city. For those services we would be dressed up in really good clothes, with little hats on.

One thing I always loved was swimming. All the girls from Raukkan were good swimmers because we lived on the lake and spent our summers diving off the jetty and swimming down at the Kurangk. In summer every year around February the Salvation Army used to hold an aquatic display and the girls from the Home would go down to

3 ~ Suffer the Little Children

Unley pool to practice for this. When I first went to Fullarton I didn't know what a pool was, but to me it was a treat, so I didn't mind walking all the way from Fullarton to Unley. All we took with us was our towel and bathers. The towels were white and, like the grey blankets and all the linen in the Home, had 'Government' written right down the middle of them. Pansy and I used to spread them over our backs as an advertisement that we belonged to the government!

Along the way we would take any fruit that was hanging over the fences and we'd stuff our towels full. There were nice juicy peaches, apricots and plums. Coming from Raukkan where we couldn't afford to buy much fruit, it was a real treat. We weren't supposed to eat before swimming, but we couldn't help ourselves. One day one of the white girls rushed to the toilets when we got there because she'd eaten too much fruit. She wasn't allowed to train that day and she got reported to the Matron and we all got into trouble for it because they found stains on our towels.

After the training season they would have the aquatic display in the Adelaide City Baths, which was where the Festival Theatre is now. There was a big swimming pool with dressing rooms and diving boards and a smaller one for little children. The second year I was in the Home, the aquatic display was to be held in Melbourne and I was really excited about it, because I was one of the best swimmers. But I didn't get to go, because I decided I wanted some passionfruit from the vine in the yard and when I climbed up for them I fell and broke my wrist, so that ended my swimming career.

On Saturday afternoons we would go for hikes into the foothills, about four or five kilometres away, to pick blackberries. On the way we passed an abbey with monks walking around in brown hooded gowns with their arms folded like they didn't know where they were going. I never heard them talk, and when they saw us they would stop and let us kids pass. We were told they were Catholic, and it made me think of the Woods children from Raukkan, who were put into Goodwood Orphanage when their parents split up — that was run by Catholics. I don't know why they went there; their mother was still alive. But they were very fair-skinned, and all the Aboriginal kids in Goodwood would pass for white kids, so I think they wanted to separate them and bring them up as white kids. It didn't make any difference. They did the same as us — went straight out to work as domestics and station workers.

Outings

We had a lot of outings and sporting events with the Mount Barker Boys' Home and the Kent Town Boys' Home, and there were Salvation Army events, like Congress meetings, where we used to meet with those two particular Homes. We got friendly with most of the Aboriginal boys who were at Mount Barker and Kent Town, and it was like a treat just to get away from the Home. I would be so excited the minute I knew one of these events was coming up, I didn't do a thing wrong, never raised my voice, never stepped out of line when I was marching, never stole any fruit. I was perfect because I didn't want to miss out. We also met up with the Goodwood Orphanage, Semaphore and St Francis Boys' Home kids once or twice on special occasions. That's where I got to know John Moriarty, Charlie Perkins, Wally McCarthy, Laurie Bryant and Steve Dodd.

There'd be turnouts where all the Homes in Adelaide were invited to attend, like the Christmas Pageant. We would have to watch the parade in our designated area and didn't get to mix with the other children. Colebrook Home had their area, and I was always anxious to see if Doris was there, but she was probably too small to come down.

I met up with a lot of the people from Colebrook at the Lord Mayor's party after the pageant, like Faith Coulthard, Lois O'Donoghue, who I found out later was Doris's special carer, Amy and Eileen O'Donoghue, George Tongerie and the Brumby sisters, Muriel and Daisy. They were in Colebrook and yet their younger sister Rosie had been placed in Fullarton. Rosie was always glad to see her two sisters. I never thought much of it at the time, but later as a teenager I realised that the government really did what it could to split families up. Colebrook Home was more for children from the far north of South Australia, particularly Oodnadatta way, so I didn't understand why a little

Ngarrindjeri baby like Doris was in there. Doris grew up knowing Pitjantjatjara more than her own language.

Some fun in the home

After a while I decided to stop worrying about getting out and going home and I started to try harder to be a good girl, but it didn't always work. I was still angry with the system. There were more white girls there than Aboriginal girls, but us *nunga* [Aboriginal] kids had a special bond. I wasn't the youngest one there, but I was one of the smaller ones and we used to get up to mischief together.

I must have been about twelve when one Saturday afternoon we came back from our hike into the foothills and we were sitting down talking about how we always got away with things. The white girls were getting a little bit hostile with us because they were jealous of how cocky we were. So they dared us to go over to Kent Town Boys Home that night and bring something back to prove we'd been there.

After tea all the *nunga* kids got together, and most of them wanted to take on the dare. I was making excuses that it was too far and we were too tired from our hike that day, but the others were all keen to show those white kids what we were made of. Not everybody agreed; June Campbell, Rosie Brumby and my cousin Edie Rigney wouldn't come, but somehow the others talked me into it.

We all went to bed fully dressed and waited till they had called lights out, and the captain on night duty had done her patrol up and down between the beds. Then we all slipped out quietly. Ruby and I went down the side balcony steps from our dormitory. The bigger girls had to climb down over the front verandah, but we were all like little monkeys at climbing.

The main gate was locked every night, but we knew how to get over the fence because we had classes at Miss Hogarth's gymnasium in Grote Street in the city and we were all very agile. We made a pyramid with three bigger girls on the bottom on their hands and knees, two smaller ones on top of them and the littlest girl would climb up this human stepladder and slide over the top. I was the smallest, so the first over the fence! I prayed to God there was no-one waiting on the other side, and when I got over I made a sound like a bird to let them know it was all clear. Once a couple of the bigger girls were over, they made another ladder on the other side until the last girl was over the fence. It was hilarious and we couldn't stop giggling. The instruction all the way to Kent Town was, 'Don't make a noise, be quiet'.

It was about six or seven kilometres to Kent Town and we cut through the Parkside Asylum (now Glenside Hospital). Every time we'd see a car light coming we'd hide behind a tree. One of the girls rang a relative who rang one of the boys in Kent Town to let them know what was happening, and Maxie Deacon and Johnny Tamberlin were there looking out for us. They gave us some things to take back.

The round trip took about four and a half hours, and we got back to Fullarton pretty late that night. We went back up the balcony steps and the girls inside had left the bolt unlatched so we could get in. Ruby and I were the only ones from our dormitory, and when we got in we heard Patty Unger sobbing in her bed, as she often did. We got undressed quickly, put on our nighties, messed up our beds and ruffled our hair. Then Patty saw us and she woke up properly, looking very confused. She started to cry. When she cried she made very loud, roaring sounds. I've never heard a kid cry like that before, poor little thing. Ruby and I went over to her bed and tried to quieten her down, when the duty officer heard her and came into the dormitory. We pretended we were just up comforting Patty and she fell for it. Ruby and I sighed with relief.

Johnny had got a message back to one of the girls that we'd been there. We got away with it, and I don't remember them giving us any more dares after that.

Army celebrations

Whenever a big donation was received, the Brigadier would visit and we would have a day off school to give thanks. Everyone was dressed up to the hilt and our shoes were polished till you could see your face in them. The children were lined up at the front of the building to greet the officials as their cars pulled into the drive. We would all clap and say together, 'Thank you, Brigadier'. It was like a little party, with cordial and cakes and the brass band played and the children sang for our visitors. The *nunga* girls always sang particularly well and one of the main songs was always 'Ever is the war cry victory, victory and ever is the war cry victory'. I'll never forget that song; I still know all the words.

On occasions like this the officers wore special uniforms with all the regalia, and when I saw all their medals I was transfixed. My mind went flying back to Raukkan and my Nanna gently stroking her son's First World War medal.

Holidays at Raukkan

When school holidays were coming up I'd be on my best behaviour, saying please, excuse me and I beg your pardon all the time, so there'd be no excuse not to let me go home to Raukkan. At Christmas, before we left the Home there was a little gift for each of us to open on Christmas Day. The first year I got a pretty bangle, but it was too big for my wrist and I soon lost it. The second year I got some hankies, a few ribbons and a couple of nice little hair clasps. Most of the items were donated from the People's Stores on Victoria Square.

I had it in for Sister McKenzie. Marj Angas, who took over Sister McKenzie's position, said years later, 'She was a very cold type of person…and totally unsuited to deal with [Aboriginal people]'s problems'.[7] The way I saw it, she didn't help with our problems, she caused them. So every chance I got I made sure I got revenge back on Sister McKenzie. And I did it on quite a lot of occasions. Like one time I visited the Protector's Office. I was waiting for Sister McKenzie at her desk when a man came over and filled up her inkwell and left it on top of her desk. So I pretended to rest on the desk and knocked it over with my elbow. The ink went all over. Another time I remember her taking me somewhere in a taxi. She put me in first and then got in herself. I said, 'Oh I dropped something outside. I've got to get out and get it'. So rather than let me get out myself, she held me back and said she would get it. So when she got round the other side of the taxi,

I pulled the handle up and locked the door. I was sitting there trying not to laugh. I was punished every time, but I just couldn't help myself.

When I got home to Raukkan for the school holidays my Nanna was so glad to see me. Although there wasn't much spare money, we always got Christmas presents at home. Bathers was a regular present or a nice towel to go down to the lake.

At the end of the first year when I returned to Fullarton, we were taken into Adelaide to be fitted for school clothes at a shop called Cravens in Rundle Street. We had to visit the Protector's office first and we saw Sister McKenzie there. I reminded her she said she would let me visit Doris, and she said she would see what she could do.

First visit to Doris

Eventually when I was old enough to be allowed out for the day, I got permission to go and see Doris. I was so dumbfounded I couldn't even cry. I had waited so long for this I couldn't wait. Normally I could go off to sleep quite easily, but after that news every night was restless till the day arrived a week later.

I remember walking over to the Unley railway station. I was excited. I didn't know what to expect. June Campbell took me and Rosie Brumby came along because she was going to see her sisters. She kept saying to me, 'Are you all right Doreen?' I still couldn't believe it was real. I thought it was some kind of trap. Every time the train stopped at a station it seemed to take forever. When we got off the train there was a steep hill, but I was running.

We got to Colebrook Home and Faith Coulthard brought Doris out to see me. I just trembled. She was a little baby, and I sat down with her there on the verandah and told her I was her sister, but she wouldn't accept that. She kept saying that the other girls in the Home were her sisters, not me. No matter how hard I tried to explain that I was her 'real' sister, she wouldn't have it. She didn't know me. I broke down and cried, and Sister Hyde came out and took me inside and gave me a snack. I was allowed to spend about half an hour with Doris and then I walked back down to the Eden Hills station to catch the train back.

It was a sad and confusing journey. After that I was allowed to go up to Eden Hills and see Doris about once every three months.

Return to Fullarton

At the end of my second year, Sister McKenzie came and picked up all the girls and took us back to Raukkan for the Christmas holidays. After the holidays she came back to return us to Fullarton. My cousin Pat Rigney and a couple of other girls were in the same carriage making their way back to work, but again Sister McKenzie made me sit next to her, and I was boiling with rage all the way to Adelaide.

Sister McKenzie was wearing a light knitted top. She used to do a lot of knitting as she was travelling in the train, and she made all her own clothes. She had plenty of time for this because she was always travelling to the different missions to take away the children. Just before we got to Murray Bridge I looked down and spotted a loose strand hanging from the bottom of her jumper. I leaned over and pulled it a little bit. I saw a couple of stitches coming out so I pulled it a bit more and then a bit more. Then I started to quietly roll it. She was reading her pattern book and doing her knitting, so she didn't notice what was going on. It wasn't a very smooth ride on the train and I pretended I was falling over. Every time we were thrown to and fro I'd lean up against her I'd say, 'Oh sorry Sister McKenzie'. Then I'd sit up again and pull the ball around behind her.

I must have done about four or five rows and all of a sudden she started feeling a bit of a chill around her middle. I could see her looking uncomfortable so I thought I'd better stop, so I tucked the ball of wool in behind the seat.

She tried to pull her jumper down but she couldn't. I sat up straight and tapped my feet like I wasn't taking any notice. All of a sudden I heard her shout, 'Oh my goodness!' Half her top was missing and her corset was showing round her midriff. Keeping a straight face, I said, 'Sister McKenzie, what happened to your jumper?' I just cracked innocent, played it cool. I tell you, I ought to have had an Oscar. Then three or four girls sitting a couple of seats back looked round and saw what was happening and they all burst out laughing.

She had a light coat and she reached up to the luggage rack for it. She pulled it on and round her middle and she sat there for the rest of the journey like that. I was thinking that once she gets up she'll find the wool tucked behind the seat and I'll be in strife, so I tried to pull it out and got enough that I could break it and slipped the loose end in her pocket.

We got back to Fullarton without further incident. I thought I got away with it. Then the following Wednesday evening after I'd finished my duties in scullery, I was heading up to bed, and when I got to the landing the officer on duty told me that Sister McKenzie was in the lounge and wanted to see me. I thought, 'Here it comes'. She gave me a big lecture about undoing her jumper and then she told me to go and see Matron Watkins for my punishment. So I went and knocked on Matron's door and she told me to come in and sit down. She was sitting at her desk writing and I sat there waiting for her to explode. She didn't say a word. It seemed like I waited an hour and then she said, 'It's getting into warmer weather'. Then she went back to writing. So I sat there, fidgetty with nothing to fiddle with. After a long time she put her pen down, looked up at me and said, 'The balcony'. I looked at her. She said, 'You know the lino was pulled up last week?' I said, 'Yes Matron'. She said, 'The whole balcony is going to have to be scrubbed. We're looking for volunteers'.

Now Fullarton Girls' Home is a big building, and the verandah at the top went right round the whole Home. 'I'm not offering my services', I thought, 'I'll sit and play dumb'. I sat there twiddling my thumbs, picking at my fingernails. She said, 'I think after what you did to Sister McKenzie, wouldn't you be happy to volunteer, Doreen?' I said, 'No, not really, Matron'. She said, 'Well, I think you'd better do it', and I asked, 'Or else?' She said, 'Or else'. So I had to do it.

Punishment

Normally when the floors were washed there were four girls. Two would wash the floor with hot water and soap, and another two would come behind and mop it up. That was quite easy, but I had to do this all by myself and it was just bare floorboards covered in lots of marks where the lino had been pulled up. I was given a big broom and a scrubbing brush, and I had two and a half days each week for three weeks to do the work. I had to get down on my hands and knees with a little bladed knife to remove all the little pieces of lino, and I was supervised by Captain Goodwin. I finished up with splinters in my hands and they were sore and red and my nails were all broken.

The whole time I was scrubbing the balcony I was talking to myself and growling myself, hating myself that Dad and Nanna would be upset with me and telling myself I'd just have to put up with it. Despite all this, I didn't regret the incident with Sister McKenzie and I still couldn't bring myself to be civil to her.

Trouble

Other girls got into trouble there, but I was trying to get back at the system because I couldn't see why I wasn't allowed to stay at home. If I could work like that at Fullarton, why couldn't I do it in my own home and help Nanna? I kept asking that question of people, but nobody was giving me any answers. On top of that, the white girls used to bully the Aboriginal girls, and the other Aboriginal girls would put up with it because they were scared of getting into trouble. If anything went wrong, the white girls would all point their fingers at the nearest Aboriginal kid and it was impossible to defend ourselves. Nine out of ten times I'd be the one to get blamed, along with an Aboriginal girl from the Port Augusta area. There were two Alice Springs girls there. They were Lilly and Rosie Kunoth. Rosie later acted as Ngarla in the movie 'Jedda'. They were *Anangu* [from the far north of South Australia] and we were *nungas* [from southern South Australia], and some of the white girls were frightened of them. But the older white kids were setting traps and I didn't realise it until I got caught in those traps.

I remember one typical incident in school. We didn't have pens; we were using chalk, crayons and pencils to work with. One of the girls used to turn and poke her tongue out at me and one day she called me 'blacky'. So I stuck her in the leg with a pencil. Of course I got into trouble for that, but I got back at her. Even though she was older and bigger than me, I caught her one day and hit her a couple of times. She didn't hit me back, but she went crying to the officers. This was the white system and you had to get used to it.

The *nunga* kids always got caught if we broke the rules, because the *gunya* [non-Aboriginal] kids would dob us in, so we would have to go to bed early, stand in the corner or have our privileges stopped. Of course every time an Aboriginal girl got into trouble for something they would get reported to the Protector, who would let the superintendent of the mission know and then their parents would hear about it. Dad had to check in at the Protector's office for permission to come and see me and Elsie, and my cousin Edith too after she came into the Home, but if I was bad, he wasn't allowed to visit. But sometimes we could go out for the day and we'd leave just before lunch and be back before tea. We just went down to the Torrens River and sat down there and watched the ducks and swans and then we'd catch the tram back. I loved his visits. He would bring us a little packet of licorice allsorts which was a real treat. But his visits were not often enough for me. Each time he left he'd give me a hug and a kiss and say, 'Be a good girl, my baby'.

Leaving Fullarton

I ended up getting out of Fullarton sooner than I thought.

There were a couple of little girls there called Betty and Shirley Milson. They were nice kids and they had nice ways, but they were starved for friendship, so the *nunga* girls used to look after them. Betty was very tiny with big hips and she wasn't as tall as she should have been for her age. They'd both had polio and they were crippled. Shirley was crippled in her joints and her hands were permanently clenched. It took all her strength to pick anything up. I remember one Christmas they couldn't go home because their mother got sick. Shirley's bed was opposite mine, and she was lying there sobbing, because she was very upset about her mother, so I went over and comforted her until she fell asleep.

Some of the bigger girls would take their lollies from them and make those two girls do their chores and I objected to that. One day I saw them lifting some big buckets of water. I knew they were not supposed to be lifting anything heavy like that, so I asked Shirley what was going on. She wouldn't tell me, so I went over to one of the girls and told her, 'If I catch you making Shirley and Betty do them things, I'm going to dob you in to Matron'.

Without me seeing it, one of the other girls pushed Betty over and the bucket of water went all over her. She looked like a drowned rat. I heard her screaming so I ran round the corner and I saw one of the other girls running. I picked Betty up and got a couple of other Aboriginal girls to take her into the bathroom and wipe her down. Then the lieutenant came out and asked what was going on. The white girls said, 'Doreen's fighting the bigger kids'. Round the corner she came, and sure enough there I was belting those girls.

The Aboriginal girls held the others back while I had one of them nailed to the ground, pulping into her. I heard Lieutenant Jones say, 'Doreen, stop that at once'. She went to grab hold of me and I pulled my arm away. With that she lost her balance and tried to steady herself against the gate leading down to the cellar. Someone must have forgotten to bolt it shut that day, and the gate swung open and down the steps she went. She managed to stop herself from rolling right down, thank goodness, but she broke her arm.

This time I was in big trouble. I was called to Matron Watson's office and told I was going to be expelled because I was uncontrollable. I asked her what 'expelled' meant, and she said I would have to leave the Home. Well I was really glad; I thought that meant they would be sending me back to Raukkan.

4

Unexpected Kindness

The Weekend Australian, 11–12 March 1995

... Ms Kartinyeri tells of the effects on her of the events.

We Ngarrindjeri women decided to reveal we had secrets concerning the Lower Murray River in South Australia, where our people used to live, when it became clear last year the new State Government was determined to build a bridge to Kumarangk (Hindmarsh Island).

They voted unanimously for me to speak for them, because I knew the stories. They voted for me to tell the stories because it was the only way to stop the bridge.

My aunt Rosie, my mother's older sister, and my grandmother told me everything, and that is how I learned about our genealogy.

I sat with my aunt during seventeen years, until she died in 1981 in her early nineties. Some of the other women feel they should have stopped me telling the stories. They're blaming themselves, too.

A lot of Ngarrindjeri people did not know of the women's business and you can blame the Government for converting the people [to Christianity] in the nineteenth century.

I am slowly and gradually putting family trees together now so people can claim their identity.

In the past, people lost their heritage. They could not stop desecration because the whites could stop their rations, or sack them. The old people just had to cry.

But our oral history, they can't take that away. They can't say the black fellas have no culture, because they have their stories, and they are reality, not myth. They are now trying to take them away, by demeaning and talking about our oral history as if it is nothing.

In olden days people would have been punished by killing for breaking Aboriginal law by revealing secrets. I don't thing [sic] that would happen now but people remember stories of these punishments, they date back hundreds of years.

But there are other consequences for us, sickness or possibly death may come. I never experienced them myself but it's what can happen to you when you know things have occurred, when you know any kind of law has been broken.

This is women's business. Men aren't supposed to know about these things. My biggest fear since I told of the secrets has been men finding out. I had to wonder, do I tell? Will they respect the confidence of it? I realised I could only tell if the secrets were kept safe.

Mr Robert Tickner, the federal Minister for Aboriginal Affairs, who had promised to keep the secrets safe, sent them back to Adelaide for the Federal Court case in which the developers, the Chapmans, were appealing against Mr Tickner's ban on the bridge to Kumarangk.

It's white man's law, they had to be presented in the event the judge wanted a woman lawyer to read them.

I got a call last year from Dr Deane Fergie, the woman anthropologist who prepared a report on the women's business for Professor Cheryl Saunders, who in turn reported to Mr Tickner. She told me Professor Saunders felt I hadn't given her the full story, that I was withholding something.

So I stated everything to Professor Saunders in the Aboriginal Legal Rights Movement offices in Adelaide. Those words became the basis of the two confidential letters attached to Dr Fergie's report to Professor Saunders.

I feared Mr Tickner would read the secrets but he promised he would not. But I still had a doubt, that something like the letters getting into the wrong hands would happen.

The public needs to know the full story of our struggle, they know only little parts. It affects all women around Australia. It's been twisted, no one can understand it.

If those who breached the women's confidence were white people in olden days, blackfellas would have speared them for invading women's business.

I'd like to see Mr Ian McLachlan and the Coalition's Aboriginal affairs spokeswoman, Ms Chris Gallus, sacked from Parliament, and the man who did the copying sacked as well.

Getting sacked from Parliament would be only minor compared with what they would have got under our old law. I can only hope although this dreadful thing has happened, these people will be punished.

Where they want to build the bridge is all we've got left. Otherwise they might as well poison us off. The Government has gone everywhere with roads and bridges. Our people have a voice now — don't build that bridge.

The bridge must be stopped. I think the Government owes me that. I am feeling guilty for all my people.

Kumarangk and the surrounding area is the most sacred site we Ngarrindjeri have ever had, it's our Ayers Rock, and we cannot sit back and see it destroyed. I don't want to see our grandchildren deprived of their heritage.

1949

It was just before the school year was about to start in 1949, and I had been given pencils for the first time and a pen and nibs for writing with ink, because I was going into Grade 4. This was a big step up for me, but I never got to use that pen. I had just turned thirteen and I was feeling really good. Not only had I stood up for two little white disabled girls, but I was going home to my family at last. I was sorry that Lieutenant Jones had hurt her arm, but it wasn't my fault that the gate swung open. To me that was an accident.

4 ~ Unexpected Kindness

After breakfast, Lieutenant Appleton made an announcement that I would be leaving that day. All the other Aboriginal girls were hugging and kissing me because they were happy for me that I was going back to Raukkan but sad they weren't going home too. That afternoon Sister McKenzie came for me and all the kids stood on the verandah and waved goodbye.

When she was in Adelaide, Sister McKenzie used to be driven around in a car like a queen. Usually she sat in the front, but that day she got in the back with me and I watched the waving girls through the back window. She sat silent in the car and kept me quiet all the way. I thought she was taking me down to the railway station. It wasn't until we went past it and headed towards North Adelaide that I realised that something was wrong. We pulled up outside a big church in Sussex Street. I saw some high gates and then I knew it was another Home. The caretaker, Mrs Mills, came out of the door of Sussex Street, as it used to be known. She took me into her office and had me stand there while Sister McKenzie told her that I would be there for two weeks. I thought that wasn't so bad, I could hack that for two weeks if I was going home.

Sussex Street was a place where Aboriginal women would live when they came to Adelaide for medical treatment, and I knew some of the women who were there. Aunty Joycie Rigney and her sister Aunty Kate from Raukkan were there at that time, and a couple of women from Point Pearce. There were a couple of tribal women from the far north as well. They spoke to me in English, but when they talked together I couldn't understand them because they spoke in Pitjantjatjara or Antakirinja or Yankunytjatjara.

I stayed at Sussex Street for several days before Sister McKenzie came and picked me up and took me in to the Protector's office. I remember watching Mr Penhall's secretary, a little old lady, sitting there typing on a great big typewriter. I was thinking I must be at the office to get a pass to go home on the train. Sister McKenzie interrupted my thoughts. 'Come this way, Doreen. Mr Penhall will see you now.' We went into Mr Penhall's office and they talked to one another about me. It didn't seem to matter that I was sitting there listening to them.

I heard Sister McKenzie say, 'Barton Vale would be the appropriate place'. Mr Penhall said, 'No I don't think so. She comes from good stock'. I was puzzled by their conversation.

But I knew what Barton Vale meant. It was a girls' reformatory. A couple of people I knew were in Barton Vale. Confusion was setting in again. Eventually Mr Penhall said to Sister McKenzie, 'As soon as I hear I'll notify you', and that was the end of their conversation. Sister McKenzie took me back to Sussex Street.

A few days later she took me into Cox Foyers, a department store in the city, and got me a suitcase and some clothes and a pair of lace-up shoes. Then she took me to the Adelaide bus terminal. She paid for my ticket and told the driver that someone would be at the other end to meet me. As I stepped onto the bus, she handed me a letter and I put it in my pocket. I didn't know anything about what was happening.

Once the bus had started off I took out the letter. On the envelope was written, 'Mr and Mrs George Dunn, per Doreen Kartinyeri'. I didn't know what this meant either, so I put it back in my pocket and forgot about it. It was a warm afternoon so I dozed off a bit, and before I knew it the bus had stopped. I got off and looked around. I thought, 'This doesn't look like Tailem Bend. Where's my Dad?' There was something wrong, but I just couldn't work it out. A nice-looking couple came over to me and politely asked if I was Doreen. They introduced themselves as Joan and George Dunn, and told me that I was in Charleston in the Adelaide Hills and that I was going to be staying with them for a little while. Charleston was only a tiny town with a store, post office, garage and a few houses. They said they would take me back to their farm a few miles out of Charleston for a nice hot drink and a good sleep.

Getting to know the Dunns

They were complete strangers, but they spoke to me so nicely I didn't try to fight them. I got in their car and before long we were in the country and pulling into their farm. By now it was evening, so I couldn't see very much, but when they took me inside, their house looked like a real home. There were family photos on the walls, just

4 ~ Unexpected Kindness

like Mum had at home at Raukkan. Although I didn't know any of the people in them, it made me feel comfortable. They gave me a hot cocoa. I wasn't in the mood to eat anything so we went upstairs and they showed me to my room. It was a small room with a bed, a dressing table, a little wardrobe and a chair. Mr Dunn put my case on the bed and said he had some work to do downstairs and wished me goodnight. I think I answered him, but I was still trying to work out where I was and what was going on.

After he left, Mrs Dunn helped me unpack and she said, 'I suppose I'll get instructions about you tomorrow', and it was then I remembered the envelope. I pulled it out of my jacket pocket and said, 'This must be for you'. So I sat on the bed and she sat on the chair while she opened the envelope and read the letter. Then she folded it and put it back in the envelope and said, 'I'll show you where the bathroom is'. When she'd done this she said, 'You might as well go to bed. You must be exhausted you dear little thing'.

I didn't know what to think. I wasn't used to white people being so nice to me. I thought maybe that meant they were going to put me on the train home the next day.

I didn't sleep well that night; I kept on waking up. I got up and opened the curtains and looked out over the paddocks. I opened the window a little bit and I could hear the cows mooing. It looked like familiar country and I was trying to work out where I could be. I wondered how far from Raukkan I was. Charleston is only about 30 kilometres from Adelaide and 120 kilometres from Raukkan, but it could have been another world away as far as I was concerned. I worked out it was too high for me to jump out of the window, so I sat on the big windowsill and just stared out the window. Next morning Mrs Dunn came and got me for breakfast and when we'd finished eating, she told me what the letter from Sister McKenzie was about. She said, 'You have been placed in our care and control for two years and you will be working here as a domestic'.

I was stunned. I could not think, I could not ask questions. She went on reading, but I didn't hear the words she was saying. All I could hear was that first sentence. She went on and on, referring to the letter in her hand. I wanted to snatch the letter away, but I didn't have the strength to do that. I couldn't even lift my arm. I wanted to see for myself what Sister McKenzie had written about me, but I never did.

Mrs Dunn talked to me about Fullarton. She told me I should be very grateful that I hadn't been put in a reformatory after all the trouble I'd been in. She didn't understand what it was like for me to be in the Home and that I was only in trouble because I had been taken away from my family. Lovely voice, lovely woman telling me these things, but I felt like tearing her hair out. She said that her family made lots of trips into Adelaide and Matron had given permission for me to visit my relatives in Fullarton. She also said that if I was very, very good, I might be allowed to go back home to Raukkan to visit. That's when I realised I wasn't anywhere near home.

She didn't have very much for me to do that day, so she showed me where the library was if I wanted to do some reading, told me to help myself to the fruit basket and left me to look around while she went upstairs for the children. You couldn't have asked for anything better than that from a woman. Rosemary was about five and John was a toddler. They looked at me and smiled, but I wasn't in the mood for smiling. I was too confused. Rosemary wanted to chase me and hung onto my hand with a beautiful little smile on her face, but I just wanted to get away. I was to help keep an eye on them, because Mr and Mrs Dunn were going to be busy with the farm. I was to make my bed and do the dishes. These weren't strenuous duties considering what I'd had to do in Fullarton.

Home away from home

Despite my confusion and disappointment at not going home, in their home I felt kindness, acceptance, protection and respect. I hadn't felt any of those things since I left Raukkan. The Dunns' place was like a home. Fullarton was like a concentration camp to me, because I felt as if I was being punished and I didn't know what I had done wrong.

Mrs Dunn showed me around the farm. In the afternoon Mr Dunn's mother came to meet me from her adjoining farm. She smiled and talked very nice to me and told me she also had one of the girls from

Fullarton with her. I wish I'd known then it was Rosie Brumby. She said she thought Fullarton Girls' Home was bringing up the Aboriginal children very well. I thought to myself, 'Fullarton never brought kids up that well. Some of them finished up in the reformatory, some of them finished up on the streets, some of them finished up going back to broken homes, so that wasn't a good result'.

At that stage no Aboriginal girls from the Fullarton Home had gotten anywhere academically. If my treatment was any example, they had no chance to. Some time after I began to work for Mr and Mrs Dunn, there was an article on the front page of *The Advertiser* about my cousins Una and Pat Rigney, who were at Fullarton. They had been given an IQ test and came out with flying colours.[1] Una was a brilliant student, and those girls opened doors for Aboriginal people to get a better education, because after that the Protector's Department started to talk about letting some of the girls go beyond Grade 7. Una and Pat were allowed to go to high school and high hopes were held for their futures, but they both eventually went out to work like the rest of us. They finished up going back to Raukkan and marrying local fellas there.

I settled in to life with the Dunns. Mrs Dunn was the first white woman who had ever said 'please' and 'thank you' to me. Mr and Mrs Dunn senior were also nice to me. All of a sudden my whole attitude towards white people started to change. Mrs Dunn used to take me into Woodside Library and get me books and I finally really read *Anne of Green Gables* and *Gulliver's Travels*. She encouraged me to read and to get into other things, like tennis and basketball. She used to take me along when she went to Country Women's Association meetings. She would introduce me, but none of them could say 'Kartinyeri' right. She'd say, 'This is Doreen; she's here doing domestic work for us'.

Old Mrs Dunn was really good at knitting and I remember her showing me how to make gloves. On Saturday nights she would pick me up and take me into Woodside to the movies. I told her how when I was up at Tailem Bend we would have to come in the side door and sit in the front seats, separate from the white people in the cinema. She thought that was terrible, but she didn't understand much about how it was for Aboriginal people then. I thought going to the movies was a real treat, but it was also convenient for old Mrs Dunn, who needed a companion.

One time she took me to see a movie about black slaves. They had these black people tied up with cane yokes and they were being forced to dig up the ground. If they slowed down a bit they were flogging them. I watched them blackfellas being flogged in front of their wives and children and I got really upset. Old Mrs Dunn said, 'It's all right dear. It's only a movie'. But she apologised and told me she shouldn't have brought me to see that movie.

When I was with the Dunns for about a week, I overheard Mr and Mrs Dunn talking about Sister McKenzie. Mrs Dunn said, 'I cannot believe they've got a woman of that manner working in Welfare with young children'. To Mrs Dunn, she was always 'that woman'. This put me more at ease with the Dunns because they agreed with me about Sister McKenzie!

One day they took me down to the suburb of Kings Park in Adelaide, where Mrs Dunn's parents, Mr and Mrs Walter Motteram, lived. They too were different to all the white people I knew in my childhood, like all the superintendents and mission workers, not to mention Sister McKenzie. It had got to the point where every time I saw a white face I just felt sick, and I was only a little girl. No child should have to have so much hate in their body, but I had it for white people, and I wasn't brought up to hate. But gradually I came to be glad I had been expelled. Much as I couldn't bear to leave Elsie, I got away from the environment I hated so much and into a kind and friendly family.

The only hitch in this arrangement was when the phone would ring or a letter came from Sister McKenzie or Mr Penhall. It would make me shiver. One of the reasons for my anxiety was that one time Sister McKenzie wrote to Mrs Dunn to let me know that one of the elderly ladies from Raukkan had died. It was a relation to my grandmother Sally, but Sister McKenzie didn't say who it was. I tossed and turned in bed every night wondering who it was. Was it Aunty Martha? Was it one of my other aunties? I was beside myself. It wasn't until Pearl Wilson went back to work for old Mrs Dunn about a month later that she told me who it was. But Sister McKenzie wouldn't give me permission to go back for the funeral.

Visits to Adelaide

In the time I was with Mr and Mrs Dunn I got the chance to go into Adelaide with them often, and I was able to meet up with Elsie. She was working for a Mrs Shannon over near Norwood and would come to stay the night with me at the Motterams, or I could go and spend the night with her, but I wasn't allowed to go out anywhere alone. The Protector still had tight control over me. I met a lot of Mrs Dunn's relatives, and when her sister Mary married I attended her wedding. I also met a lot of white kids in the neighbourhood of Kings Park and made friends with them, and yet I could not get on with a single one of them in the Home.

I was allowed to catch the tram out to the Fullarton Girls' Home to visit the girls. On one trip a young white girl got on the tram and the conductor asked me to stand up and give her my seat. She was about the same age as me and the same size, so I didn't see why I had to stand for her. I said, 'No, if she was pregnant or an older woman I would get out of my chair for her, but I got here before her; I don't have to get up for her'. So the conductor just pulled the cord. I heard, 'Cling, cling' and the tram pulled up. The conductor said, 'Would you mind getting off the tram?' I said no. He said, 'If you don't get off I will have to put you off by force'. So I got off the tram and walked the rest of the way to the Home, just because I wouldn't stand for a white girl.

Mrs Dunn would ask me to do something for her and when I'd done it and done it well she'd say, 'Thanks. That's wonderful'. And I deserved this, because I was never a lazy person. Even as a kid I was always tidying up behind my brothers and sisters and behind Nanna, because Nanna used to have that habit of dropping clothes here and there. Everything I did at Raukkan for my Nanna and my aunties and my father, they'd always say, 'Thank you, my girl'. It was like that on Raukkan. Sometimes *Mutha* Bessie would ask me to pick up her mail for her. I'd drop it off to her and she'd say, 'Oh thank you, my girl. I didn't feel like that little walk today'. All of the boys and girls did things like that and we were thanked for it, so it was nice to be appreciated again, and their recognition gave me back a lot of confidence in myself, even if it didn't stop me crying myself to sleep at night because I missed my family.

I got two shillings and sixpence a week, my first pay. I was still getting clothes by order from the Protector's office, so during that time I saved up enough to buy myself a Box brownie camera and a pushbike. I felt good about this until years later when I was talking to some of the other older girls. They told me that their employers were paying their wages and that when they turned sixteen they got paid their Child Endowment for the time they were in service. So when I turned sixteen I went down to the Protector's Office and they told me that my Child Endowment was going towards my pay, so I was actually working for my own Child Endowment entitlement. Not only did they have an unfair system for Aboriginal people, but some Aboriginal people got more than others.

Visiting Doris

In the Fullarton Home I had been able to visit Doris every three months. Then after I was with the Dunns for a while, I visited her again. She was about three years old now and she still didn't know me as her sister. Years later I found out that all the kids in Colebrook were taught to think of the others as their own brothers and sisters, but I couldn't understand why Doris wasn't told about her biological family as well. It was the church people who put those ideas in the kids' heads, but I was so hurt that my little sister didn't own me.

Lois O'Donoghue tried to explain to Doris that although all the children in Colebrook were her brothers and sisters, she and I had the same mummy and daddy, and over time Doris came to understand, but seeing Doris just occasionally just wasn't enough to help me heal from that terrible rejection.

While I was with the Dunns I was also allowed to go home to Raukkan for holidays, but I still had to write and ask permission of the Protector first. This made me angry because I would have to abide by whatever conditions the Protector laid down. When I went home,

I got hold of some old photos, and next time I visited Doris I took them with me and I showed her. I showed her the one of Mum, me, Connie, Ronnie and Nancy. She didn't want to look at it, but when she finally did, she wasn't in the photo because she hadn't been born, and that made her sure she wasn't my sister.

When I got older I understood how hard it must have been for her, but at that time I was still only young myself. Oscar told me that when he went to see her he got the same reaction. It wasn't until she had left Colebrook and was out working for a couple of years that Doris really acknowledged me as her sister. She would have been about sixteen and I was a young married woman by then, with a couple of kids of my own.

My time with Mr and Mrs Dunn was really good. I got to realise that the hate in my heart shouldn't be there. I stopped blaming God for taking Mummy and Nancy away. I started to feel different, but I kept it to myself, because blackfellas never used to show their feelings in the olden days. You just lived day to day and only got emotional when you lost someone in the family. By now Dad started to see there were nice white people too. He was sent out to work on the railways at Coonalpyn where he worked with some German immigrants. He told us all, 'I never thought I'd ever meet a white man that I could shake their hand. By gee I met a lot of mates up there'.

Move to Adelaide

After two years and two months the Dunns asked me if I would like to go into Adelaide and work for the Motterams in Kings Park. Mrs Motteram wasn't well and needed someone young in the house to look after her. I liked Mrs Motteram so I agreed, but as usual I had to ask Mr Penhall's permission. I was fifteen now and so fed up with having to get his approval for everything, I simply told him this was my plan.

Mrs Motteram had a gardener and a woman who would come in and do all the heavy work, like stripping the beds and doing the washing. I was more or less there for company, and she was great to be with. She had a really good sense of humour and was very easy going, but she used to become frustrated at having to get about in a wheelchair.

I'd say, 'Come on, I'll take you out for a little spin in the yard', and she'd say, 'No, you're a dangerous driver', but she enjoyed it. They had a lovely garden and a beautiful big home. Mr Motteram used to bring home packets of broken biscuits for me, and when I went back to Raukkan I took a tin of these chipped biscuits for my family and they thought it was wonderful.

I would read to Mrs Motteram. When I struggled with a big word she would tell me how to pronounce it, and in that way she helped me a great deal with the education I had previously been denied. I was also taken along to social occasions. I would sit quietly and watch people and I didn't talk much. Sometimes they would ask me questions about where I was from and what the mission was like and I'd tell them that when my mother died I was taken away by the government and put in a Home.

On weekends I was allowed to go into Adelaide and meet up with Elsie and Pansy Wilson and some Point Pearce girls who were working at St Peter's College and Prince Alfred College. Some girls were also working in the Queen Victoria Hospital, which was known as 'The Queen's Home' then. We used to meet at Beehive Corner on Rundle Street (Rundle Mall now) and spend our Saturdays and Sundays down at the River Torrens as well as the Botanic Gardens and the Zoo. In those days Aboriginal people didn't have to pay to get into the Zoo. I don't know how that rule came about, but later on when I was researching the archives I was reading the government expenditures for 1889 and I found that the Adelaide Zoo received more funding than the Aboriginal Protection Board that year. No wonder Aboriginal people didn't have to pay to go into the Zoo; we were obviously considered less important than the animals!

In those days there was a koala farm near the Zoo and some Aboriginal boys worked there, including my cousins Theo Kartinyeri, Jimmy Rankine (Coco) and Henry Long. Apart from koalas, they had some other small animals and a giraffe there, because that's where sick animals from the Zoo were kept while they recovered. One time, one of the Aboriginal workers took some time off when he was sick, and he wasn't paid for it because he didn't realise he had to produce a doctor's certificate. So all the Aboriginal workers got angry. In retaliation they let the animals out and there were all these animals running around Adelaide.

A lot of the Aboriginal girls were really nice-looking girls, and men would like to come and talk to them, particularly men in uniform — soldiers, sailors and airmen. I was the youngest and I wasn't interested in boys, so the older girls would want to get rid of me. I always had to be home early anyway, so some girls would walk me up King William Street and I'd catch the tram back to Kings Park.

Back to Raukkan

I was with the Motterams for about three months when my Nanna became ill. She wrote to me and asked if I could go home to Raukkan to look after her. I showed the letter to Mrs Motteram and just like that she agreed to let me go. I stayed at Raukkan for a couple of weeks to care for Nanna and then returned to Kings Park, but it was only a couple of months later that Nanna took another turn for the worse, and Mrs Motteram and I decided I was needed at home permanently. I arranged for Edie Rigney to take my job. It was September 1950, and at fifteen and a half years old I was finally returning home. The Protector still had charge and control over me, so I don't know why he let me go at this point, but I think my Nanna might have finally persuaded him she really needed me. I was happy enough with the Dunns and the Motterams and it changed my outlook on life, but there was nothing like going back to my family and my home again. It was wonderful to be back with my grandparents. I sat with my grandmother a lot, and her sister, Granny Ada we used to call her, as well as her brother Gerry, both of whom were now living with us at Raukkan.

They told me that my mother's mother grew up on Poonindie and moved to Raukkan with her parents when she was thirteen years old. The superintendent got my grandmother a job with a Dr Wigby in Glenelg, and apparently she fell pregnant for him so they returned her to Raukkan where my Auntie Connie was born. My grandmother would have only been about fourteen or fifteen at the time. This was the sort of thing that was happening to a lot of young Aboriginal girls in those days and they just had to accept it. The Aboriginal families had to deal with it and the white bosses were never charged with any offence.

There wasn't much to go around on Raukkan, so if only I'd known at the time that I had three pounds eight shillings and eight pence in a bank account [about $1000 in today's terms]. I only found this out when I was doing research for this book and came across a letter in the Protector's records from the manager of the Savings Bank of South Australia at Strathalbyn to Mr Penhall, dated 18 January 1950. The bank manager wrote to advise that the Narrung and Point McLeay bank agencies had been closed and amalgamated with the Tailem Bend branch. He asked whether the amounts in the accounts should be paid out to us, or whether we wanted new accounts opened at the Tailem Bend branch. There is no record of Mr Penhall's reply, but there were twenty-five of us on that list, and to this day I have never seen a penny of that money. Whatever happened to it, I have no idea.

Mother's Day

Mother's Day was a very special day at Raukkan. The church was packed. It was entirely different from any other service I ever went to. Outside on the verandah there were big buckets of white chrysanthemums standing in water, and everyone who was walking in would be given a flower and a dress-making pin. On the front of the altar was the word 'Mother' written in a light green material in block letters, and we would all file in and pin up our flowers on the fabric, and when it was all filled in the word 'Mother' would be spelt out in white chrysanthemums. The hall would be packed, with the kids up the front and the parents behind and a few white people from Narrung and Poltalloch would join in. It was all very beautiful, a sing-and-rejoice sort of thing, but it was very emotional for me, having lost my mother.

Salvation Army again

About this time the Salvation Army came in to Raukkan and took over from the Congregationalists, and their church services were entirely different. I didn't like the change because the Salvation Army introduced confession, which didn't sit right with me. You'd have a minister standing up in the pulpit preaching to the people about all the things people have done wrong in this world, all the sins and all the crimes that have been committed, and how God Almighty was the one to forgive you for this. There would be a break in the service for anyone who felt they had sinned to make a confession to God and ask his forgiveness and become converted.

I didn't feel as if I needed to go and ask God to forgive me for my sins. I didn't think I'd committed any. The Salvation Army way made me feel bad. At home my family all prayed and said our prayers at night and we always said grace before each meal. That was what Christianity meant to me, what we'd do in the home and how we'd respect one another, not converting and confessing. I preferred to look at the way old *Mainu* David [Unaipon] lived and the other old men like Ricken McHughes and Dulcie Wilson's grandfather Ted Rigney. They were good-living Christian men. They'd always help people and lived like real gentlemen.

I liked the old way of having church, because you'd hear the prayers and they'd ask you if you'd like to read something from the bible. We'd get up and we'd read a passage, and it left you leaving the church feeling good.

Three Miles

On weekends I would go with my brother and sister to visit Aunty Connie, who lived at the Three Miles out from Tailem Bend, and it was a really nice little outing. I remember one time I had something my brother Squashy and my cousins Wilfie and Mattie Kartinyeri wanted, but I wouldn't let them have it. I was just about to dive into the river at our swimming hole and they sang out, 'Sister McKenzie's coming!' I got such a fright I scampered up the tree, grabbed the willow branches and swung out and dived right into the middle of the river so that Sister McKenzie wouldn't see me. I didn't know what she might be coming for, but I wasn't going to wait around to find out.

Just as this was happening, my cousin Mavis was coming down the cliff and saw me diving into the water. I wasn't in any difficulty, but I was too far out when I surfaced. We were never allowed to swim where we couldn't grab hold of the willow roots if we got a cramp or got caught in the current. When I eventually swam back into shore, Mavis was sitting on the bank waiting for me. She said, 'You know you're not allowed to do that. I'll have to tell my mummy and Aunty Connie'. I said, 'Where's Sister McKenzie?' She didn't know what I was talking about. Then we heard the boys laughing. They had been pulling my leg because I hadn't given them what they wanted. Mavis understood why I had dived out into the deep water, so she said she wouldn't tell. She felt sorry for me. She had never been taken away from her family; none of Aunty Laura's children were, even though Sister McKenzie did keep an eye on them.

From time to time I would go into Adelaide, usually to sign papers required by the Protector. Once I was returning home when the train was delayed because of an obstruction on the line, and I didn't get into Tailem Bend until it was too late to catch the Mail, so I stayed overnight with Mavis. Mavis was keeping company with Keith Humphries who drove the Mail, and next day she told me they were heading down to Marangoon and asked me if I wanted to go along. Mavis said she would make sure they got me on the Mail that afternoon.

So we jumped in Keith's little old battered ute, and when we got to Marangoon there were some men waiting there with a dinghy. Next minute I see Keith Humphries pulling the old leather car seat forward and he dug out six or seven flagons of wine. I was shocked. Aboriginal people weren't allowed to drink and they weren't allowed to be in possession of alcohol unless they were exempted. Mavis was exempt, but I wasn't, and I was scared, I tell you. Next minute I see them pull out a big chaff bag. They put the flagons in the bag, tied the bag off the back of the boat so it was towed along unseen under the water, and they rowed into Raukkan with all this alcohol.

I was very eager to get on that bus, so Keith and Mavis drove me over to the main road. I saw a vehicle coming down the road. It was the bloody police from Meningie. My body just went limp. Mavis said,

4 ~ Unexpected Kindness

'Put a smile on your face, Dodo'. The police car pulled up and Mavis said, 'How are you going, sergeant? We just pulled up so Doreen can catch the Mail. Has it left Tailem Bend yet?' I was too frightened to open my mouth, not knowing what might come out of it. I looked at Mavis and she was so calm and talking nice to the police officer. He said, 'No, it's on its way. Will you girls be all right?' 'Yeah, we're right. See you sarge.' I still couldn't speak as they drove away.

I was really upset with Mavis, but then the Mail arrived. Mavis gave me a hug and a kiss and said, 'See you, my *thatha* [sister]', and I said, 'Yeah, and next time I'll make sure I'm not in this position again'.

When the Mail got to the punt, I'll be blowed if the police weren't there searching blackfellas for drink. They were pulling all their things out of the cars. They looked in the bus, but found no alcohol and the bus was allowed to go through. We drove onto the ferry and I was sitting there feeling guilty as hell. While we were waiting, Aunty Dorrie Kartinyeri, who was also on the bus, started to get cross with the police. She said, 'Those bloody *kainggaiparis* [policemen] are always searching us for *muthu* [wine]'. Then as the ferry takes off she reaches under her blouse and pulls out a little bottle filled with wine and takes a little nip! Well I was going weak at the knees, because Aunty Dorrie wasn't exempted, so she would have gone to jail if she'd been caught.

The ferry reached the other side with a big jerk as it hit the bank, and I fell over. Aunty Dorrie said, 'Look out, don't fall on that bread there, Dodo; nobody wants squashed bread'. Once the bus was driving off the ferry, Aunty Dorrie asked young Paddy Rankine to pass over her two high-top loaves. The bus continued on and Aunty Dorrie had those two loaves clutched in her arms. Then I saw her pull the two loaves apart and take out two bottles of wine!

By the time we got into Raukkan I was ready to collapse, I was so scared. Aunty Dorrie wrapped up the bottles of wine in something, put them in her bag and packed it at her feet until the bus stopped outside her house and she got off. I was pleased to see the back of her.

As we headed down towards the Post Office I was thinking, 'All I need now is to see that bloody dinghy pull up and them fellas walk over that hill there from the jetty with their flagons and I'll faint'.

I was terrified because there I was, not yet sixteen, watching them smuggle alcohol into Raukkan. I allowed myself one look up the hill they'd be coming over, and I thanked God that I couldn't see any sign of those men.

The men obviously got their haul in okay, because that night a big fight started up. We all got up out of bed to see what the commotion was. Nanna said to Dad, 'Don't you go down there now son, that's *mendhun* [fighting] going on'. It wasn't often that I saw people under the influence of alcohol on Raukkan, but when people got hold of drink they couldn't seem to handle it sociably and the men would get aggressive. I was too tired to care by then. After my day I should have slept for a month.

I really enjoyed the social interaction with the other teenagers on the mission. To go down to the lake for a swim, we would have to climb Big Hill, and at the top of the hill we used to stop and sit around and we'd be *yanun* [talking]. The girls were up there one beautiful sunny afternoon and we were looking out towards the hills at Mount Barker and Mount Lofty. We all knew the story about the *krawi ko:mi* [big man] lying in the initiation position in the landscape and that Mount Barker and Mount Lofty represented his knees. Sitting over on the hill on Raukkan on a nice clear day you can see it as plain as anything. You can even see the formation of his stomach, chest, head and neck. You can also see another part of his anatomy! The girls started to giggle.

The next minute we heard some boys coming up the hill on what we call Lovers' Lane. It's a little track with *kathari* [prickle] bushes growing on either side. There was Robert Walker, Jack Sumner, Fred Sumner, Spencer Rigney and Clarrie Long and a few others. The boys came up and were kicking around with us giggling girls and they said, 'Oh, *nakun* [look] over there at the *krawi mra:ni*'. We knew what they were saying. Then they said, 'We've got *krawi* ones like that too', and were carrying on. The girls were all gushing and laughing and acting childish. I was getting shamed. I said, 'You fellas shouldn't talk like that in front of us girls', and we became so embarrassed we decided

4 ~ Unexpected Kindness

it was time for our swim, so we all ran down to the lake and jumped straight into the water.

When I was sixteen, Jack Sumner became my first boyfriend. I adored him and he adored me. Then Dad told me that we were related (our mothers were first cousins) and forbade me to see Jack. I was heartbroken, but my interest in kinship and genealogies blossomed after that. I was intrigued with who could see who, and hungry to find out as much about family trees as I could. I didn't write anything down; I just kept it all in my head.

My first job after I returned to live with my Nanna and *Mainu* at Raukkan was working for Mr and Mrs Ross Swalling. He was the superintendent then and I worked for them as a domestic. I wasn't earning much, but at least it was a job. I didn't like them; I was their little black lackey. Most of my pay would go to buy whatever was needed in the store because my father was working off the mission and my grandparents were only living on rations. They couldn't get a pension because they were Aboriginal, and although they got Child Endowment for my younger brother and sister, that was controlled by the superintendent on the mission. I used to supplement my wages by making feather flowers, baskets and mats and selling them.

It was while I was working for the Swallings that the Sturt Re-enactment took place in early 1951. Mr Swalling was asked if the Raukkan people would like to be involved. It was to finish with the opening of the Sturt monument, which stands at Raukkan today on top of the hill. The journey was to be enacted the way it was described day by day in Sturt's diaries as he travelled down the river in 1830 from the other side of Mildura with a small crew of men. When the party reached Raukkan they were met by a band of Ngarrindjeri men who were dressed in body paint and threw spears at them. The superintendent agreed that the mission people would participate, despite what the blackfellas on Raukkan thought of Sturt. They saw him as an invader just like Captain Cook, and they were very unhappy about what had happened to Aboriginal people since that invasion took place.

Grannie Pinkie Mack was the cultural advisor to the men who were performing, so they sat down with her and she taught them the right corroboree songs and the *pata winema* dance. None of the women were allowed to take part.

It was a lovely day that the re-enactment party reached Raukkan, and it was a beautiful turnout. The event was recorded by ABC Radio and appeared on the news in Adelaide. That night we all listened to the radio and it came over very clear. The highlight of the event was the landing at Raukkan. The Army was there to accompany the boat, and we stood on the shore watching as they came in. We saw the main boat and then these army boats coming towards the shore. Then all of a sudden these big boats kept coming up onto the sand and kept on going. We'd never seen an army duck before, so we all screamed and scattered everywhere. The old ladies tried to run, but kept falling over in the sand, and the children were covered in sand and crying because they were so frightened. They didn't realise a boat could also be driven up onto land. Cameras were clicking everywhere. I told Mr Swalling afterwards that we should have been informed about this, because some of the little boys ran away and hid and couldn't be found for quite some time.

The role of Sturt was played by an English actor, Grant Taylor. The evening before, he and about sixteen other cast members came for dinner at the Swallings' and I helped prepare the meal and waited on them at the table. He and the other cast members were very nice to the Raukkan people. Mr Swalling asked me to read some of the script for the following day, and I was horrified that the men were going to throw spears at Grant Taylor, but Mr Swalling assured me that it was all pretend. I was hoping that the men — who included my brother Oscar — would remember this!

After the re-enactment was over we all went across the barrage to Kumarangk, where we had a big feed and a corroboree and a sing-song.

I finished up working for the Swallings, and became a foster mother to my cousins Ron, Heather and Bobby Rankine at age sixteen. And Heather still called me Mum to the day she passed away suddenly not long ago.

5

A Hollywood Life

1995

If I had known what was to happen, before I got involved with the Kumarangk bridge business, I would absolutely have done the same thing no matter what. I'm a fighter. But one thing that bothered me was that I could feel my hatred for white people coming back. Over the years I have got to know a lot of white people and I have many white friends. But I never knew people could be so narrow-minded, ignorant and nasty. My supporters and I were getting racist hate mail and the media turned on us. They took to calling me 'Mrs' Kartinyeri, even though it wouldn't take much to find out that Kartinyeri is my birth name. At the same time I was an 'activist' and making all the women's knowledge up. What for? Some had it that the men had put words in my mouth. It just wasn't possible for the white public to accept that I was a custodian of traditional women's knowledge.

I thought there was a lot of prejudice against blackfellas when I was growing up, but it's still here. And the minute Aboriginal people start speaking out for their culture and heritage and history, the first thing white people say is, 'Oh they just want the land'. They're only concerned they might lose what they wrongfully took from us all those years ago when Captain Cook came to Australia. When Native Title came in, there was a big fuss because white people thought they were going to be kicked off their properties. But Aboriginal people just want access to go to their hunting grounds and the farmers was bolting the gates and keeping them out. People in the cities thought that their homes would be claimed, but that isn't going to happen. Aboriginal people are only asking for respect for our culture. We just want to be able to share the land that has always been so precious to us, not take it away. All I was asking was that they don't desecrate the land and waters that my tradition says must be treated with great care.

I prayed to God that my hate wouldn't come back like it used to, and because I had been all over the country in recent years and seen all the things I'd seen and talked to the people I'd talked to, I realised there will always be black and white in this world and I was brought up not to hate.

1951

Looking after Ron, Bobby and Heather was just the beginning of my fostering career. I started looking after my cousin Topsy's three boys, Eddie, Dick and Wayne, while Topsy was expecting the birth of her next baby. Topsy and Lester Rigney were living in a de facto relationship and therefore weren't allowed to live on Raukkan, and she wasn't allowed to go into the hospital to have her baby, so she did what a lot of the women did and went to Aunty Laura's shack at Three Miles so Aunty Laura could deliver her baby.

At the same time my cousin Sarah Jackson (née Rankine) was also expecting a baby, and I was helping her out as well. I was running down to her place every day doing the washing in an old hand-pump washing machine and hanging it out. I'd hang up her things, take Nanna's and Eddie, Dick and Wayne's clothes back to our house and hang them up to dry. Come half past three in the afternoon I'd be running down to Sarah's again to bring the clothes inside and wait for the big kids to come home from school. I was constantly going all day, and about six o'clock every night I'd grab the kids and throw them in the big old tub. I used to have to fill the copper outside, strip the kids down and argue them into the bath. Then I'd get them into bed.

After that I'd go and tend to Nanna and my grandfather, and by the time I'd finished that and emptied the water out and propped the tub up against the wall, I was exhausted. That was my routine for about nine months.

But I loved them to think that they trusted me to look after their children and I looked after them well. Topsy and I were always dearest sisters and friends until she died. I was only sixteen, but my mothering instincts were always there, even though I'd never had a steady bloke, never had sex. I wasn't worried about that. I believed I would know when the time was right for that and when it was I would get on with my own life.

After a while, my cousin Stella's husband Jim Cross called in at Raukkan on his way back from shearing, and he suggested I go with him to see Point Pearce play in the football grand final. I needed a holiday, so I decided to go. It was my second trip to Point Pearce since my sister Nancy died in 1943. Aunty Rosie wasn't yet exempted, so she and Uncle Nat still lived on the mission. I met up with her and my Nanna's brother, great-uncle Wilf Varcoe, and his wife Holly and a lot of other people.

Back at Raukkan, in the second week of December, Bruce Rumbelow brought me a message from Topsy to take her boys up to Three Miles because the baby was due. Aunty Laura sent the big boys away for a few days, so there was just us women and the kids. I got out my *Phantom* and *Felix the Cat* comics and read them while I waited.

That night Eddie and Dick went to sleep, but Wayne played up. So I brought him outside with me and I set an old rug on the floor and he and I played knucklebones with stones while I waited. Next minute Aunty Laura said, 'Light up that fire, my girl'. Aunty Laura had put some nice big chunks of charcoal in an old screw-top biscuit tin and poured some kerosene over them. To start the fire quickly, I poured the coals over the pine cones and stacked wood and lit it, and immediately there was a lovely fire.

I was nervous because I'd never ever seen a baby born in my life. Then Daughter was born. She was named Janice, but always known as Daughter. Aunty Laura called me in to have a *nakun* [look]. I picked her up and put her in the little box that was her crib. Aunty Laura told me to soak the sheets in the cold water drum. I had to stir them with a big broom handle. Then I went back into the caravan and I saw something near the windowsill at the back of the caravan and I went to see what it was. Aunty Laura said, 'Leave that alone. Don't touch that'. It was the afterbirth. Aunty Laura showed me the cord that connects the baby to the mother's *pulangi* [navel].

Aunty Laura was an excellent *puthari* (midwife). She had all her own equipment, the women had faith in her and she coped very well. We were all very excited. Topsy already had eight children and now another little girl. I thanked God I had only been there for the one! It was quite an eye-opener for a young teenage girl.

It was a wonderful experience to be there when Daughter was born, but that was it for me and mothering for the time being. I thought if I was meant to be mothering I might as well get married and have my own children! Of course that didn't mean I wanted to rush off and get married. All in good time and in my own way. But Sarah had her baby soon after Daughter was born, and I thought it was time for me to move on.

The opportunity came up to go over to Point Pearce again, and I snapped up the chance. By this time Aunty Rosie had got exempted, so she and Uncle Nat were living off the mission. Aunty Rosie had a bad hip, and they told her if she got exempted she would be able to go in and get treatment to correct it. So she got her exemption and went into the hospital, but they said there was nothing they could do for her because the bone had already set. So she was dismissed from the hospital and she had to wait until all the exemptions was actually abolished in 1962 before she was able to go back onto the mission. That old lady spent more than ten years away from her family because of that.

Along with a number of other Aboriginal families, they were living at Hollywood, near Reef Point, right on the beach front. Hollywood got its name because a lot of the exempted people thought they were big shots — like movie stars. They all lived in little tin shacks, which were very nicely done out. They had no electricity, so they used wood stoves, and a couple of the women had kerosene fridges. Aunty Rosie had an old ice box and they had to go into Port Victoria to get blocks of ice for it.

I stopped on the mission with my cousin Aileen Wilson and her husband Mark. Aileen's father, my mother and Aunty Rosie were brother and sisters, and Aileen and I were very close. On the weekends all the young boys and girls would jump on the horses and ride out to Hollywood, and I'd spend the weekend with Aunty Rosie. That's when I really began to get to know her well. Kim Kropinyeri said that we were two of a kind. My sisters Doris and Connie are like our Mum, but I'm more like Aunty Rosie, and there was a wonderful bond between us.

She had the most marvellous way of expressing herself, and as we worked together on the weaving or making feather flowers she would teach me many things. She started at that time to talk to me about kinship, all the people on Raukkan and other yarns. She taught me all about the old ways. She told me how they used to initiate the young girls to get them ready for sex. She told me boys were prepared for first sex too, but women had no details of that. Aunty Rosie told me Auntie Laura knew these things too, even though she was a bit younger. She had been through the initiation and all the girls a bit younger than her, before it was stopped by the white staff on Raukkan. Just Aunty Rosie and me, weaving and yarning. She made it very, very clear I was not allowed to tell anyone else any of this information.

It was on those rides down to Hollywood that I also first met Terry Wanganeen, who was to become my husband and the father of my nine children.

While I was at Point Pearce I kept myself by getting a job at the Maitland Hotel, where they were taking on Aboriginal girls in the kitchen, cleaning rooms and doing the laundry, so I did a few of those kind of jobs.

During this visit to Point Pearce, I experienced the death of Aunty Rosie's grandson Jimmy, who was a twin to Joy. I remember Mark and

Cyril came running down for Aileen. So we ran up there and Jimmy was dead. They had him laid out on the bed. They sent someone down to Hollywood to pick up Aunty Rosie and bring her to the house. It was so sad. He was a corker little kid, and Aunty Rosie was quite hysterical.

When I returned home after a couple of months, I knew I just had to get away from Raukkan, because though I loved my Nanna dearly, I couldn't handle her continuous crying. I used to jump into bed behind her and she'd stroke me and pat my hair and talk to me, but it was really starting to get to me, so I talked to Aunty Martha one day and asked her what I should do. Aunty Martha told me there was nothing more I could do for Nanna; that I just had to let her go.

When I look back now, I'm upset Nanna never got proper treatment for her depression. There should have been more done to help her. She shouldn't have suffered like that all those years.

Grape picking

After Christmas and my seventeenth birthday in February 1952, I headed up the river to go grape picking. Lila and Elsie were living down on the flats by the river just over a mile out of Berri, where there was quite a lot of work fruit picking, and Lila had written to tell me about it. The pay was a bit better than I'd had before, so I decided to give it a go. Soon after I got there, Nanna's youngest son, Uncle Francie (nicknamed Uncle Buddha), got into a fight, and when he fell, his head hit the corner of a brick and he died from his wounds. Nobody had any money to take him back to Raukkan, so they buried him in Mildura. I could just imagine my Nanna's grief then.

I stayed with Elsie and her husband Freddie in their little wood-framed house with hessian walls. Paint was hard to come by so the walls were painted with calcimine. It was a powdery substance that you mixed up into a paste, and we used crepe paper to dye it and paint the walls in different colours. Photographs were pretty scarce in those days, so we got little packets of chewing gum in the shop with pictures of all the old movie stars. I would tie sticks together to frame the pictures and then cover them with cellophane and hang them up to decorate the walls of the house. It looked really nice. We didn't have much, so we became quite clever at using what we had to brighten up our surroundings.

I worked at grape-picking from the end of February to about June. Then I got a job in Percy Slaughter's packing shed at Barmera. We dried the grapes to sultanas, currants and raisins, and they had to be packed into boxes to go to the markets. There was a big conveyor belt and I packed the fruit into boxes, someone else sealed them and another person stencilled the boxes. It was back-breaking work, especially for me because I was a *minya* [little] one and I had to stand up to reach the table. And I couldn't stand the dried fruit anyway.

So I moved over to Barmera and stopped with Aunty Gertie Goldsmith, who was a cousin to my Dad. The boss of the shed was Bob Bickmore. I became friendly with his daughter Wendy, and her brother Graham and I became very pally.

We used to go to the movies together and Graham took me out to the block [orchard] on his motorbike. One Easter weekend Graham and Wendy and I were down at Lake Bonney. It's a pretty spot. At Easter time they had a showground down there, a big ferris wheel, lucky dips, darts, knock-em-downs and all that, and it was a really lovely turn. We were sitting down looking out over the lake. At the time I knew a bit about sacred sites around there, but I didn't say anything to those whitefellas about what I knew. Then Graham told me that a couple of years earlier after a big storm, some Aboriginal people's remains were found floating in the lake. When they were taken into Adelaide by the police for forensic analysis they were found to be about a hundred years old. According to Graham it was well known that when white people first came to the area, they used to get rid of the blackfellas by knocking them on the head and throwing them into the lake to drown. He said he'd heard his father talking about this when he was a little boy.

I was angry that those *gunyas* had kept quiet about it, and I told Graham how I felt. Well that scared him, and he made me promise not to tell anyone he told me.

Graham wanted to marry me. He bought me a nice little ring and I threw it in Lake Bonney. It must still be there.

Relationship with Terry

While I was working in Barmera I ran into Terry Wanganeen again. There were a lot of Point Pearce young people doing seasonal work in the Riverland, and I got to know them very well, including Terry's sister May and his cousin Pearl Goldsmith. Terry and Peter Goldsmith both had motorbikes. One Saturday I was sitting down by the lake listening to Aunty Sudi sing. Aunty Sudi was Gwen Natoon from Raukkan, and she had a beautiful singing voice. They used to call her the Black Melba. She often sat down there on the shores, and people would stand round and listen to her. She was really a beautiful, happy-go-lucky woman and we were always glad to see her. I was wearing a pair of shoes that were hurting my heels. So I took my shoes off on the lawn. When Aunty Sudi finished singing she got up and left without me realising she was wearing my shoes!

Some of the guys from Norm Smith's block arrived, so I asked Terry if he'd go and pick up a pair of shoes from Aunty Gertie's for me. So all the girls waited there and Terry brought my shoes back for me. We finished up sitting together in the pictures that day. It was such a simple thing.

In 1953 we borrowed Peter Goldsmith's car and made a trip over to Raukkan. It was good to catch up with my grandparents and family again. Connie and Ronnie had grown up quite a bit, but it was sad to see my grandmother's health failing and I couldn't be there for her.

Then in early 1954 I found out I was pregnant. I was proud that now I was to be a mother. Terry and I decided to get married, but I wasn't going to have the wedding at Raukkan, because I was still carrying resentment towards some members of my family who I believed didn't want me after Mummy died. This was another way the Protector affected Aboriginal families. Taking children away caused divisions in families that often took many years to resolve, if at all. So because Terry was from Point Pearce and I now had many happy associations there, we decided to get married at Point Pearce and live there.

Point Pearce

Terry was earning good money compared to other Aboriginal people at the time, so he gave me the money to send to Raukkan to bring my grandparents over for the wedding. I had to go into town and get a money order, and I sent it to Raukkan with a letter explaining to them how to get it cashed at the office. They wouldn't have known what a money order was; they lived off rations and barely ever handled money. I wasn't much more experienced myself. With one of my cousins along to help them, my grandparents and younger brother and sister caught the train into Adelaide and the bus to Point Pearce, and they thought it was wonderful being taken all that way.

Doris was only nine and still in Colebrook Home, so I had to apply to the Protector to bring her over for the wedding, but he wouldn't grant me the permission. Earlier when I was working at Berri I made a bit of money and put a few bob away because I wanted to take Doris to Raukkan to see Nanna and *Mainu*. The Protector didn't grant me the permission then either. As a result my Nanna died not even meeting Doris. It was so cruel.

My cousin stayed for the wedding and then went back to Raukkan, but we organised for my grandparents' rations to be transferred to the store at Point Pearce, and they stayed on for about two months. They loved it. They lived with Aileen (their eldest grandchild) and Mark. Aileen was a woman you could look up to and admire. She was always involved with meetings on the mission and she was there to give me the support I needed.

It was a nice quiet little wedding, on 23 October 1954, a lovely spring day. We got married in the Methodist church in Maitland and my father gave me away. My cousin Elva was my bridesmaid and my brother Oscar was Terry's groomsman. At that time Oscar was shearing around the Point Pearce district, and was starting to see Terry's cousin Ellen Milera, who he later married. I wore a nice pale blue suit and a little cling hat with a tiny little veil. I had short hair that curled up at the edges of the hat and I sewed a couple of pearl beads at the back which hung down over my hair. Terry wore a black suit and a smart white shirt.

We had our reception at Aunty Sarah Graham's place, because she had a lovely great big lounge room and could fit quite a lot of people around the table. When they had a turnout like that, everybody would throw in for it. They were good like that at Point Pearce. Aunty Sarah decorated a nice little cake for us, but we weren't allowed to have alcohol, so wedding ceremonies weren't toasted with champagne like they were in the white community. It was a quiet luncheon at the table, and friends and relatives popped in to congratulate us. But my biggest pleasure was having my grandparents and Connie and Squashy there.

Nobody had honeymoons in those days, so it was straight back to work for Terry, and I went about setting up home in the two front rooms of Terry's father's house while we waited for our baby to be born. Terry's father, brother Raymond and sisters Lorna and Kathy shared three of the other four rooms of their six-room house. I got on very well with them. Kathleen was a delicate little girl, nice looking with a good sense of humour, and Raymond was a lovely boy. He just did everything he could to please his brother and me. May was away working and Terry's brother Everett was in hospital with tuberculosis, but on the whole I thought they were lucky they hadn't been taken away when their mother died, like I was.

There was still no electricity on the mission for another nine years, so there were no fridges, no washing machines, no televisions. We had a wood stove, same as at Raukkan, and the men would go out to where the stump pickers had finished working, and using great big handsaws they'd cut the wood and deliver a percentage of it to each household. The four-room houses also had an open fireplace, but people couldn't afford any floor coverings like lino, so the floors were just cement. Water was carted from the various wells around the mission and we had a copper to heat it for washing.

The running of Point Pearce was very much the same as Raukkan, but there wasn't quite as much religion. On Raukkan there was just the Congregational church, and then in later years Salvation Army, and services were conducted during the week and all day on Sunday. On Point Pearce they had Lutheran, Methodist and Church of

England ministers from the district coming in to conduct Sunday services only. Some things were similar, but the social life was better on Raukkan. On the other hand, Point Pearce wasn't so isolated as Raukkan and there was a lot more interaction with the local white community.

Most of the men on the mission worked as shearers, and with the help of shearing contractors Aboriginal men were in demand. The farmers didn't have to pay as much as for white shearers because Aboriginal people were the lowest paid workers in Australia, they put in a full day's work and they weren't getting drunk after their shed was finished like a lot of the other shearers were. I sometimes try to imagine if Terry had earned the same as the white shearers how much better off we would have been.

Although he had no formal training, carpentry came quite easily to Terry. There were no traineeships or anything like that for Aboriginal people then. You either learned to do a job and do it properly or you didn't get the work. It was funny, one time the superintendent brought in a 'qualified' white carpenter to train the Aboriginal people in this line of work. One day Terry came home cursing because he had to explain to the white carpenter how to make sash windows. Terry was actually more experienced. But the carpenter didn't like Terry telling him how to do things when he had a certificate and Terry didn't.

It made me proud when my son Brenton got his certificate for carpentry. Then Klynton got one for welding, after being an apprentice under his brother Jamie, and yet Jamie wasn't qualified to have apprentices under him. I talked to Marj Tripp in the Department of Aboriginal Affairs about this, so they rushed Jamie into trade school for three days and gave him his certificate. When you think about it, it stinks, because if the skilled men had been given a certificate they could have made a life for themselves outside the mission. There were capable plumbers, carpenters and electricians there, but because they didn't have a certificate they couldn't get a job in the white community and they couldn't claim the basic wage for that particular job. That was a way of keeping Aboriginal people down and out of the white communities.

All Terry's work was seasonal. He was a gun [fast] shearer and could shear 280 to 290 sheep in a day, which was a big tally in those days of shearing with small shears. When Terry was bag sewing [hessian bags full of grain], my brother-in-law would drive me down to the wharf and I'd thread the needles for Terry, so he would get twice as many done. Eventually I was able to buy good furniture and a fridge. Bag sewing became redundant with the construction of silos in the 1960s, but Terry still held the record for shearing and for bag sewing when he died.

Aboriginal people weren't allowed into hotels, but that didn't always stop them from drinking. My brother Oscar got picked up a couple of times for being 'an Aboriginal under the influence' when he went to drink with one of the boys from the shearing shed he was at in the south-east. But on the missions, when the shearing was done that was it. No ice-cold beer for hard-working men. I know a lot of the white farmers in the district would have gladly sat down for a beer with the boys, but they were too bloody frightened of being charged for it.

It was the same for the footballers. Even when Point Pearce won the Grand Final (as they often did), the players couldn't celebrate with a beer like their opponents, or they'd get locked up.

Four men did all the mission farming — ploughing, sowing the crops of wheat, barley and oats, cultivating and reaping them. The soil was good and the men worked hard, so the farming at Point Pearce was a successful enterprise, whereas it was hard going in the sandy soil at Raukkan.

We all enjoyed keeping up with what was going on in the world. We never used to buy the newspaper, but we'd get it the day after from one of the white officers, or a group of us would throw in for it. That's how very poor the salary was on Point Pearce.

The roads on Point Pearce were not maintained and there were potholes everywhere that just got deeper and deeper each year after the mid-year rains. I remember writing a letter to the Point Pearce Council saying they had to do something about the roads because getting to Port Victoria to do your shopping was becoming so difficult.

I reckoned that instead of using a car to get to Port Vic, we needed a boat!

I hadn't been married long when I had a visit from Mr Earl, the stock overseer, who told me there had been a bit of trouble over at Raukkan and my brother Squashy (Ron) was arrested for hitting old Bill Robinson after a bit of a dispute. It didn't take much to provoke Squashy, and I understood how he felt, because those white staff watched our every move and treated us like criminals. So Squashy just lost it. Apparently when my Dad tried to step in, Dad copped the second punch that was thrown, so Squashy knocked my father out too!

The police came down from Tailem Bend and arrested Squashy, and after he'd done three months in jail they expelled him from Raukkan and he wasn't allowed to go back there any more. He was only sixteen or seventeen years old and barred for life from his home, where all his relatives lived. The Protector put him out on a farm north of Port Augusta, and about six months later when a relative died Squashy wasn't allowed on the mission for her funeral. So he decided to sneak in and got a seat on the Mail. But as the ferry pulled in to take them over to Narrung, the police searched the Mail and Squashy was arrested and he had to serve twenty-one days in jail. When he got out of jail he went back to Port Augusta where he had made a few friends, and eventually he ended up in Kalgoorlie where he stayed for about fifteen years. He didn't want to come back because he was afraid of being arrested again, so we didn't see him for all that time.

Hollywood and Aunty Rosie

Aunty Rosie and Uncle Nat were raising six of their grandchildren rather than let them be taken away, after their daughters Stella and Winnie died in childbirth. This was a struggle for them and we helped where we could. Uncle Nat got to the stage where he couldn't pull in the big rope fishing net by himself, so Terry helped him with the nets he used to catch fish to feed his family.

While they were doing this I would help Aunty Rose make feather flowers and prepare rushes for weaving, and I learnt a lot more from her about our culture. Because I was too young to learn much from my Mummy, Aunty Rosie showed me how to how to weave properly, and she was teaching me about kinship and culture at the same time. She said the rushes were like members of a family; you can't have them all the same size. She would say, 'Don't make them too loose. Pull them together with little stitches like a nice, tight-knit family'. She started bringing these things into it and I soon realised there was more happening than just making mats and baskets. These were the times when she taught me a lot about traditional women's things — how to improve your chances of getting pregnant or about how to use contraception. She told me how the women from Raukkan used to go down to the Coorong to have their babies. Before I even got married I used to always wonder why people were having babies down the Coorong and Aunty Rosie explained to me why.

We also talked a lot about genealogies. Aunty Rosie would ask me about people on Raukkan and she'd say, 'Oh she's my cousin', or something like that. So that would get me thinking about how they were her cousin and she would explain that to me. And all the time we were weaving so I started connecting genealogies up with weaving, in my mind, just like Aunty Rosie did too.

Aunty Rosie showed me how to make cradles for babies. I'd never seen them on Raukkan, so she told me about their shape and how to make them. When you come to turn the side up, that's when you've got to do a different stitch. And you need to add more rushes then, to give it more strength — like the strength of a family. No matter what she told me it all went back to family. And within a week I was making them.

Then one day I was down at Hollywood cooking a damper cake for her in the ashes of the fire and Aunty Rosie started to tell me how to deliver a baby if you're there on the spot. She said you tie the cord on the side next to the baby once the palpitations stopped and you cut it right in the middle. You keep that cord on the outside, but you let the other end go back into the mother. You leave the cord on the baby's *pulangi* [navel] to dry and when it falls off you keep it and use it for ceremonies.

She explained all that to me and I listened and remembered it all. As it happens, when I went back over to the Three Miles, I asked Aunty Laura about these things and she told me exactly the same things as Aunty Rosie, which didn't surprise me because Aunty Laura used to deliver babies of all the *mundhana* [pregnant] women at Raukkan and at the camps around Meningie and the Three Miles, and she had a lot of experience.

This education in Aboriginal culture and history went on all through summer. I would go out with Aunty Rosie to pick rushes for weaving. After we'd picked them, we'd dry them out, then soak them in water in an old kerosene tin, then dry them out and soak them again until they turned a yellow colour, when they're ready to use. The rushes at Point Pearce weren't as good as the ones at Raukkan, they were thicker and they would split. So we tried all sorts of ways to make them more pliable, and they still weren't good enough to weave with. That's why any of the men that were going shearing over Raukkan way would call in there to pick up rushes to take back to Point Pearce for Aunty Rosie. We'd use the rushes that weren't as good for the stuffing on the inside and the really good ones for the lacing around them to make our mats and baskets. The lacing has to be very tight and close so as to completely hide the stuffing and this takes quite a bit of skill too.

While Aunty Rosie and I were working together, she taught me about what to expect with the birth of my baby. She told me how to manage the pain of labour in the ways of our old people. Aunty Rosie would make sure I listened and learned from her properly, and she would poke me with her stick to emphasise the fact she would only tell me things once. Often she would clasp her hand to her heart when she told me to listen and learn. It must have been that Aunty Rosie chose me as the one to be given the knowledge, because even her own kids weren't told the things I was.

Toy-boy

Eventually it was time for the birth. The nearest hospital was in Maitland, but Aboriginal women were not allowed to have their children there, so we had to go straight through Maitland all the way to Wallaroo Hospital [about 80 kilometres away]. The mission had a little old government-supplied van to take us, and the roads were in bad shape, so it was a rough ride. As a result of all this, I think as many babies were born on the side of the road as they were in Wallaroo Hospital. Of Nyumsi Wilson's sixteen children, eight were born on the road. Fortunately the closest I came to this was when Dibby came in the Wallaroo Hospital passage and Robin was born on the barouche while they wheeled me inside. Even so, Aboriginal women weren't allowed in the labour ward. I had five of my children in the small room set aside there for Aboriginal women.

My little son Terrence Oswald Wangangeen was born two months before my twentieth birthday on 4 December 1954. He was so perfect we nicknamed him Toy-boy because he looked like a little doll. Aunty Ivy Karpany came with me, as a friend and a *puthari*, and she is the one the Maitland Hospital still acknowledges for her midwifery work. Named after his father and my father, Terry-boy was a beautiful baby and I was overjoyed. I couldn't wait to get him back home to show him off, I was so proud. When I did get back to Point Pearce I was determined to be the best mother I could. With the experience I'd already had in looking after little children, I knew what to do and I did it well.

It was summer and I spent a lot more time with Aunty Rosie on the beach down at Hollywood. Getting around in the sand was the hardest thing for her with her *krawi taraki* [her extra leg, her crutch]. Aunty Rosie had an old wooden chair she liked to sit in on the beach, but it sank into the sand and was uncomfortable for her, so Terry cut the bottom of the legs off and nailed a board across to make it firmer for her. So she was in her glory like a queen on her throne. She loved that old chair. I'd be lying on a blanket with Terry-boy and we'd while away the time yarning. One time we did this I had Toy-boy lying on his bunny rug and I was breastfeeding him. It was warm and relaxing and I was starting to doze off, when I felt Aunty Rosie nudge me with her walking stick. She said, 'Dodo, don't go to sleep now. You shouldn't lie there with your *ngumpari* [breast] uncovered. *Krayi* [snake] will come.' I didn't know what she was talking about, so she said, 'I'll have to tell you about your mother', and she started to tell me a story.

Mum was born on 18 November 1910. One day my grandmother was lying on the floor of the *wurley* they had built down by Lake Alexandrina, breastfeeding Mum, when they both fell asleep. It happened to be, Aunty Rosie told me, she and my grandfather were just about to go into the *wurley* when they noticed a snake inside drinking from my grandmother's breast. My grandfather told Aunty Rosie not to move and to be quiet so she wouldn't frighten the snake. Aunty Rosie was paralysed with fear. They stood there still together and when the snake had enough to drink, it just crawled over my mother and out of the *wurley*.

I would never have believed that a snake would go to a woman's breast, but after Aunty Rosie told me that story I never lay down with my breast out again and I'd never sit near reeds or rushes where snakes might be.

As the months went by, Toy-boy was growing and he was a picture of health. He had a little dimple in his chin very much like his father, and at five months he was sitting up. In July 1955 it was winter and we had a bit of rain. One day a group of us were waiting for the store to open and Toy-boy's aunties were all fussing over him and one of them took him out of the pram. He was wearing little felt slippers with a bunny face on the front and she stood him up and he started pushing his pram. It was the first time I had seen him walking, so of course we were all pretty thrilled about it, watching him walking through the puddles. But he got his feet wet.

Next morning I noticed he had a bit of a sniffle when he woke up, but nothing really serious. We had no doctors on the mission, although there was a male nurse named Petrov. Again, we would have to drive past the Maitland Hospital to get to the doctor in Ardrossan or Wallaroo. Terry-boy didn't seem so sick to me; he was laughing and playing around and his Aunty May was teasing and joking with him. But he had a bit of a temperature and a runny nose, so I thought to be on the safe side I should get him some attention, but Dr Meldrum in Ardrossan was booked out and I couldn't get to see him that day.

Terry arrived home from shearing about half past five that evening and went straight to the pram to talk to his little son. Suddenly he sang out to May and I, so we ran up to the front room. It was then we realised there was something wrong. His little body shook and his eyes rolled in his head. Terry's brother Tiny ran for the help of one of the old ladies, but it was too late. The baby died there in my arms. He was seven months old.

I had seen people taking fits before, but not like the convulsion my son took that day. I always wondered why he died. I blame the government for it, because there were about eighty to a hundred people living on Point Pearce in those days, and considering the poor conditions we were living under, we should have been provided with better medical facilities. We were controlled by the government, but not provided for adequately, and this was just another one of the terrible injustices we had to suffer.

Dr Meldrum eventually came, but all he could do was sign a death certificate. About eight or nine o'clock that night Mr Earl, the farm overseer, brought a police officer from Port Victoria over to the house. He told me they wanted to do an autopsy on the baby to find out why he died. I didn't know what an autopsy was, but in any case Terry said no. My mind was blank, so I let Terry make all the decisions. Because it was summertime they took his body to Maitland and put him in the morgue. We buried him a week later; it was the saddest thing. I was crippled with grief.

Funerals are always very important events in Aboriginal communities, and no more so than for a little child. It was a big funeral; everybody at Point Pearce turned up. We had a little service for him at Terry's sister Stella's place and then Terry carried his little coffin and placed it in the grave. Very simple, sad funeral. Terry didn't ever want me to put a headstone up because he didn't believe in putting cement on top of his baby's grave, but just recently our kids got together and had one put up for me. He's buried near my brother Oscar, just down from Auntie Rosie.

Just after Toy-boy died, my cousin Sandra Power's daughter Eugena died and I just didn't want to know. I couldn't bring myself to go over and see Sandy until the day of the funeral. It was the hardest thing for me then.

A month after that, my cousin May's little Laura died. They put it down to a heart murmur, but me and May thinks that it was because she fretted for my son. In November, just before Toy-boy was born, May's husband Matt was killed going home from his job on the highways in a taxi. Mattie and I grew up like brother and sister. We used to jump on the same horse together and we married brother and sister, Terry and May. Mattie died in November, Toy-boy was born in December, Laura was born in January, Toy-boy died in July and Laura died in August. It was like my whole world was torn apart again.

Aunty Rosie's comfort

That's when I used to go crying to Aunty Rosie. I kept on going down to Hollywood in Stella and Ron Newchurch's horse and cart to be with her. She comforted me and explained why these things happened. She told me not to get too upset, because I already knew I was pregnant with my second child. Toy-boy's death got me talking more to Aunty Rosie about childbirth, marriage and death and different little sicknesses people could get without realising it. I spent even more time with Aunty Rosie because Aileen and Mark had moved over to Murray Bridge and I missed them. I was really scared about my second pregnancy. I couldn't take the thought of bearing another beautiful little baby and risk losing it again. I knew how to bring on miscarriages; I had learnt that from Aunty Laura. But I couldn't possibly do that.

I looked forward to those weekends with Aunty Rosie all that summer while I was pregnant with Ron. The only thing I didn't like was cleaning and cooking the fish. It was my job for too many years.

Aunty Rosie was sixteen years older than my mother. She was the third eldest child and the eldest daughter in her family, and she had a lot of knowledge. I already knew a bit about my father's side of the family, but I wanted to learn about her side. Aunty Rosie was a remarkable woman with a fantastic memory, and she taught me how to use my mind. If I got something wrong, she would correct me, and I'd have to memorise everything she told me. She could tell me who's related to who without even stopping to think about it, and I learnt more from her than I think I would from reading any book.

Then to learn more about my father's side of the family I went to talk to Nanna Sally's brother, Uncle Wilfie Varcoe, and he gave me information on his brothers and sisters and who they married. I already knew who my grandmother and grandfather's children were and I knew my grandfather was from Bundaleer station, because he often talked about Bundaleer and how much he would like to go back there one day, but he never had the means to get there. I knew his mother's name was Ellen Armstrong and his two aunties were Joanne and Amelia, because that was given to me when I was very young.

It was while I spent time with Aunty Rosie that she put it all together for me, telling me in the kinship way. She would often draw initials in the sand to illustrate what she was telling me, and then when I had got it she would rub it out again. She was straightforward. If she was talking about her cousin — and she and Mum had lots of cousins — she would explain how that person came to be a cousin.

Aunty Rosie moved to Point Pearce in 1931 so she knew as much about the people there as she did about her family and relatives and people living at Raukkan. She filled me in on all her friends and I kept it in my head, except when she talked about the old missionaries and superintendents and Protectors. I couldn't seem to remember the whitefellas' names, so I wrote them down and kept them inside the plastic cover of a little book.

Another thing Aunty Rosie did was teach me how to cook nice meals economically, so my children wouldn't be without. If we had a little bit of meat, she'd mince it up to make it go further for her and Uncle Nat and the kids. I learned a lot by listening and watching and Auntie Rosie told me exactly what position to sit in to watch.

Being with Aunty Rosie was the best thing that ever happened to me. I liked Uncle Nat, he was a lovely quiet man, but Aunty Rosie was very outspoken and she wouldn't be frightened to tell you what she thought. She had a lot of sadness in her life too. She lost her only two daughters and a little grandson, and when she got exempted she couldn't go into the mission to see her family. But she was my mentor and I thank God I had the opportunity to spend a lot of time with her.

Children

My next son, Ronald Douglas Wanganeen (known as Jamie), was born on 5 December 1955. Ron was also a beautiful healthy baby, so he replaced the loss of Terry-boy and helped fill the gap of not having a baby around. I was a mother again and I enjoyed the responsibilities that entailed.

Darryl James (Snacka) was born on 11 November 1957, by which time we moved out of my father-in-law's house and into a two-room house of our own. A family moved off the mission, so the house became available, but we had to apply to the Point Pearce Council for it. There weren't a lot of houses there in those days, but there were more people, and a lot of them had quite large families living in four or six room houses. Our first house was just a bedroom and kitchen and like all the houses, had outdoor toilets and showers and baths. I had a double bed and a single bed in the bedroom, with the two boys sleeping head to foot in the single bed.

Klynton Bruce (Kandy) came along on 17 October 1959 in Wallaroo Hospital with the help of a *puthari* from Raukkan, Beryl Rankine. There was exactly one year, eleven months and five days between each of those three boys, so I had my work cut out and the house was cramped.

After we had been married about three years, we got our first car, a little Holden, from the car dealer at Maitland, Don Gunning. His garage is still there, along with Nixon's. This was a real treat because we were able to pack a lunch, put the kids in the back and go to the football and basketball matches. Terry was still playing football and I used to like to watch the girls play basketball (which is called netball now). Before we had a car it was impossible to take the kids to sport on the mission truck. The Yorke Valley Association sports were really enjoyed by the Aboriginal community, and Point Pearce players excelled at them, like they still do today. Terry's cousin Ellen Weetra was a record-breaking goal shooter, and Keith Warrior, was a star footballer who also didn't get the recognition in the white community he deserved. There was one thing for the whites and one thing for the blacks. Point Pearce was the only Aboriginal team in the Association, but they won more grand finals than most of the white teams. This tradition continues today in the national football league, where many of the top footballers are Aboriginal men, but at least they're recognised better for it now.

More foster children

After I had had a few of my own children I started to help others out when there was sickness and death in the family. One of the main reasons I did it was because I still had that bitterness in me about Doris being taken away when Mummy died. I'm sure there was relatives there that would have helped Nanna and Dad out with her. So I felt an obligation towards those kids; I didn't want to see them go through what I went through, being taken away and finishing up in a Home.

Starting with Eddie, Dick and Wayne at Raukkan, I eventually also looked after Daughter and many others over the years. For example, when Tiny (Edward) Wanganeen's wife died leaving ten children and a new-born baby, I took Wendy and I had Wendy for four years. Terry's cousin Keith Weetra and his wife had fourteen children when she got cancer, so I took Kenny and Trevor. And then another time, when Terry's sister Kathleen Taylor died, I took Irene, Yvonne, Dianne and Alex. I had five of Sarah Jackson's children — Charmaine, Stuart, Nelson, Warren and Meredith. Then there was Heather, Robert (Pubelie) and Ronald Rankine, Harry Newchurch, Clifford and Trevor Wanganeen and Cheryl Travis. I was strict with my foster kids because I didn't want them to go out and get into trouble.

I didn't get any financial support for any of my foster children except Cheryl, and when I did apply for Endowment for Ron and Kathleen's children, I was accused of only taking them for the money. That really made me angry. I was so hurt to be accused by my own people of doing it for the money, especially since I was washing and scrubbing and working my hands to the bone for those kids.

Life goes on

We lived in the two-room house for about five years before we were able to move into a four-room house, and it was there that my first daughter, Lydia Dawn (Dibby) was born on 26 October 1961 at Wallaroo, with the help of Aunty Sarah Graham, a younger woman who was learning midwifery from Aunty Ivy and Aunty Beryl.

Aunty Sarah was also with me for the birth of Robin Grant on 7 August 1963, Brenton Clark (Dooley) on 17 June 1965 and Ricky Keith on 3 July 1967. My youngest child, Christabel Violet, was born in Adelaide because there were complications. I was sent into the Queen Victoria Hospital in January 1969 for observation and I was worried I might lose her, but fortunately all went well and she was born on 5 February.

Apart from Klynton, Robin and Ricky, all my other children were named for relatives. Robin was a name I was always going to have for one of my boys because of my close cousin Mattie, Aunty Laura's son who had passed away. When we were young he developed appendicitis and I had to help him walk in to Barmera to have his appendix out. All the way there he sang, 'Poor little Robin walkin' walkin' walkin' to Missouri', and he was still singing it as we walked through the hospital doors. The nurses thought it was hilarious and said, 'That's the first patient we've seen come in singing a song!' And we always laughed about it, so I told Mattie I'd call one of my sons Robin.

Juggling the kids took a lot of organisation. I had a different coloured towel for each child and those who were around the same size would fight over underwear. I unpicked second-hand clothes from the Salvation Army, and out of one adult shirt I would make three little shirts for Kandy, Darryl and Brenton, and I used to write my kids' initials on their clothes with chain stitch. Once I lost Darryl at the show and I told the police he was dressed exactly like Kandy and they were able to find him in no time at all. I made dresses for the girls and shirts and shorts for the boys and they looked very smart.

* * *

Around this time Aunty Rosie's grandchildren were of marriageable age and I chipped in and helped with cooking and preparation for the weddings of Joy, Peggy, Janice and Rosie. Aunty Rosie and I didn't just socialise because we loved one another's company, but we also worked really well together. During our talks Aunty Rosie would often get very angry and growl about the government and things like that as well, but I wasn't into politics. We talked about what the Protector was doing and she'd go into a lot of detail about the olden days and compare it with what was happening in the present.

Dad's asthma got worse, so Terry and I went over to Raukkan and brought him back to Point Pearce because the doctor said the climate was drier and better for asthmatics than a damp area like Raukkan. It was nice for the children to have their grandfather around and he would look after them sometimes.

Around this time I was going on to all the committees on the mission, including the Community Council, because a lot of the older women, like Aunty Hilda Wilson, Aunty Doris Graham and Aunty Viney Weetra, were starting to move out into the white communities, owing to the government's assimilation policies. Terry and I decided to stay on because he was a jack of all trades and had plenty of guaranteed work. Terry's cousin Elaine Newchurch, who is about the same age as me and had children of the same age, became very a good friend, and the older ladies persuaded us to join the School Welfare Club and the Christmas Cheer Committee that would make up things for the children for Christmas time. I had some experience because when I was younger I started the Young Group on Point Pearce. So we had fancy dress balls and lovely little evenings in the hall. Whenever Lainie and I went shopping we'd take a little bit of petty cash or sometimes with our own money we'd buy little presents as prizes for sporting events. We raised money by making toffee apples and having cake stalls.

Lainie and I started to change things because we felt things were too set in the old ways. I was Secretary and Lainie was Chairperson and we'd invite other school welfare committees to share ideas. We formed a good working group with Linda Angie, my sister-in-law Ellen

Kartinyeri and Rita Angie and other young mothers on the mission, and we got a kindergarten started. Before that the children didn't go to school on the mission until they were about six years old. So there were a lot of little children running around with little supervision because their mothers had so much to do. Once the kindergarten was up and running that made life a lot easier for everyone.

We also started the Point Pearce Women's Centre, which is still going today and I was on the committee to allocate housing on the mission. That system has changed and housing is now allocated through the Aboriginal Housing Authority. In 2005 when I applied for housing, I was told I would have to provide a letter verifying my Aboriginality! Can you believe that? After all I've been through in my life for the colour of my skin, having set up the kindergarten and the Women's Centre and lived on Point Pearce for over thirty years on and off, now I have to prove I am Aboriginal in order to get somewhere to live!

To get funding to write this book I had to get a letter proving my Aboriginality and as my son Klynton was then South Australian Commissioner for ATSIC [Aboriginal and Torres Strait Islander Commission], I was given verification that I am Aboriginal by my own son! I never did understand the white system.

Don Dunstan and his first wife Gretel came out to Point Pearce in January 1968, when we had an 'Open Village' for three days to celebrate the mission's centenary, and I was in charge of catering for the luncheon. That was the first time I appeared in the newspaper. They had a photo of me mixing up cake mix in a bowl. This was just after the 1967 Referendum which led to Aboriginal people getting the vote (previously we weren't considered citizens of our own country). Don Dunstan was very big on Aboriginal issues and was friends with many of the people in our community, none more so than my brother Oscar, who he spent a lot of time with. Don Dunstan used to love to hear Oscar sing the rude songs he entertained people with, and even recorded them. As a result of all this new era, lots of Aboriginal people were starting to get involved in politics, and when Don Dunstan became Premier of South Australia, we were very happy.

When I was working for the Dunns, I remembered a debutante ball I saw held at Woodside. We had never had anything like that in Aboriginal communities, so we decided to have a deb ball at Point Pearce. We got in touch with Mrs Stan Davies, a white woman who lived at Port Victoria, and she came out and helped us organise it. She told us what the procedure would be, how to train the debs and their partners, how they were to be presented. Mrs Davies helped a lot of the girls make their dresses, and the debs were presented to Don Dunstan. It was a huge occasion and there was a big article in the paper about it.

The first deb ball was such a success, I was keen to have a second one for the younger girls, and that was held in the same week as Neil Armstrong walked on the moon in 1969. I made Dibby's little frock and helped Lainie's sister Pam make her daughter's dress. Then we had little swallowtail suits for the boys, and I ran up two little jackets. I became very artistic and was very pleased with the job I did of decorating the hall, because it looked beautiful.

By now I was carrying so much information about kinship in my head, it was starting to hurt, so I decided to try and put it down on paper. Jamie made me up a partition, and I pinned little cards on it and connected them all up with string. This was my first attempt at putting genealogies on paper and little did I know that it would lead to much bigger things later on.

It was 9 July 1975 when I lost all my material possessions when my house burnt up. The worst part was losing all my photos: photos of Mum's and a few little photos of my own. Aunty Rosie was wonderful and gave me back all the photos that I had given her over the years. I also lost some memorabilia of my mother's, like the eiderdown she made for me. Luckily I had lent Mum's sewing machine to my sister Connie, so apart from my memories, that and her ring were all I had left to remind me of her.

Then I had a big blue with Terry. By this stage the ban on alcohol had been lifted, but because people weren't used to it, it caused all sorts of problems. That's when the women used to get bashed up and many of them, including me, ended up in hospital sometimes. The doctors would patch us up and send us back to Point Pearce, to our husbands, the same environment. These were the worst times for me, when Terry drank and got abusive. I've never been big, and couldn't hold him off or stop his rage. At that time I had eight children, and was also fostering Wendy Wanganeen and Kenny and Trevor Weetra. It got worse and worse, until it was difficult for me to care for all those little kids. Terry's brothers and sisters tried to stop him, but he was just so violent and I don't know why. I was home all the time cooking, cleaning, washing, knitting, crocheting, sewing. I did everything a housewife and mother should do. But nothing was right for Terry. One time he threw a whole leg of roast lamb out the door because he said I hadn't cooked it right. It didn't make sense. Eventually I couldn't take it any more. In a rage I smashed a bottle on the table and stabbed him.

They took Terry up to Maitland Hospital, and the doctor told me he either had to lay charges of attempted murder against me – even though Terry didn't want to — or I could go to Hillcrest Psychiatric Hospital for six weeks' treatment and I wouldn't be charged. They decided I had an anger problem, but it was Terry's drinking that needed treatment, not me. They said I would have to go voluntarily, and so for the sake of my kids that's what I did.

6

From Madwoman to Historian

May 1994

It was at home at Baroota in early 1994 that I first heard about the proposed bridge to Kumarangk. One morning, all of a sudden I woke up and sat right up in bed. I had a dream where I saw my Dad telling me I had to do something, but I didn't know what it was. We got up and Syd put the TV on. There it was on the news. They were going to build a bridge to Hindmarsh Island. They can't do that!

I couldn't see why they'd need a bridge. My mind went back to my childhood when we spent holidays at Kumarangk. We used to walk across to the island from Mark's Point. Mark's Point was named after Mark Wilson, because he was a *thampamaldi*, the one that has to do the tribal punishment on the people who done wrong. I remembered camping at Kumarangk next to Mark's brother Dan and his wife, Rebecca Wilson. It was a big happy family, and in the evening us kids would listen to the old ladies singing corroboree songs led by Granny Pinkie Mack. I took this upbringing for granted, and now it felt like it was all being threatened. All this was going through my mind — why did they need a bridge?

I rang Tom Trevorrow [chair of the Ngarrindjeri Lands and Progress Association] and he told me what he knew about it and that there was going to be a meeting of Ngarrindjeri people over Kumarangk. I told him I had information about knowledge sacred to women and I wanted to be part of any meeting.

I thought they must be planning to build the bridge from Mark's Point, so when Tom told me they were planning to build it from Goolwa to Kumarangk I started cursing [Doreen Kartinyeri's great-great-grandmother Malpurini is thought to have been buried opposite Goolwa]. I knew there were sacred sites all around Kumarangk every five or six kilometres. And then there's the stories about Kumarangk, the water all round it and the mainland. I asked Tom to tell me all about it. He told me the developers Tom and Wendy Chapman, who had a marina on the island, were going to build the bridge together with the State Government. Tom didn't know any more, so he got Victor Wilson to ring me.

Victor and I was yarning about what he remembered his father telling him about Kumarangk, and then he asked me if I knew any history about it. I said yeah and he wanted to know what it was. I told him about the sites in the area and the families that come from there and that's all. I told him they couldn't build a bridge there because we had too many people buried there and he knew this much because he said the older ones had told him that. But he was confused because he could sense I was holding something back. He said, 'If you know anything traditional way about the lifestyle of the people you might need to tell us'. That's when I told him I couldn't speak to him about it because he was a man.

Well, that triggered everything off. They wouldn't leave me alone after that. They got Aunty Maggie Jacobs to ring me, and that's when Aunty Maggie and I realised we had some of the same knowledge about Kumarangk and the Murray Mouth. Likewise with Sheila Goldsmith. Then Victor asked if he could come over and pick me up to take me down to the Kurangk, because they'd organised a Ngarrindjeri meeting. So I went with Victor to the meeting at the Pines [dormitory-style accommodation] and the Mouth House [on Kumarangk at the mouth of the Murray, owned by Anne Lucas].

1975

I couldn't believe a perfectly sane person like me should have to spend six weeks in a mental institution. It's a wonder it didn't *send* me crazy! Bert Clark was working with the Aboriginal Health Agency in Adelaide and he took me in to Hillcrest. I don't know why they didn't give me a female Aboriginal social worker, when Lowitja O'Donoghue and Ruby Hammond were available, but Bertie was kind and arrangements were made to foster out my children for a while with their aunties and uncles.

There were about eight patients in the ward and they had me in the middle bed. I asked if I could go into a private ward or at least to the end of the room so I wouldn't be surrounded by them. There was a woman who cradled a bundle in her arms. I thought she had a baby, but when I looked closer I saw she only had a doll. Then there was a woman who thought she was a big opera singer and she'd be singing scales all the time. She would just stand tall — no words — just warbling, and she got on everyone's nerves.

The worst of it was having to go to group therapy. You had to sit down and talk about your problems and how you're feeling. I didn't think that it was anybody else's business. I was the only Aboriginal person there, and the others were uninhibited because of their mental illness and not afraid to be as racist as they liked towards me. At one of these sessions I lost it and they ended up putting me in a straitjacket. But it was all them whitefellas that were mental cases, not me.

Eventually I decided I'd play the game at group therapy, so I told them how I felt. I said, 'If I stay in here any longer, they're going to put me into a cell. I can't survive with all you fellas around me like this. You fellas are like you're letting it get the best of you'. I was lecturing to the patients and telling them just what I thought. Well the male nurse came in and ran me out of the room. He said, 'How dare you speak to those people like that. They've got a sickness'. So I said, 'Well what the fucking hell am I doing here? There's nothing wrong with my mind; I just got sick of taking punches from my husband and I hit him back'. You see, I did feel sorry for those people, but I just couldn't hack it.

There was one high point while I was in Hillcrest. Snacka was working as a strapper for Bart Cummings. It was early November and the Melbourne Cup was coming up, and Snacka was strapping a horse called Think Big. I was so excited about it I asked permission from the doctor to go to Victoria Park Race Course to watch the race being broadcast. They say the whole country stops still for the Melbourne Cup. Permission was granted, and I was given into the charge of Ally McNamara and Terry's niece Tumsie. We met up with lots of blackfellas there. Of course I backed Think Big and it won! I was over the moon with pride when I saw my son leading that horse. Well after the race Tumsie and I started banging into the drink, and although Ally McNamara took me back on time, I was drunk.

Well I got back to Hillcrest with a whole lot of banknotes wrapped up in my *mundi* [breast, in my bra]. Sixteen hundred dollars I won. I didn't put it in my purse because they'd search that to see if you were taking anything in. Because I was drunk they decided to put me under the shower, and when the nurse pulled off my clothes, out flew all this money.

They stopped me from going out after that. I never used to be a drinker in them days; even when the ban was lifted I never took it on. But I did drink that day, and who could blame me. My son strapped the winner of the biggest horse race in the country and afterwards I was going back to a psychiatric hospital.

I was so frustrated and angry. I refused to see any visitors because I didn't want anyone to see me in that place, and I played up in Hillcrest because I just wanted to get out of there. They were giving me medication to sedate me and I hated it, but they would stand over me until I had taken it. So one day I told the nurse I had to go to the toilet first, so she said she'd come back afterwards with the medication. I locked myself in the toilet and sat there for a long time just to spite them. The nurse started banging on the door saying, 'Mrs Wanganeen are you in there?' I said, 'No, I've just gone to the Regency Theatre and seen this movie, *Gone With The Wind*'.

I rang Bertie Clark so often about getting out that he started to avoid my calls, but eventually he felt sorry for me and told me he would do what he could to get me out. I asked him to get hold of Maude Tongerie because she was working in the same Department, but George and Maude [both Aboriginal social workers] were up in Oodnadatta at the time. They had been very supportive of me, because they saw me with black eyes and all beat up and knew what my situation was. They also knew that I was a good mother to all my children, so they did what they could. Eventually, after six weeks had passed (and it seemed like forever), Bertie came and took me out. And when I went back to Terry it was entirely different. His whole attitude changed. He became the husband and father that he should have been, so it seems that that drastic measure actually had some effect.

Assimilation

These were the days of assimilation policies, and exemptions had been abolished in 1962. When the assimilation policies started it was just crazy. I thought, 'What the hell is going on?' There I was with six kids and then all of a sudden now we've got to get assimilated into the white community after they had lived all their lives in the mission environment. The government was doing surveys in places like Murray Bridge, Port Lincoln and Port Augusta — near a mission but not right next door — about bringing Aboriginal people into these towns. They went around to the white people and asked if they would object to Aboriginal people living next door to them. Then the government began buying homes in these towns for Aboriginal people, whereas one time if an Aboriginal man went off a mission to work, he'd be put out in the bush in a little railway siding or something to keep him away from the towns.

Quite a lot of people went into Adelaide, but a few went into small communities like Murray Bridge, Ceduna, and Port Pirie. I remember in 1961 my brother Oscar's daughter Eileen was born, and I went up to Port Pirie where they were living, to look after the children. Oscar was working at the railway siding just out from Pirie, and Ellen was one of the first Aboriginal women allowed to go to the Pirie Hospital. Previously they'd have to have their babies in their house.

The prejudice in Maitland was terrible, with bad newspaper reports about the conduct of the local Aboriginal children. We wanted something better for our children and a better education for them, and to do that we decided we needed to move. Terry didn't really want to go, but I thought leaving Point Pearce could be a fresh start for us. So Terry got a job with the Highways Department at Pooraka, and the family moved up to Kapunda to live.

After Terry

But our marriage was effectively over. We had been together twenty-one years, but too much had happened and I realised it couldn't be saved. We could not agree on anything; the friendship was gone. I also felt isolated. My asthmatic Dad was living with us and I couldn't leave him on his own. I didn't make many friends in Kapunda, the kids had a bit of a walk to school, and Terry started work too early in the morning to drive them. I've never, ever driven a car since I ran over Robin in my backyard. He was about seven when I reversed out and hit him. Fortunately he was only bruised a little bit but that put the wind up me. Then Kandy got sick, and we decided living out in the community without our support networks was too hard. So we moved back to Point Pearce. But nothing had changed in the relationship between Terry and me, so I decided to leave.

I moved to Adelaide to a house in First Avenue, Wingfield. The three biggest children, who had started work, stayed with Terry, and I had my youngest five living with me. I was still fostering Kenny and Trevor Weetra and Wendy Wanganeen. Kenny and Trevor didn't want to leave Point Pearce, so they stayed with another aunt, but Wendy came with me.

I also started taking in Point Pearce children who had run away from the mission and had committed low-level offences in Adelaide. As a result I needed a bigger house, so I moved to Cheltenham to cater for looking after another two boys, Trevor and Clifford Wanganeen. Then there was the time seven of the boys held up the pub at Port Victoria. I went to court to fight for them and Elaine Traeger, the social worker with Welfare, got them placed in my care. I needed a bigger house but they didn't get me one, so I did the shed up so they could sleep in there. I had them for seven or eight months until Welfare came and took them and got them jobs or sent them home.

I also had baby Rachael. Her father, Matthew Kartinyeri [Doreen Kartinyeri's uncle] was also boarding with me. When the mother got out of hospital she went out drinking and left her baby. I was furious to hear this, so I marched down to her house to find everything dirty and in a mess. So I took Rachael home. I had to buy her clothes and bottles and things because I hadn't had such a little one for a while, and I told them not to bother to come for her until they had cleaned up their act. I had that little girl for about seven months until her mother did clean up her act. Now Rachael's children come in and see their 'Nanna' in my house at Point Pearce.

My father worried that he was a burden on me, but I'd tell him how much his grannies loved having him around. Brenton would go to sleep with his little head on Dad's chest every night. Then one night Dad's lungs collapsed and he was rushed to the Queen Elizabeth Hospital. Before I left him in the hospital he told me to get Squashy to come home. I think Dad probably thought he was on his last legs and he wanted to see his son, who had been in Western Australia for many years. It took about three months to find him and for Squashy to raise the money to come back to Adelaide. When he got back then my father sort of recovered, and Squashy thought it was all a set-up to get him home.

It wasn't until 1979 that Dad had another severe attack that was his last. He died in his bed because he couldn't manage to find his puffer, and when the ambulance came they found it wedged between his pillows. I think he died a very sad man; there was only me, Oscar, Connie and Doris left of his family. I don't think he ever really got over Mum's death. We had his funeral at Raukkan and buried him with our Mum. By this time Squashy's ban had been lifted, so he could attend his father's funeral.

It was while I was living at Cheltenham that I met Syd Chamberlain in 1978 at the Globe Hotel. That was the first pub to let the blackfellas in after the drinking ban was lifted, and we all used to meet up there. Donny and May Karpany took me down for a drink, and Syd was a good friend of my cousin, Cliffie Wilson. Syd moved in with me in October of that year when I had moved to Davoren Park. A Pitjantjatjara man with four children of his own — Kym, Wayne, Pam and Jenny — Syd and I have been together ever since. Syd worked as a station hand, and after we got together he'd go out to the different stations to work. He would stay away for a month at a time and he was driving very long distances. Sometimes the car would break down and this just wasn't the best situation. Then he secured a shearing job north of Port Lincoln, so we decided to buy a house at Cummins on the Eyre Peninsula. I loved it there. There was another two Aboriginal families living there, and they were working on the railways, even though that sort of work was dwindling off by then. When Syd wasn't shearing he worked for the local council. I looked after his kids and we grew to have a close loving relationship.

Syd and the kids and I liked to travel down to the Coorong from time to time for summer holidays. We really enjoyed ourselves on those trips. I showed them different places and told them where they could and couldn't go. We had our little tent up and just opened the back of the station wagon out and put the water bottle and a big bottle of cordial into a tuckerbox full of ice so the kids could have cool drinks. Sitting down there throwing the line out, memories would come. I'd just close my eyes and I could hear the birds and the bushes. Every time I heard the whistling sound of the wind through the reeds I would think about Aunty Rosie. She used to make that sound. So did other people back home at Raukkan. It was a beautiful time.

In the meantime Aunty Rosie was getting on in years. She was really active and then all of a sudden her health started to deteriorate. She was stopping with her granddaughter Peggy and her husband Robert Weetra, and every time she'd get sick, Peggy would take her to hospital. Then Dibby would ring and let me know, and Syd and I would go over to the Maitland Hospital to see her.

One particular time we were looking at old photos when I came across one of Aunty Rosie as a young girl with a handsome young man in World War One uniform. So when Syd and I went in to see Aunty Rosie at the hospital, I took the photo with me. I asked her who was in the photo and tears came to her eyes. She said, 'That's me with my brother Rufus'. She told me she had made the beautiful dress she was wearing especially for the occasion. Uncle Rufus was on one week embarkment leave before he was shipped out to the war. She said he was her baby brother and shouldn't have gone to war because he was too young. Her eldest brother Cyril also fought in that war, and both of them died.

Then she started telling me about the other men. I knew that my mother lost two brothers and my father lost a brother in the First World War, because every Anzac Day we'd have a service in the church and their photos would be put up and we would lay wreaths. Mum's uncle, Grandfather Gordon, was a returned soldier, and he used to come down to Adelaide for Anzac Day, and there have been photos of him in *The Advertiser* laying wreaths for his nephews at the War Memorial in Kintore Avenue.

My Grandmother Sally, who lost her eldest son, used to say, 'All they sent me was a letter'. Later on when I was researching in the archives for my book *Ngarrindjeri Anzacs*, I found that letter.

Aunty Rosie died in 1981 of old age. She was eighty-seven. We went up to Maitland Hospital to see her and she didn't want me to leave, but visiting hours were over and we wasn't allowed to stay. That night she passed away. When I got there next day all her grannies were there already and I was the last one to know. I think because she and I were so close they were frightened to tell me. That was another painful loss for me.

The beginnings of my formal genealogical work

Syd and I were living at Devon Park when one day Lewis O'Brien[1] came out to see me. We got talking, and he was asking me about relationships and kinships to old people from Point Pearce. I knew all the connections to Raukkan people, and Lewis talked to me about the kinship between his wife and my now ex-husband Terry. Aunty Pauline was the daughter of Pappa Eddie's second wife, so it makes her a half-sister to Terry's mother. But Aboriginal people don't look at 'half' or 'step'. Everyone is taken into your family; it doesn't matter who they are.

Lewis knew how important it is for Aboriginal people to know their kinship. It is the basis of our identity, especially for the ones that were taken away and lost touch with their families. He also knew that I had been doing a lot of work putting genealogies on paper for Aboriginal people who asked for them. So Lewis organised a little room at the University of South Australia's David Unaipon School at Underdale, and I started recording genealogies. With the help of Peter Willis, my first project I called 'Finding my People'. Paul Hughes[2] was teaching there and he and Lewis talked to Fay Gale[3] about how to get funding for my work. At that time Fay was in the Geography Department of the University of Adelaide, but she had done a lot of work with Aboriginal people, including Aunty Olga Fudge, Aunty Gladdie Elphick and Aunty Laura Agius. These women were greatly admired in the community. So in 1979 Fay applied for a grant from the Australian Institute of Aboriginal Studies[4] in Canberra. After looking into this it was decided that it would be best for me to fly to Canberra to talk to Dr Peter Ucko.

Now I've never been one for heights. I can't walk up or down stairs that aren't filled in, and you'll never ever get me into a lift. I'd certainly never been on a plane before and I didn't want to go on one now. But I knew I had to do it.

Dr Ucko asked me questions about Ngarrindjeri families from older generations than mine. And I was giving him the exact information to match the archives he had — who was related to who and who married who and from what family or what tribe did they come. I was able to answer all of his questions, so he said yes, we will fund you.

So I came back to Adelaide and moved into the Geography Department with Fay. The knowledge was there in my head. I just needed to put it on paper and I didn't know how to do that and I didn't know how to search the archives for other materials. Fay had Joy Wundersitz working for her, and she asked Joy and one of Fay's students, Jane Jacobs, to help me with research. They took me to

State Records and taught me how to use archives. We went into the Protector's records, and I was introduced to the 'Letter Book'. That was one of the biggest books I'd ever seen in my life. Joy showed me how to search the index and I thought, 'Oh my God, how am I going to get through all this?' It just spun me out.

During this research I came across all sorts of interesting information, including the records of all the births, deaths and marriages on Raukkan. People were dying of all sorts of things in the old days. Pneumonia was a big one, because it used to be really cold in winter time and all they had was an open fire or an old wood stove. There were children dying in infancy from 'malnutrition'. If you look at the ration supplies the families were getting, you could see that there wasn't much to go around for many of the families. Then of course they would take the other children away if one died of malnutrition.

After a while I started to get used to it. By the time Jane and Joy finished with me they taught me where I could get almost anything from, and I really do appreciate the work that they did with me. We went into the police records of court trials and criminal convictions of Aboriginal people. Most of them were only minor offences under the Aborigines' Act, but people were recorded as criminals for things like being under the influence.

There I was going into work that white people had written on Aboriginal people. I saw my Aunty Martha's name — Martha Isabel Rankine — and we got copies of the letters that were actually written by the superintendent concerning my aunt. I was shocked. The superintendent accused her of horrible stuff. I thought, 'No, no. That can't be my Aunty; it must be someone else with the same name'. I couldn't believe that they was writing things like that about my lovely, kind, generous Aunty Martha. I was very, very upset. But I had to get used to it because I would read many more letters like this about lovely people I knew. Women were accused of having affairs, so they would be 'bound down to the mission' (not allowed out). Men got expelled off the mission for fighting the white officers, bringing alcohol into the mission and other offences. These letters were the official record of how Aboriginal people's lives and bodies were being controlled and it was a shock to be witness to them.

I decided to try and work out a family tree on the Rigneys, which is my mother's family and gives me my Ngarrindjeri connection, so this is where I wanted to start. Joy showed me the way whitefellas do genealogies on paper, but I didn't like it. So instead of doing it as a family 'tree', I began recording them in a linear way. I did it that way because it was a way my people could understand and follow more easily, but it did take up a lot of room.

I published the *Rigney Family* genealogies in 1983. I still have in my possession the genealogy I produced for this, which is 44 feet long. I had it pinned up around the wall. That year I was inspired to make a whole lot of feather flowers for the launch of that book. We had a lovely launch at the Museum, with a little stage set up outdoors and there were speeches and the press came and took photos.

Dot Shaw had her copy of the book at a workshop and a whitefella picked it up and was looking through it. He said to Dot, 'My wife Meryl's great-grandfather's in here, Benjamin Challenger'. That's my great-grandfather, who had one son named Samuel from his white wife. Samuel Challenger had a son called Melrose (after the town they lived in) and Mel's daughter was Meryl. So Dot just looked at him and said they'd better get in touch with me. Meryl rang me up and I had a meeting with them. Meryl and I have the same great-grandfather, so she's my white relation. It's a small world!

Because my way of doing the genealogies was different from what people were used to, we couldn't get the Rigney book typed. The next book, the Wanganeen family, was typed, and the rest were all done for me on computer. I never learned to type, and by the time I was doing all this I had enough on my plate. My tools of trade are reams of writing paper, boxes and boxes of pencils, rulers and lots of erasers. My genealogy books came out quite well, and I have published seven of them now, some of them up to four volumes.

That year I also wrote an article for a book Fay was editing called *We Are Bosses Ourselves*.[5] The article described all these processes and how my work was progressing. I also attended my first COMA [Conference of Museum Anthropologists] conference in Canberra, where I met Jackie Huggins. Later on when I was in the Museum I went to my second COMA conference, in Brisbane, and I met up with Jackie there again. This time I took with me all the records for Cape York and Cherbourg, and Jackie and the others didn't know they existed. People looked at the photos and there was lots of crying. I talked about Tindale and wanting to take his work back to the people. Those women put me on a pedestal for the work I was doing, and since that time I have had lots of meetings with Jackie, and we get on really well together.

Prison visits

One of the boys who appears in the Rigney book was at the time of its publication doing quite a long stretch in Adelaide jail. Working in the Welfare Office, Marj Angas got to know the families very well, especially when they've got children in trouble. She used to visit me about once a week in the Museum. I was looking at the welfare system and children being taken away from their parents, and she was giving me information. In return I offered to give her photos to show to the boys in jail. Eventually one of the boys asked if I would go in and talk to them about their genealogies. So I made up some big posters with all the old photos and went out there and talked to the boys. The guards on duty reckoned the reactions from the prisoners was remarkable and that that's all they were talking about.

Then the word got around, so I was asked also to go to Cadell, where they were doing shorter terms, and also Mobilong jail at Murray Bridge, where there were a lot of *nungas*. I continued making these visits until there was a bit of a riot at Adelaide jail and I decided it was too dangerous to go back again. It was a hard decision. But I made a note of who was where and I made sure those prisoners were told each time I published another book so they could get a copy if they wanted to.

More room

It soon became clear that my little room wasn't big enough for me to spread all my work out, so Fay then found me a bigger room over at the old medical building across Frome Road and I set up my office there. Fay got her husband Milton Gale to come in and work with me. I had started by writing up names on little cards and I had cotton running down to each child. Then Joy thought of using the old-style computer paper which was continuous folding pages, and these were very long. Milton wasn't happy with the way I was doing things. He wanted me to write the little tiny ones — mother, father, children, their marriages and their children — and if it was more than three generations, I had to put it on another page. But I wanted it going from the oldest down to the youngest. So Milton and I didn't work very well together, although I put up with it for about four months. I thought I would turn it around. So I put the first generation second, the second generation third, the third generation fourth and it worked out really great. And Fay went along with what I decided.

But Milton wanted me to do it the other way and to my mind he was being very pushy about it. So I told him he wasn't telling me how to do my history of my people. But he wouldn't let it go and he just kept on pushing me to change my whole format, so I let him have it and I punched him. Joy ran all the way down to the Geography Department and told Fay I was getting stuck into Milton. That's when Fay realised Milton and I couldn't work together, and he left.

The Tindale collection

It was while I was here that I was introduced to Norman Tindale's material. Norman Tindale[6] was the anthropologist at the South Australian Museum for many decades and he did many fieldwork trips to Aboriginal and Torres Strait Island communities right around Australia. Among the information he recorded was hundreds of pages of genealogies. Fay thought I would be just the person to go through them and update them, add to them, record who has since been deceased and so on.

However because of the sensitive nature of these papers (which included records of illegitimate children and so on) they were under restriction. So we decided to approach Norman Tindale to get his permission for me to do this. In 1984 Fay spoke to Graham Pretty at the Museum, who looked up some of the information I had written from memory, and it matched what Norman Tindale had recorded in 1938–9, so he was very impressed. So he got in touch with Norman Tindale, who was living in California. He wrote back giving me permission. I was the first Aboriginal person to get access to these materials.

Wow! That day opened a lot of doors for me. I went downstairs in the Museum and met Steve Hemming, who was then Curator of Ethnology. His assistant was Philip Clarke, who, together with Philip Jones had previously been volunteers in the Ethnology Department with Steve as their boss, and then employed on various government grants Steve had applied for. I always worked well with Steve. And it was great. It was magnificent. I couldn't believe that old man Norman Tindale done so much work.

We sat at the table and Steve got some genealogies out and I was going through all these names. There was my family! And there was me, recorded as being three at the time. And then I would see a name I knew, so I started to name people with brothers and sisters to them and children to them and grandchildren to them and great-grandchildren to them. After that Steve asked Fay if the Museum could take me over with my work. Jean Rankine had been pushing Steve to do this and Fay felt it was best for me to get into the Museum as part of the staff. Vince Buckskin was hired to work as Aboriginal Liaison Officer in the Anthropology Department, and the Aboriginal anthropologist, Dr Suzi Hutchings, was working there for a while with Kaurna custodian Georgina Williams on the Tjilbruke project.[7]

In 1985 I published the *Wanganeen Family* genealogies.

The following year Steve became Curator of Anthropology, Philip Jones became Curator of Archives and Philip Clarke Assistant Curator of Archives at the Museum. Philip Clarke was registering and captioning artefacts that were stored in the boxes in the back till then. He really only got interested in all this stuff when he got to work with Steve and me on field trips. He never participated; he just sat in the back taking notes. I got on well with Steve and Peter Sutton and also Philip Clarke in the early days, but I never took to Philip Jones. I had the feeling he thought I was a threat and he acted all superior. He might have been a bit more educated, but knowledgeable, no. I told him so one day and that put the end to our relationship.

The only time I'd really see Jones and Clarke was round about lunchtime when we'd meet in the downstairs staff room. I'd also see Joan Murphy there; she used to be secretary to Norman Tindale. I came to rely on Joan because she was one of the few people who could read Norman Tindale's writing really well. Those genealogies were no easy reading, and it took hours of poring over them to make sense of them. My work was progressing so well that in 1987 Steve applied for a further large grant from the Department of Aboriginal Affairs to keep me going.

Steve had put in a request for a big room for me at the Museum. There was one on the first floor that they got cleaned out for me, and I liked it. In 1987 I walked into that room with only memories and a vision. Six months later it was full of Australian Aboriginal history. And that is how I began the Aboriginal Family History Unit at the South Australian Museum. In an article published in the *Records of the South Australian Museum*, Steve Hemming recorded my role like this:

> Ms Doreen Kartinyeri was well known to the Museum at that time and her employment on the project was seen as essential. Her knowledge of southern South Australian Aboriginal families is very detailed and her familiarity with early photographs an invaluable skill when dealing with the Museum's large collection. Ms Kartinyeri had been working towards publishing genealogies of all the southern South Australian Aboriginal families and had already published the genealogies of the Rigney and Wanganeen families. Her skills and her research plans complemented the resources the Museum had to offer the Aboriginal community. It was therefore decided to employ her as an Aboriginal Research Officer with the Museum's Aboriginal Family History Project...South Australia is fortunate to have an experienced Aboriginal history researcher such as Ms Kartinyeri...[8]

I still had three young children going to primary school, and Robin was just starting high school, so I had to get home by three o'clock in the afternoon because I didn't want them going home to an empty house. Graham and Steve were happy to leave it at that arrangement. When I got to the Museum, Steve was the only staff member that was actually doing anything on the family histories, and he was my boss. The work started to become too much for me, so it was decided to employ an assistant and we settled on Neva Wilson. Barry Craig also joined the Museum at this time and he was a great help. By 1988 Peter Sutton was Head of Division and had to approve every decision, and it was Steve and Peter Sutton that encouraged me in my work.

Researching the records

I needed to study Norman Tindale's records so closely, I asked Steve if I could get them photocopied. Again we had to ask Norman Tindale's permission, and again he agreed. When I got photocopies of the Raukkan and Point Pearce genealogies, I brought over my collection of records that Joy and Jane had helped me photocopy from the archives, and I had what was in my head. With those resources I published the *Kartinyeri Family* genealogies in 1989. I sent a copy to Norman Tindale in America and he wrote back to say that he never ever dreamt there would be a publication like this and that I had done a magnificent job. So he was very encouraging too.

Poonindie book

I was also working at this time with Peggy Brock on a book on the first Aboriginal mission in South Australia, Poonindie. Peggy is a historian, and she and *Kunamara* Ware,[9] who was with the Aboriginal Heritage Branch of the Department of Environment and Planning, approached me because *Kunamara* Ware knew I had collected a lot of archival material on that mission because my Nanna Sally was born there. So I got a little bit of time away from the Museum to spend with Peggy, and we used an office provided by the Department, and they gave me a small salary.

Because of my interest in Poonindie, while I went through the archives I kept my eye out for information on it, but I found very little, particularly about the time of the first missionary, Mathew Hale.

Doreen demonstrating how to commence weaving at Hindmarsh Island during the consultations with Professor Cheryl Saunders, 1995. Photo by Diane Bell.

Small mat woven by Doreen in the Ngarrindjeri style. Photo by Sue Anderson.

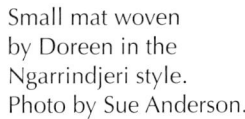

Feather flowers made by Doreen for the launch of the Rigney genealogies, 1983. Photo by Doreen Kartinyeri, 1983.

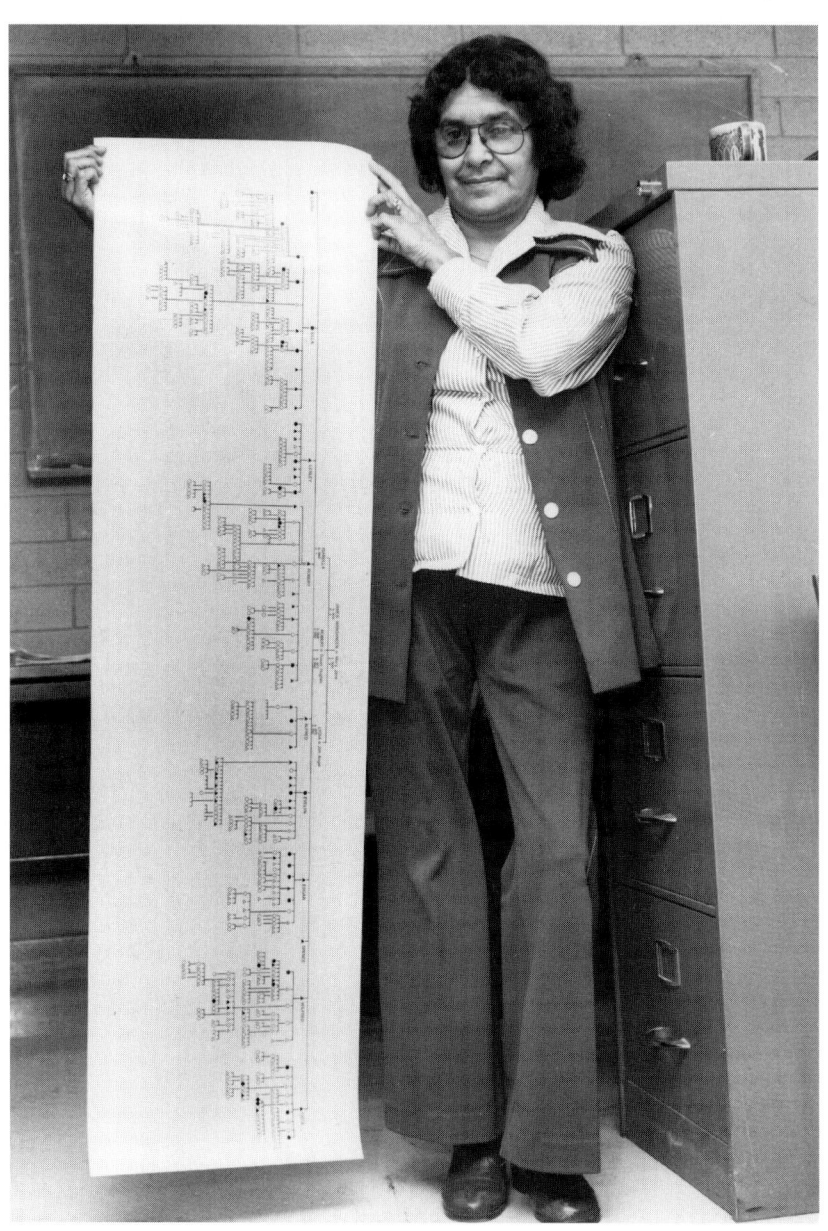

Doreen and one of her early genealogies, c. 1980. Photo courtesy Advertiser Newspapers Ltd.

Doreen and her sister Doris Kartinyeri displaying historic photographs from Doreen's collection at the Point Pearce school, c. 1980. Photo courtesy Doris Kartinyeri.

Doreen and Sue at Doreen's house in Point Pearce on South Australia's Yorke Peninisula, 2004. Photo courtesy Doris Kartinyeri.

Doreen after receiving her honorary doctorate from the University of South Australia, 29 May 1995. Photo courtesy Lydia Rankine.

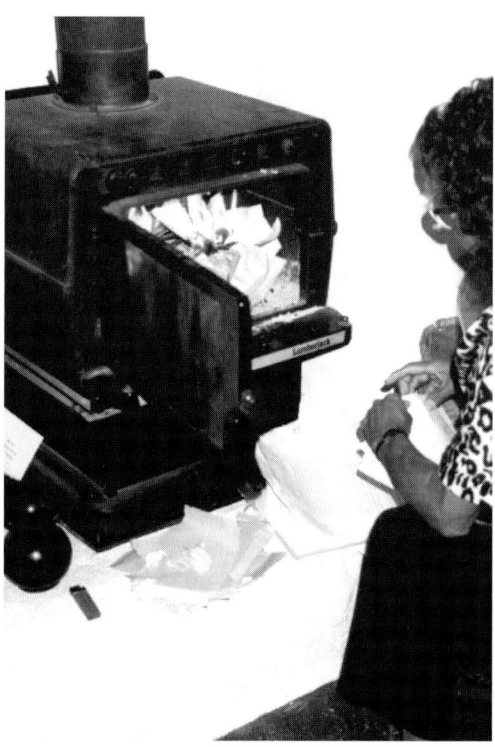

Doreen burning envelopes at Sandra Saunder's home, 1995. Photo courtesy Sandra Saunders.

Raising the Ngarrindjeri flag on Hindmarsh Island 1995. Photo courtesy Sandra Saunders.

Ngarrindjeri demonstration against the Royal Commission, Adelaide 1995. Photo courtesy Sandra Saunders.

Sandra Saunder's *Callinan sits on the High Court 1998*, acrylic on hardboard, 2001. Justice Ian Callinan was challenged because he had provided draft terms of reference for the Royal Commission and had advised Minister Herron on the Hindmarsh Island Bridge Bill. Courtesy private collection.

Doreen being supported by her son Klynton after the von Doussa judgment in 2001.
Photo courtesy Advertiser Newspapers Ltd.

Doreen Kartinyeri, August 2001, at a post-Federal Court media conference.
Photo courtesy News Ltd.

I thought that a man like Mathew Hale would have some very good records, but they weren't to be found. Then I thought he most probably would have taken all his stuff with him when he returned to England. So I wrote to the London Archives. They wrote back and told me Hale's records were in the Bristol Archives, and they would release them to an established archive in Adelaide, so I arranged this with Valma Ankel of State Records.

With his records I was able to help identify the Aboriginal subjects of two paintings by artist Michael Crossland (1800–58) of Poonindie cricketers that no-one had previously known. They were Samuel Cornwillan (or Kandwillan) and Nannultera. That was really good, because they never used to give Aboriginal people names in the old pictures. Historian John Tregenza had been trying to identify them for some time, so he was very pleased and ended up writing about my discovery in a history journal.[10]

I worked with Peggy for about six months or more in late 1988, and *Poonindie: The Rise and Destruction of an Aboriginal Agricultural Community* was published in 1989. I contributed a lot of personal photos, as well as others from my collection that I got from the Mortlock Library and the Public Records Office, and I drew up a genealogy that we put at the back of the book. It would have taken Peggy years of research without my help and I dedicated myself to this book because it was my grandmother's place, so I was upset that Peggy was just going to say 'with the assistance of Doreen Kartinyeri' or something like that. *Kunamara* Ware had to talk to her before she agreed to make me a co-author. We launched it over at the Poonindie church and Peggy gave me nine copies — one for me and each of my children.

Researching further afield

Although I started with the local genealogies, these began to take me across borders. Researching the families of people who had gone to other States, one of whom was Mrs Connie Hart, I found that one of her forebears, Nicodemus Wilson, went over to Victoria. Steve Hemming, Philip Clarke and I planned a trip to Melbourne to talk to her. Steve did some taping with her because she still had Ngarrindjeri knowledge passed down from her father, even though she was born in Victoria and married into Cumeragunja mission. She said she always wished she could have come over to see Raukkan, but she didn't know who to contact or how to go about it. It was lovely to see her. She had some rushes growing in her backyard and had been taught the weaving of the Ngarrindjeri people and she showed us some little things that she made.

The biggest problem I had in that job was getting the information back into the Aboriginal communities where it was so needed and wanted. So after I completed the Rigney book I started to make field trips with Norman Tindale's records. Oscar was living with us and Squashy came to stay a lot too. Then Syd got a job on the Woodville Council, so I was able to go away on my field trips without a worry in the world, because I knew that my two brothers and Syd would look after my children.

My first field trip was to Raukkan. Now there weren't very many people left that remembered Tindale when he visited there in 1938–9, but there were a few, so we went and met with Aunty Marj Koolmatrie, Vivien Lovegrove and Lyndsay Wilson (Dulcie's husband), who remembered his visit.

Some of them didn't want to give me names of their illegitimate children. I told them they didn't have to; that that was a permission only they can give me, fair enough. That's how I printed it. But some of them are now saying to me that they should have given me permission for that, because that little girl they had who was not her husband's doesn't appear in there with her half-brothers and sisters. She appears in the father's line, because he gave me permission to put her in his book, which is another title by another name.

So you see it took me a lot of heartache, a lot of travelling, a lot of time, a very little bit of money, because I didn't have a lot of money to do this. They were giving us cars and petrol and setting us up accommodation, but I was still getting my same salary. It never changed for three years — $260 a week. I gave up my pension, which was a little bit more, for that. But I was so determined to do it.

Sometimes I got told off, I got cursed, told I shouldn't be doing this and it's not my fucking business and sometimes I got beer thrown in my face. But I just stood my ground, because if I didn't do it now, our grandchildren would not know anything. But some of the meetings we had were really great and we video-recorded some of them.

My second field trip was to Point Pearce and then from there I went to Bendigo in Victoria because most of the Lake Condah and Lake Ebenezer people all finished up round there. The Victorians wanted all of Tindale's original books; they insisted. So Steve Hemming, Philip Clarke and I went over there and told them we could not give them the originals, but we'd be happy to photocopy every one of them and give them back to each Aboriginal group. After big negotiations we did that. We had to bring in a couple of students on work experience to do the photocopying because it was such a big job. And it still took a lot of time because we had to explain what we wanted done and how. They weren't genealogies that you could just run through the machine and put together in a heap; they had to be put together the way Tindale did it and we weren't able to unpick his books to make it easier.

Steve Hemming joined me on most of the trips and then, around the time he started to negotiate about the Ngurunderi film [about an ancestor whose Dreaming story is pivotal to Ngarrindjeri life] he was producing for the Museum, Philip Clarke started to become involved as well. Philip Clarke had only ever come up to the Aboriginal Family History room from time to time, but apart from that he had nothing to do with it.

At the same time, all these people were learning a lot from me. Steve I just took under my wing, and I taught Philip Clarke many of the things I had already taught Steve. I taught him the proper pronunciations of Ngarrindjeri words and a lot of the kinship. He learned a lot from me.

I told him about Ngurunderi, who was our Ngarrindjeri God, and the story about him and his life on Raukkan with his two wives. His wives ran away and he chased them down through the Coorong and

Goolwa and all that area. And then when he died he went up to the sky and he's one of the bright stars in the Milky Way.

They decided at the Museum to do an exhibition on Ngurunderi and Ngarrindjeri culture, which opened in 1988, and when Winston Head was setting it up I had a look at the exhibit, and had to tell them they got some things wrong. First of all they had the *wurley* set up so that the fire outside was in the wrong position for the wind direction. In the position they had it, the wind would blow the fire back towards the *wurley* and it would be burnt down. It's simple; if your wind's coming from the west you'd have to have your fire on the east side of your *wurley*. You had to take notice of all of that. If they didn't have the benefit of my advice on that, that would have been wrong, and all the Ngarrindjeri people would have picked it up. I also had to tell Steve the Ngarrindjeri woman figure was in the wrong sitting position. I told Steve I couldn't tell him why, because I wasn't able to tell a man that, but I told him how they should have her sitting for the scenario she was in. Steve would have worked it out then that there was women's business.

But we had plenty of sad times too. When Neva Wilson started working with me she asked me how I did it. I said I didn't know, but I knew it was important that I do it and that I do it right.

Still, there was one person who thought I wasn't doing it right. I'll never forget the time Mac Lawrie, old W.T.'s son, came in to see me in the Museum there to have a yarn and look at photos. He said his father would not like someone like me doing Aboriginal history. He reckoned his mother and father would have known more than me, and I told him that if they weren't dead I would have talked to them. It seemed to me he was upset that a little Aboriginal woman was researching her own culture. But I resented the fact that he thought I didn't know what I was doing.

I asked him if he had any photographs we could use; after all, his father was on the mission for thirty-seven years and would have collected a lot of stuff. I asked him if I could have copies made. But he said he couldn't do that because his parents had left them for him and Enid. So I had a big argument with Mac. Then I said, 'There's the door. Close it on your way out'.

Stolen Generation searches

Finding Stolen Generation families was a priority. With the Stolen Generations it's very hard to describe in words what effect it had on the people who came in to look at these records, as well as the effect on me. In South Australia amongst the Protector's papers were records of all the children that were placed in the Homes. People would ring up and make an appointment and we would always find time to talk to them. They'd come in and we'd sit down and I'd explain all Norman Tindale's genealogies to them and how he used to obtain them, sitting down in the most unpredictable places with people wherever he found them.

Then I realised there were photos taken of people who had actually been taken away from their families by the Protector of Aborigines in the 1930s. I started to find and reconnect a lot of the Stolen Generation people with their families. Even today I can't stop doing this. When I was working for the Native Title Unit at the Aboriginal Legal Rights Movement in Adelaide, about 1998 I got a phone call from a woman wanting to see me. She and her two sisters didn't marry into Aboriginal families when they left Raukkan and now she wanted to find out about hers. We made an appointment and she came to see me and she told me who her mother was. I knew her. I gave her a copy of her family's genealogies. She said, 'I remember my Mum talking about Uncle Vivien and Uncle Albert and Uncle Frank and Aunty Heather'. And there she was singing names of people she never met.

Then there was the case of one of my foster daughters. Her adoptive mother had her from when she was a baby, but when she was a twelve-year-old she was playing up something terrible in school. She knew she was Aboriginal and she knew she was adopted, but she didn't know who her birth parents were. Her adoptive mother wouldn't tell her, but got in touch with the Welfare and told them that the girl didn't want to mix with any of her white friends or family any more. So Elaine Traeger asked me if I would take her for a while.

She was playing merry hell. I put her in Croydon Park School with Christabel and Ricky and when they mixed with white friends, she belted them. She was really having problems. She said she wanted to know who was her mother and father. So I rang Elaine Traeger up and I said that she loves her adoptive family, but she just needs to identify with her black family. It took us about three months to negotiate, but Elaine eventually gave me the name of the mother and I contacted her. She was happy to come down and meet her daughter.

The mother drove herself a long way down to Adelaide and said she should be arriving by about five p.m. that day. I waited and waited but she didn't turn up. And then a couple of the boys came in and they said, 'Mum, there's a car outside, *nunga* woman in it'. She did get into Adelaide about five, but she was too frightened to come and knock on the door.

So I went out and introduced myself. I said to her, 'Look, you've come all this way. Come and meet her. What happens from then is entirely up to you fellas'. So she came in, and I told the girls to put the kettle on, and I took that girl into the lounge and they met for the first time. It was so emotional. What the mother was frightened of was the fact that her husband might find out, and to me this was very sad. I felt so sorry for that poor girl and she was so disappointed.

But anyway, after a few months she rang me up and said they'd talked about it and her other kids wanted to meet their sister. So we agreed to let her go and spend some time with them, but it didn't work out and she doesn't have much to do with her mother now.

Still, I had to be grateful for what happened out of that little case, because I was told by Elaine Traeger that I shouldn't do that work because I was not a welfare worker. But I believed I knew more about the way these Aboriginal families felt than the welfare workers would ever know.

If we thought we were busy in the Aboriginal Family History Unit, then there was an international women's conference held at the

Festival Theatre in the early 1990s. Aboriginal people came from all over the country, but most of them ended up spending their time at the Museum with me. There were people crying all over the place, and I had to ring downstairs for the white staff to come up and help me. I couldn't cope with all those people coming in from the conference. Zola Betts rang beforehand from Brisbane and asked if she could pop in to see me. I had also met with Henrietta Fourmile in Brisbane when Neva and I attended a conference there, and she came and got photocopies of genealogies to take back to her people.

Some people didn't understand the sensitivities of the material. I saw that and I acted in the best way I could possibly do to give it back to the people, but still a lot of them were in shock. Some people were saying that Tindale had no right to write their family's stuff down or to take their photos. He often wrote in comments and he was very good at referencing where these comments came from — a Protector's report, or a welfare report or whatever — but a lot of these reports said things about people that were very nasty and I didn't want them getting out.

While I was busy with other things, Vincent and Steve had a meeting with Josie Agius and the Port Adelaide mob. Next thing I go to the bloody football on Saturday and I get cursed because all this material's flying around and I'm working in the Museum with it. So I went and ripped a strip off Steve and Vince Buckskin because the people blamed me for it. What Vincent and Steve didn't know was Tindale had a particular mark for illegitimacy. Because of that they didn't see that they were giving out information about illegitimate children without knowing it. They should have discussed it with me first.

To me the material Norman Tindale collected is a treasure. Even if some of what was written down is offensive to some people and he did make some mistakes, when I first read in black and white off Tindale's handwritten material what I was already told about the old people, I just thought, 'Wow!' And he did a massive amount of work.

But if people thought Norman Tindale's written comments were bad, they weren't as bad as those written by Ron and Catherine Berndt.[11] I first met the Berndts when I was with Fay Gale. After that meeting

Ron Berndt sent his assistant, Dr John Stanton, to give me a copy of their genealogies. I didn't like the way they talked about the people on the mission, particularly the women. They talked about incest and sexuality and it looked very 'dirty' to me. And some of it was wrong. For example, my Grandfather Gordon married twice, but they didn't have that. I felt like I wanted to burn it. When the Berndts came over to Adelaide again from Perth, I told them how I felt and they told me that was the information they got from Albert Karloan. Now Tindale got a lot of his information from Clarence Long (Milerum), who I vaguely remember, but I don't remember Albert Karloan. I did hear there was a bit of conflict between the two of them, Albert and Clarence, I think because they were giving stories to the two different anthropologists. Even so, I find it very difficult to believe that Albert Karloan talked to Catherine Berndt about things like that. I don't believe he would have had women's information, let alone given it to them.

For all the criticism I might have got, the good side of my work made up for it many times over. So many people were so excited by what I could tell them, it was a joy. I never threw out TAB tickets because I would often meet people in the TAB and we'd get talking about their genealogies and they might fill in a couple of little gaps for me. So I'd write it down on the TAB ticket and take it back with me. I did a lot of work in the TAB. I also missed many buses. I would be standing at the bus-stop and someone would stop to talk to me about their family line and two hours later we'd still be there talking!

Aunty Doris Sandel

Then there was the story of Aunty Doris Sandel (née Kropinyeri), a Ngarrindjeri woman from Raukkan. She was never part of the Stolen Generations but she was frightened her two children would be taken away, so she ran away. The white father of her children set her up in Victoria and kept her and her children for many years. Never married her, but he still provided for her and for this she'd always be grateful, she said.

As it happened, her daughter Pam was involved in Aboriginal things in Victoria, and she came over for a conference and came into the Museum to see me. She said who her mum was and who her mum's parents was. I must have sounded crazy to her, but I just named every one of her family off to her like I usually do. She was standing there in shock. That's when I realised that Aunty Doris would be the oldest living person then that was born on Raukkan, and that she would remember Raukkan in the early 1900s. I told her I would try to get some money together to go and meet her. So Steve and I and Philip Clarke went to Melbourne to visit her. She was seventeen when she left Raukkan and she was in her seventies when we caught up with her. When we sat at the table with her, she was able to tell us exactly how Raukkan was in the days when she was there, and they drew up a map of it from what she told them. The good thing was that Steve had already put a display together in the Museum using a map drawn up by Uncle Lyndsay Wilson. He put down on paper what he remembered and who was living where. Aunty Doris was the generation before him and I was the generation after (and Steve got me to do it too). So there we've got Aunty Doris, Lyndsay and me — three different people of different generations very knowledgeable about their culture — showing how Raukkan changed over time.

When Tandanya [National Aboriginal Cultural Institute] was about to open on 1 October 1989, we made arrangements for Aunty Doris to come over for the opening ceremony, and she brought her two daughters — Pam and Susan — and her granddaughter Katherine with her. We took them to the West Terrace cemetery, and Doris explained to us about her mother being buried in a pauper's grave that's not marked. So I went into the office and found out exactly whereabouts it was. I felt so excited for her, and we decided it would be nice to get a rock from down Raukkan and place it on the grave, so Philip Clarke volunteered to do this.

Aunty Doris is in some of the photos of the opening of Tandanya with John Bannon [then Premier of South Australia] and the other officials. I wrote the Introduction to the Opening Day Souvenir

Program, about Perna Adjunda Rudkee (King James Rodney) of the Kaurna people. I was able to introduce her to people like Aunty Hilda Wilson, Aunty Doris Graham, Mary Williams and the other older ones that was there. She was so excited to meet her mother's people from Raukkan after all those years.

I gave Pam a nice photograph of Aunty Doris's great-grandfather and they were just overwhelmed about that. And I told her the little story about how they *millin-ed* [killed] him. When George Taplin [the missionary who started up Point McLeay mission (Raukkan)] brought William Kropinyeri and Jean Parry to officially get married in the church, the family of Jane, William's other wife, got very offended, so by traditional law they had to *millin* his father, old William Kropinyeri, as punishment. Taplin recorded that in his own diaries, and yet he was still christianising people and encouraging them to get married in the churches, even though he knew that there was going to be a tribal punishment.

I wasn't sure how Aunty Doris would take this story but she remembered a lot of things herself, so it all fell into place. She remembered he was buried over at Raukkan, and I told her he most probably had a Christian funeral. I could hear the anger in her reaction to that. I told her how her mother's older brother Matthew was very good at shorthand and how his views on the Boer War and the First World War were quoted in *The Advertiser*. Aunty Doris was very happy to know that her aunties and uncles were really good survivors and achievers.

It was great to be able to make these connections for Aunty Doris, because I knew about her from talking to the older people when I was very young. Later I got Aunty Laura on tape and I would have liked to have recorded Aunty Rosie, but she would never let me tape her. But I did have a special skill for listening, learning and understanding. Sometimes I might see something that reminds me of something Aunty Rosie told me, and I shut my eyes and I can visualise it all going through my head like a film clip.

The way Aunty Rosie would tell me things; she used to do a lot of actions and I laughed at her. I'd say, 'I'm not going to be doing actions like that' and she'd say, 'No, you don't have to do them, my girl; they don't do them things any more, but these are the actions that go with these stories'. There's a lot I know about movements and positions you sit and the way you act and the way you hold your head up and who you look at and who you don't have eye contact with. There's a lot of things that she taught me. She was a lovely personality, always happy, laughing. But then if she really got angry she could lash you with her tongue pretty good. I loved her like the mother I lost and so did my brother Oscar and when he passed away we buried him at the foot of her grave, just as he asked.

Interstate fieldtrips

With this work I went to every state except Western Australia. I conducted workshops and I would pin up the regional family genealogies. We took with us copies of the photographs in albums so the people could look at them. We had their names, the tribe they belonged to and how old they were.

I made another field trip to Yalata on the far west coast of South Australia, and because his relations were there Syd came with me for translating and driving. Barry Craig and Neva also came. We spent nearly four weeks on the road, because when we left Yalata we called in to Koonibba, Ceduna Area School, Port Lincoln, Whyalla and Port Augusta before returning to Adelaide. I had already been to Yalata a number of times with Syd for funerals and for holidays to take his children to get to know all their *kamis* and *tjamus* [Pitjantjatjara for 'grandmothers' and 'grandfathers']. So this was a pleasure for us. The hard part was explaining why Tindale wrote about people like he did. The Yalata women didn't comment on this, but people at Port Lincoln, Ceduna and Koonnibba and everywhere else were angry about it, and it took me a long time to explain what Tindale was doing and how he was going about it.

Tindale took photos of every person individually and I got them reproduced minus the reference number that was printed on the front, because that made them look like mug shots. Some of the people in the photos were deceased so we weren't supposed to show them out.

But Syd would talk to people first to find out if they wanted to see them or not.

At Yalata we talked with Syd's step-mother, old *kabbarli* [old lady] Freda. Barry sat in the front seat of the station wagon taking notes and Neva sat on the ground with me and Syd and the old lady. We had a photo of *Kabbarli's* mother as a young woman, a photo of Syd's grandmother, Badlie. When Syd showed the photo to the old lady she just went off in language. '*Wantinyi, wantinyi*' ['leave it'] was all I could understand. And she covered old Badlie's face. Syd knew it was her mother, but we didn't expect that reaction. I thought, 'Oh, what have I done?' The old lady went to pull the photo out of the book and when Syd saw this, he took it out and gave it to her and she put it in her *mundi* [breast] and held it there. And she started to cry, wailing in the old way. So Syd talked to her in language and told her she could keep the photograph and she pulled her-self together. But I could see the agony in her face as she talked to Syd, all the time drawing in the sand to illustrate what she was saying.

I thought that was one of the most wonderful things to have experienced. During this meeting I was also able to get genealogical information from *Kami* Freda and later I put Syd's family tree together for him, back to the old *tjamu* from the Maralinga Pitjantjatjara people. I was very happy to do that.

But because old *Kabbarli* Freda took most of the photographs in the end (and no way Syd and I were going to ask her for them back), we had to send to Adelaide for another copy of them all. In Whyalla another old lady also took a lot of photos, so we learned for future trips to take a spare set.

At Yalata people showed a lot of emotion, but made no comment about Tindale's notes. But in Koonibba people weren't happy and started blaming me again. I had to point out that I didn't do it, that I was only three at the time. I still today get blamed by some people for some of the stuff that Tindale wrote up. What I was trying to get across to them was that this is how you can find out where ancestors originally came from. This could be a big stepping stone in getting Aboriginal people land rights, being identified as part of a tribe.

Then Syd and I and Neva went to Coober Pedy. I met with Eileen Crombie, Emily Austin, Aunty Ivy Stewart, Eileen Wingfield, Eileen Brown and Lillian Fatt and one or two of her sisters. We also had one of the descendants of the Wares living up there and she was amazed that I was her relation through my Nanna Sally.

We eventually got back to the Museum after what I would say was a very successful trip, and Steve Hemming and Peter Sutton were just amazed that I collected so much. We started working on separating one family from the other, which was a big job, so because Neva's family is from the West Coast, we gave her most of that stuff to work on. I concentrated on Point Pearce, the Riverland, Mount Gambier and Raukkan. And in between all this work, I published the *Wilson Family* genealogies in 1990.

I had to convince Norman Tindale to release the material for all the other states, and at first he was a bit reluctant, but eventually he agreed. So then we headed out for the rest of Australia. I went to Brisbane, Sydney and Melbourne. After Neva and I were completing one trip on the east coast, Marcia Langton[12] rang me up and asked me if I'd like to go over to Sydney to this conference as a speaker. I talked about how what we held in South Australia belongs to so many other places around Australia, and somehow this made me a key person in its distribution. Someone suggested to Marcia and I that we were going to re-write Aboriginal history. We both said no, and I said I wasn't here to change Australian Aboriginal history, but to make sure that in future it'll be written properly. Next day we're in the bloody paper, a photo of Marcia and me and an article saying we're wanting to change Aboriginal history!

I had a couple of trips to Darwin, which were very rewarding, because they didn't have many records at all about Aboriginal people in their archives. They had a few papers about white people who had worked with Aboriginal people, but that was all. The second trip I took Val Power [née Karpany, sister of Muriel van der Byl] and it was a great success.

I spent nearly a year getting around to the other states, all except Western Australia because there was so much information there that it was a job in itself. Eventually the Museum employed Peter Bertani to tackle Western Australia. Peter was from WA and he could talk the language, he knew skin names and had information on tribal ways that I didn't, so I was happy for him to take it on, but the WA trips ended up taking a big chunk of our budget and eventually the funds ran out because of this.

The Garnett brothers

By now a lot of people had heard about the work I had been doing, and I was in demand for radio and television interviews. Neva and I were interviewed by Geraldine Doogue for the ABC program *Life Matters*. After I published the Wanganeen book a woman in Port Lincoln saw me on TV, and she wrote to say a relative of hers married an Aboriginal man by the name of Garnett Wanganeen and they had two sons, Keith and Peter. One was in Sydney and the other was working in Africa, and she wanted to get two copies of the book to send to them, so I met up with her to give her the books. She asked me why I didn't have any information on them in the book. I told her that all I knew was that Garnett (who was a brother to my father-in-law Bob Wanganeen) married a white woman and had two sons, but I hadn't been able to find out any more. So she filled me in. She said Garnett Spencer Wanganeen changed his name to Spencer Garnett because he was light enough to pass as a white man and thought this would be best.

Peter wrote me a nice letter from Sydney and thanked me for the book and for giving him his identity because he didn't know that he was of Aboriginal descent for a long time. He sent me a photo of his five children sitting round his father's grave in the West Terrace cemetery. When Keith came back to Australia they contacted me and we had a reunion. I had helped my ex-husband Terry find two long lost cousins.

The whole time I was doing this work I wasn't getting paid the salary of another person who had a degree. But the thing is I love my work.

Kinship had been my passion since I was a teenager. Since then I've memorised thousands of names and their relationships and nothing has stopped me publishing them right up until my latest books, *Narungga Nation*, published in February 2003 and *Ngarrindjeri Nation*, published in 2006. Not even the Kumarangk affair.

7
Putting Black History on White Paper

Having published the Wilson and Rankine genealogies in 1990, I was now the author of five genealogies, the Poonindie book and an article in *We Are Bosses Ourselves*. In the six years I had been with the Museum I had given guest lectures at Adelaide University, Flinders University and the University of South Australia, as well in TAFE. I had held workshops in schools, universities and TAFE, and week-long workshops in Darwin, Brisbane, Sydney, Melbourne, Ballarat, Port Lincoln, Ceduna, Whyalla, Port Augusta, Murray Bridge, and the Riverland, as well as shorter workshops at Yalata, Coober Pedy, the Lower Murray and Camp Coorong. I had attended three national conferences and delivered papers and had them published. I had given interviews for newspapers, radio and television.

Syd and I were living in Baroota [Aboriginal Lands Trust owned community] on the northern Yorke Peninsula because Syd got work there, and again I was mostly working from home. It was lovely living there and we had some really lovely times there. After the Yalata trip, some of the West Coast women came over and stopped with us for the long weekend to talk about our different cultures. Syd's Aunty Martha Edwards welcomed everyone and Aunty Ivy Stewart spoke last and thanked me for the work I was doing. We built a big fire in the back yard and cooked wombat, sleepy lizards, kangaroo tails and rabbits that Syd had hunted, and we yarned into the night.

It was just after that in early 1994 when the issue of the bridge came to my attention. I felt that this thing was going to be the biggest destruction that they could ever do to the Ngarrindjeri people and I thought they'd done enough already, ripping off our land without compensation. I thought, 'I know the history. I might as well speak up for it now as never', because I had never been involved in something like this before. The ferry was there before I was born; I was just a baby when the barrages were built; the highways and roads were already built and the burial ground just out of Wellington had been destroyed to put in the Wellington punt so you could take a shortcut to Adelaide. This was the last straw. Enough was enough.

My mind went to a report I had seen in the Museum about the building of a bridge at Swanport in the early 1900s. When the work started on that, they uncovered a mass grave of Ngarrindjeri people. Edward Stirling from the Museum had examined the bones and said they were the victims of a nineteenth-century smallpox outbreak. But then they found bullet wounds, so they could have been the victims of a massacre, because plenty of those went on in the early days. The people were from Raukkan, and so many of them died they buried them in a mass grave just the other side of Murray Bridge. I heard rumours in the Museum that those bones they dug out of that grave were sent over to England and some to Edinburgh in Scotland, to have scientific tests done on them. I thought this was unbelievable. Some of them would have been my relations. Whitefellas wouldn't send their grandparents' bones overseas. Just damaging a headstone would be enough to get them going.

By this time the developers, Tom and Wendy Chapman, were carrying on about how they had hired Dr Lindy Warrell to do an anthropological report on the area and that they had done full consultation with the relevant Aboriginal communities. But proper consultation hadn't happened because there were so many knowledgeable people who hadn't been consulted. I hadn't been consulted, even though I was born on Raukkan, and by then I was nearly sixty years old.

I didn't know what for, but I remembered that Rod Lucas did an anthropological report on the area in 1989, because he came and talked to me. We had several conversations about how sacred that area was and he consulted me properly. And then four years later, Neale Draper, who was the government archaeologist at the time, did a report on significant sites on Kumarangk, and it seemed to me Neale Draper did what he wanted to do. He came and talked to me, but I don't think he heard me, because he went ahead and finished his report, I felt without including what I told him. He's come to me for a lot of information and I've given it to him over the years, but in my opinion he wasn't including in his reports the things that I thought were important.

The fight begins

On Sunday, 8 May 1994, Victor Wilson picked me up to drive me for a few meetings over on Kumarangk. Victor is my cousin Aileen's son, but has always owned me as a big sister and I always owned his mum as a big sister. On the trip south Victor was trying to work out what I knew. I told him he could ask me anything he liked except women's business. I used the word 'business' because I didn't want to go into details. Well now Victor was beginning to understand and realised this was something he shouldn't be getting into. It's not that long a trip, but by gee it seemed like it that day because I could see Victor wanted to talk to me about it, and yet he didn't know how to.

So to fill the silence I was talking to him about the right way to fight this bridge. I told him it was up to him and the other members of the Ngarrindjeri Heritage Committee, together with the South Australian State Heritage Committee, to act on that. By the time we got to Goolwa we realised that this had to be fronted by not only the Heritage Committees but by the people as well.

Sure enough, later in the paper they said that Victor and I had schemed up a plan to stop the developers building the bridge! But the media was not in on that conversation, was not in the car all the way from Adelaide to Goolwa, and did not hear what Victor and I said. There was no plan, no such thing. This was just the beginning of a vicious media campaign to discredit our beliefs and our reasons for wanting to stop that bridge.

We were staying at the Pines because it was cheap, and a number of us all bunked in together. There were about a dozen of us Ngarrindjeri women down there, and that night we gathered in my bunk room and I talked to them all about the things I knew that were important to women about Kumarangk. We yarned for a long time that night and they all listened very carefully to what I had to say. Some of them said they had heard little bits and pieces from their relations and what I was saying fitted with that.

Sarah and Doug Milera were living in the Mouth House, Anne Lucas's little place at the mouth of the Murray River, and the next day we had a meeting there to talk over what was happening. As well as the women I talked to the night before, Shirley and George Trevorrow, Victor and Glenys Wilson, Glenys's sister Bronwyn and their father Brucey Carter and his wife Cathy, Doug Milera and Tim Woolley from ALRM [Aboriginal Legal Rights Movement] turned up too. A few more women then arrived, including Dorothy Wilson, who took the time off from her job as Program Director at the Lower Murray Nungas' Club to drive down. I was pleased to see my cousin Billy's wife, even though they had separated, and I knew she was fighting with Victor [her brother-in-law] over things happening at the Nungas' Club.

I didn't think nothing much of it; feuds like these have been on-going in the Ngarrindjeri community, sometimes since we were kids. Certainly I had never had a good relationship with Dulcie Wilson from the time we were little. I always had the feeling that Dulcie, being a whiter coloured skin, considered herself superior to me, even though I led a very respectable life.

Tom Trevorrow chaired the meeting, and that's when it came out that Sarah Milera and I had both been separately to see David Rathman and that I had spoken to Barbara Weise. I explained that even though David Rathman was head of the Department of Aboriginal Affairs, he was still employed by white people and had to do what they wanted.

This time I talked again generally about the fact that there was some very significant women's knowledge to do with the island but I didn't go into detail in front of the men. Nobody objected or complained that it wasn't true, including Dulcie.

We spent all day discussing ways of dealing with the problem. We decided to send a letter to Alexandrina Council and elected a committee to deal with it. The decisions that the meeting made would be processed by the committee, who would represent our views to the State. We thought that was the right and proper way of doing things. I didn't want no violence.

While this was going on, Doug Milera pointed to the map and said the area represented women's internal organs. I said to Doug, 'If you know so much, how come you've missed the most important thing?' And the most important thing is that him being a man, he's not supposed to be talking about that, because it's women's business. Of course, later on the media said that the men had told the women about 'women's business'. How ridiculous. Women knew there was men's business and men knew there was women's business; just not the details. The important thing was not to talk about it.

We discussed what we could do to protect the area against them building a bridge, and Tim Woolley said the best thing to do was for us to write to Robert Tickner and ask him to put a ban on it, so that's what we decided to do. The women, including Dorrie Wilson and Sarah Milera, got together at the University of South Australia's centre at Goolwa, Ngarrindjeri Pulgi [Ngarrindjeri house], and wrote a letter, but we weren't prepared to give him any details. Tim Woolley said this wouldn't be enough; that we'd have to reveal some of the information for it to be possible for Robert Tickner to act. But that was forbidden. Over my dead body would I tell a man! I was feeling very stressed out about the thought of telling more. I left them with it. I was planning to write my own letter. But I understand that Dorrie Wilson was one of the ones that signed that letter to stop the bridge and that it was sent off in the afternoon from ALRM.

The next day, on 10 May, a protest was scheduled to block construction work from beginning. A big crowd of Aboriginal people and supporters were gathered at Amelia Park on the river front and it was a big chaos. The police were there and the media were there to record the protest. There were speeches by Matt Rigney, representing ATSIC, and Sarah Milera, who was speaking for the Ngarrindjeri Action Group which had formed to stop the bridge. Then the people all linked arms and blocked the way for the workers wanting to set up. People were jostling and shouting and Doug Milera got dragged away by the police. It was all on the television that night. I was shocked by it all. I didn't know the Ngarrindjeri people had organised such a big protest. I just didn't know all this had been going on because I had only just heard about it.

But it was this protest meeting that got the media going. Apparently the Chapmans had first proposed the bridge a few years earlier and some people saw it as Aboriginal people were only raising a stink at the last minute. I don't understand what they thought we were doing it for — whether they thought we were just being bloody-minded or what. But people don't realise how out of touch a lot of Aboriginal people can be. A lot of us live on former missions away from the cities. Aboriginal people don't have much money to make long-distance phone calls all the time. Many people don't have transport; I don't even drive, and it's hard work catching long haul buses all the time. Organising meetings and getting together costs money, something not many Aboriginal people have. So very few people knew anything about it until then. But when I spoke out I didn't know much of what had been going on in the lead up to the bridge proposal. But I didn't intend to hurt anybody; I did it because I needed to protect something that was important to my people. I actually never thought nothing much about the Chapmans at all. To me, they wasn't even worth thinking about.

Letter to Tickner

After the protest that day, I went back to Adelaide, and that's when I composed my own letter to Robert Tickner that Steve sent off from the Museum. It read:

My name is Doreen Kartinyeri. I am a descendant of the Raminyeri people of the Coorong, Hindmarsh and Mundoo Islands. I am also the Aboriginal Research Officer in the SA Museum's Family History Project.

My concern is that we need to let you know of the Women's Business associated with Hindmarsh and Mundoo Island only known by the Raminyeri and Ngarrindjeri women.

Thank you for intervening in the Hindmarsh Island issue and allowing us time to provide you with the information about this place.

I also want to bring to your attention the SA Aboriginal Heritage Act which I feel has not been followed through appropriately by the State Government. There really hasn't been a chance for women to tell about their traditions associated with Hindmarsh and Mundoo Island and the Coorong. This can only be told to women and all those involved in the Heritage process in SA have been men. I would like to talk to a senior woman in your Department about some of the details of this Women's Business.

I have always known about the stories associated with Raminyeri and Ngarrindjeri Women's Business but until recently I didn't know the exact place that they referred to. My Grandmother Sally Kartinyeri, my Great Aunt Laura Kartinyeri and my Aunty Rose Kropinyeri passed these stories about Women's Business to me.

This is really important to the Ngarrindjeri and Raminyeri people and to the whole of the River Murray and the Coorong.

There is also a lot of records about burials on Hindmarsh and Mundoo Islands which I will send to you and I am putting together family trees of the people who belong to Hindmarsh and Mundoo Islands. I need a couple of weeks to put all of this together and then I will send it to you.

The Raminyeri and Ngarrindjeri people thank you for your help and interest.

Later on I came under fire for saying that 'until recently I didn't know the exact place that they referred to'. What I meant was 'the place they referred to where the bridge was going to be built'. That lack of white education means I never learnt much grammar and it catches me out sometimes.

7 ~ Putting Black History on White Paper

After receiving my letter, Robert Tickner banned the building of the bridge for thirty days and appointed Professor Cheryl Saunders to undertake an investigation into Ngarrindjeri heritage to see whether the bridge should be permanently stopped. I didn't see why they needed an investigation, but if that's what it took, okay.

Controversy over the bridge was starting to brew into a storm. On 5 June an anti-bridge protest was held at Goolwa, attended by about 800 people. Then five days later the pro-bridge mob protested, and they got a crowd of about 600.

Cheryl Saunders was coming to talk to us, so a meeting was organised for the women to get together beforehand to talk about what we were going to say to her. The meeting was held at a conference centre called Graham's Castle in Goolwa on Saturday, 18 June. Graham, the owner, was happy to have us there.

I was getting ready for the meeting when I had a phone call saying that Rocky Marshall, a *gunya* whose family had lived in the area from the earliest times of white invasion, had published a letter to the editor, telling details of Ngarrindjeri women's business his grandmother had told him about. I got hold of a copy of the paper and I just couldn't believe what I was reading. Now that old lady must have been close to the Aboriginal women in the area and learnt a bit from them, but not enough to know she shouldn't pass things on to the men in her family. I was furious that this had been published in the paper.

We got into the minibus and headed for the island. When we got there over the ferry, I happened to see Deane Fergie. Deane was appointed by ALRM to be their anthropologist to assist Cheryl Saunders. I thought that was wonderful, but I was surprised that they appointed her to work with me, because Deane and I was good friends and we done a fair bit of work together. Deane was with the University of Adelaide and would sometimes come over to the Family History Unit. She had invited me on a trip with her to the tribal country up north, but I was too busy in Adelaide.

I had already had a couple of meetings with Deane on this stuff before the others came on the scene, and I gave her the names of other women to contact, such as Aunty Connie Roberts, Aunty Maggie

Jacobs, Aunty Laura Kartinyeri, Aunty Emmo Webster, Aunty Marj Koolmatrie, Veronica Brodie, Pansy Wilson. I even suggested Dulcie Wilson. She was older than me and because Lyndsay knew so much I just assumed Dulcie did too.

I jumped in Deane's car and told her to drive. I gave her directions to Rocky's house. I didn't know him well, but I met him through all this. Rocky and his wife were having a meeting at their house for the Friends of Goolwa. I marched in there and blasted Rocky for publicly telling our knowledge. Sarah Milera and Amelia Campbell were at that meeting. Afterwards, I wanted to talk to them about what they knew of women's business, but they wouldn't talk to me about it, so I left.

Meeting at Graham's Castle

That evening we had the meeting at Graham's Castle. The Ngarrindjeri Heritage Committee made sure as many women as possible were notified. Victor and Glenys made sure I had transport here and there. About four carloads of people came from Raukkan, a bus and several cars came from Murray Bridge, Tailem Bend and Adelaide. About 160 women were there for that meeting. Lots of strong Ngarrindjeri women were there, like Val Power (née Karpany) and her sister Muriel van der Byl, Sandra Saunders, Shirley Peisley and Vi Deuschle, who have been wonderful supporters. Daisy Rankine was there; Aunty Laura is her aunty as well as mine. Isobel Norvill[1] was there. Henry and Jean Rankine, who represented the Ngarrindjeri Council when they talked to the Chapmans and gave the bridge the go-ahead, did not come to the meeting. They must have been worried about how the Chapmans took it that they were speaking for all Ngarrindjeri people, but it's a shame they didn't come because that would have been a chance for them to explain why they had done that and clear the air.

Everybody showed interest in what was going on and it was a good meeting. It was an open meeting, no-one chairing it, no-one taking minutes, so we could all feel free to say what we wanted. There were people that were speaking at that meeting that I never ever heard speak out in any other meeting. I think a lot of them felt very strongly about the issue. Some of what were later to become known as the 'dissident women' were there, including Dorrie Wilson as well as Amelia Campbell, and they gave us nothing to believe they weren't with the rest of us. I addressed the meeting and told them I didn't really know what's going to happen, all I knew was they were looking to build a bridge over to Kumarangk and I didn't think we should let them because Kumarangk is very significant to Ngarrindjeri people. It's something that the old people used to be very, very proud of; they used to go there to teach the young ones hunting and gathering and to pass on culture and for many, many things.

I told them that a lot of the women had been raped by white settlers in the early days and that's where the women used to go to abort these babies. I didn't go into how they did that then, even though I knew it, because I didn't want the younger women to hear that. I told them that *kumari* was the word for pregnant and how that related to the name of the island as Kumarangk. They asked me how I knew and I told them about my relationship with Aunty Rosie, and her yarns about Raukkan and Kumarangk and down the Coorong. I told them she gave me the information on all the kinship relationships, and I told them the story she told me about how when she was walking over Kumarangk and went off the road to pick *mantharis* [wild tomatoes], Grandfather Ben told her not to go off the track because she wasn't allowed to dig into that soil with her crutch. This was because all those aborted foetuses were buried there.

I also told them about the story I had heard about the skeletons that were taken out when the Chapmans built that first marina. A white woman came over to me at the protest at Amelia Park to tell me that she and her son were sitting in the hotel down at Goolwa when the boy overheard some whitefella bragging about all the bones he had in the back of his ute. So the boy went outside and lifted up the canvas at the back corner of the ute and sure enough, the tray of the ute was full of skeletons. Later on that boy was having nightmares, but I told his mother he would be all right because he didn't touch them. When I heard this story I felt ripped apart. I could picture the faces of all the old people who were buried down there. It was terrible.

Eventually we had a vote and everyone there decided that even though I wasn't the oldest one with the knowledge, I should be the spokesperson for the women; that I should be the main one to speak. I knew I was strong enough to do this, and this gave the whole group a real strength about standing by that. A lot of people said this whole business caused major conflicts in the community. But as I say, they were already there; it just brought those conflicts into the public. Actually, the truth is that it brought people together. People could at last stand together for their heritage, and my commitment to get up there and say things got people saying, 'Yes, yes'. A lot of people don't know that they made me the spokesperson, but amongst us that was recognised.

There were a lot of meetings after this and it was bloody hard work getting people together to talk over the issues we needed to discuss. At some of the meetings there were 150 to 200 people from all over the place. And the strength of it was that people did get together, because if it was just individuals acting alone we would have gone under from all that pressure. I am proud that I was a major part of that.

Well, the women all were taking in what was being said, and I saw Dorrie Wilson and her sister Beryl nodding. They made comments to the effect that they had heard stories like that from their own mother. I remember directly asking Beryl, who is older than Dorrie, whether she knew anything about that and she said, 'Yeah, Aunty Dodo, I know a few things Mum told me'. She said she had also asked her Aunty Stella (who was Chirpy Campbell's mother) and she said it was true. Still I never gave the media any one of those women's names as having said they knew, just Aunty Laura, Aunty Rosie and Grandmother Sally. After we had been talking for a while I noticed Dorrie get up and walk out, but my mind was on so many other things I didn't think nothing of it.

After the meeting we went for tea in the dining room at Graham's Castle in the big lounge room, and Aunty Maggie Jacobs and I sat down there and had a yarn. Aunty Maggie wanted to suss out what I knew, and it turned out we knew much of the same things, and we were discussing what a pity it was that more people didn't have more knowledge. I suggested to Aunty Maggie maybe we'd have to tell them more. This made Aunty Maggie very nervous, so we agreed we wouldn't tell them all the details but just that we knew all about initiation of a woman, preparing her for first intercourse and for her first child. Aunty Maggie learned all that as a young girl, and it was a relief that I wasn't the only one that knew. Esther knew; Esther's dead. Julie knew; Julie's dead. Sheila Goldsmith knew; Sheila's dead. Same age group. The others were dead before but Sheila died at the beginning of all this. Leila Rankine knew, and she passed her knowledge on to her sister Veronica Brodie before she died.

But it was really good to know Aunty Maggie had the same knowledge because our paths had rarely crossed. When she married she left Raukkan and went to live in Queensland. When she lost her husband she came back and was living in Adelaide for a long time. Then she went back to Raukkan for a while and then came back to Adelaide. So me being over Point Pearce, Cummins, Port Lincoln and Baroota, I never got to see her and we weren't around for long enough to discuss anything with one another. The only time I really had a chance to sit down with Aunty Maggie before this was when Syd and I went down to Camp Coorong to show Steve Hemming how to make a *wurley* in about 1987. He made a film out of that for the Museum. Lyndsay Wilson was there and Aunty Marj Koolmatrie and Aunty Maggie was there after she came back from Queensland. People said we were getting together and building up these stories, but we never had that opportunity. We didn't have to anyway.

Next thing you know the media was saying that I said that the island and its surrounding waters represented a woman's vagina. Now I never said that and I would never have used the word 'vagina' because it's not my way to use a *gunya* word for that. I would have used the word *tjokli*, and they wouldn't have known what that was. They just wouldn't let up on that and they put it down as me saying it, which was wrong. When I got back to Adelaide there was a meeting called at ALRM and the media were there to find out what was going on. Colin James from *The Advertiser* wouldn't leave the issue alone. He kept asking me if the island represented a woman's organs and going into detail. I found this really offensive and I told him the island is sacred to women and that's all he needed to know. I said that if he asked me that question once more I would walk out of the interview. And he did ask, so that's when I walked out and I never talked to Colin James again. Much later he tried to apologise to me for that, but it was too late.

Later on that night I was talking to Isobel Norvill. Dorrie and Beryl are sisters-in-law to Isobel. We were in my room, and I asked Isobel what she thought about Dorrie walking out of the meeting. Isobel said she didn't care what Dorrie did; that she was sticking with me. I knew Isobel knew what her mother knew and I knew what Isobel's mother knew because she is my first cousin. Her father and my mother were brother and sister.

We went all round the island with Cheryl Saunders, starting at Graham's Castle. Aunty Connie Roberts, her daughter Rhonda Agius, Aunty Maggie, Daisy Rankine, Veronica Brodie and I were all interviewed separately by Cheryl Saunders, and the stories we told were pretty much the same. Sarah also talked to her, but I can't remember who else. I told Cheryl Saunders what I wanted to let her know and she asked me questions. I answered her the best way I thought. I told her the 'Seven Sisters' Dreaming story Aunty Rosie told me years ago about those stars in the sky, when seven girls went walkabout hunting. An old fella chased them and raped them and they cried, cried, cried. This made the little streams down around the Coorong and Lakes. She told me the Seven Sisters looked after all the women.

When I was going over to the island on the ferry, the puntman, John, came to talk to me. He told me he wanted us all to come round to his house because there was something he wanted to show us. He was on the Alexandrina Council and had access to plans for a road down over the Coorong, like a new freeway to Victoria. John explained that this route would cut a few hours off the trip from Adelaide to Melbourne. The plans included a bridge from Kumarangk to Mundoo Island. Now Mundoo Island is sacred to men and it's also where they smoked the bodies of the dead. I had already told people this, but the interest was all focused on Kumarangk. I was shocked that they could consider ripping up the Kurangk [Coorong] because we've got a lot of burial grounds and other important places along the Kurangk too.

After we got back to Adelaide, Deane got in touch to say Tim Woolley had asked her to do a report on the women's information and arranged to meet with me to talk about it. We met up at Legal Rights again and I sat down and told Deane what I knew. I kept saying, 'I don't want it recorded and written'. But she said Tim Woolley said we needed to record some of it if we were to have any effect. I had to make a choice; write it down or let them destroy our sites by building a bridge. I agonised over it. It seemed like a *Catch-22* situation and it sure as hell turned out to be. I finally agreed to let her write it down as long as it got put in an envelope and sealed. So that's what Deane did. I told her about the initiation practices for young girls, to prepare them for *yupun*, for their periods and for having babies. She typed that out and I watched while she put it in the envelope.

Aboriginal of the Year

While all this was going on, in early June I got a call asking if I could come down to Adelaide for the NAIDOC [National Aboriginal and Islander Day of Celebration] ball on Friday night, 9 July 1994, which I said I would be happy to do. That's when I was named South Australian Aboriginal of the Year. I took the opportunity to say I hoped there would be a favourable decision to ban the bridge permanently. There I was one minute being presented with the Award of South Australian Aboriginal of the Year by the Premier, Dean Brown, and next minute I'm in a fight with him because he wants to build the bridge at Kumarangk.

> *The Adelaide Advertiser*, 7 July 1994
>
> Ms Doreen Kartinyeri said Mr Brown's warning against federal intervention in the bridge issue on Tuesday was a 'kick in the guts' for those who were trying to protect important traditional areas near the proposed bridge site. On Monday, the Premier praised and rewarded the work of Ms Kartinyeri, a South Australian Museum historian, who was the main contributor to a report on the

significance of the site compiled for the federal Aboriginal Affairs Minister, Mr Tickner.

Now what did they give me my award for? Because of the history I had been writing. So why don't they believe the history I know about Kumarangk?

On the Sunday two days later I was at home, where Syd and I were living by then in Port Germein, when Sandra Saunders rang. She said that after receiving Cheryl Saunders' report, Robert Tickner had placed a 25-year ban on the building of the Hindmarsh Island bridge. I was glad, but I didn't feel like this was a really great victory, because that still meant a bridge could be built after twenty-five years, and I wouldn't be around to fight it again. I wanted him to ban it forever.

At this time I still kept working from home because it was too far to commute to Adelaide every day. I was working very hard and felt that the contribution I was able to make to my people was really worthwhile. The staff at the Museum had allowed me to do the work my way and had been very helpful and supportive. Apparently the Chapmans went to the Federal Court to fight Robert Tickner's ban, but I didn't know about courts and things, so that didn't mean anything to me.

A few months later, in November, I heard that Ian McLachlan was claiming we had made up the women's sacred knowledge just to stop the bridge. That made me wild, but I didn't think anything would come of that either. But sure enough, in February 1995, I hear that the Chapmans won their case in the Federal Court and Robert Tickner's ban is overturned because he didn't read what was in the secret envelopes. This didn't make any sense to me; if he was supposed to read them what was the point of making them secret? Then I hear that Robert Tickner is going to appeal. I wondered what the hell was going on with this crazy whitefellas' law. There was nothing I could do but wait and see what happened. I was working on the Sumner family genealogies and this was a big job. When it was eventually published in 1998 it ran into four volumes. So this was keeping me very busy and not allowing me much time to think about anything else.

Then the bombshell hit on Monday, 6 March 1995, the day that Sandy told me McLachlan had opened the secret envelopes and photocopied them and sent them to the media. Those envelopes had been taped up and we wrote 'To be read by women only' on them. That day my *mi:wi* [soul, spirit] was ruptured. I should never have put black words on white paper, and my punishment for breaking that Ngarrindjeri law was about to begin. The next day I was in Sandra's office, and I asked her to get some of the young girls who worked there to come into the office, and I sat on the floor with them and explained to them about what had happened about the women's information, and we were all crying. When the other women heard about his actions, the next day they all came in to ALRM, and I'll never forget the sight and sound of those thirty-five Ngarrindjeri women crying and hurting. We were sobbing and whimpering, but Auntie Maggie was roaring; she had the real Ngarrindjeri wailing. If anyone had seen us, they would have known that the biggest tragedy had just happened.

International Women's Day

I was due to give a speech at the annual International Women's Day Committee luncheon in Adelaide on Wednesday of that week. Betty Fisher[2] had asked me a couple of months earlier and I was planning to talk about my work, but this episode had me so angry and upset that I scrapped that speech and just walked up to the microphone unprepared for what I would say. The words came out really powerful. I knew I could speak well in public, but that day I even surprised myself. This is what I said:

> Most of you now would realise that there has been injustice done to the Aboriginal women in South Australia, and for that matter, all over Australia. I would have to say to you all that what happened in Parliament on Monday afternoon is unforgivable. It has absolutely crushed me and I don't think for as long as I live I will ever get over the shock of finding out that a man has photocopied my secret information on women's business down at Kumarangk. That is the island that means so much to our ancestors. You all have your beliefs. We all have ours. But the government, the politicians and the monied people of South Australia want to destroy one of the most sacred sites in South Australia. I will go down fighting to prevent this. [applause]

When Betty Fisher first asked me to speak here I wanted so much to share our Aboriginal history with you ladies, you women. The only bridge I ever want built is between the two cultures, white and Aboriginal. [applause]

I would have loved to have shared our history with you and some time in the future maybe I will, because I intend to bring back to our children and our grandchildren our ancestors' history and I will do it as long as I have breath in my body. Just recently I was told that we should not be using secret information to stop the construction of a million dollar bridge. Let me remind you that there are a lot of nationalities in this world today that have secrets. The men's lodge have secrets from even their wives. Christianity has secrets from everybody. Aboriginal people also have secrets and why, why isn't our secrets protected and respected? Today, as it was 200 years ago, there's still genocide in this country. We are not being poisoned, or we are not being killed by strychnine; we are being destroyed by policies and political people and the law of the land. We have our law and we respect it and do live under three laws under this country for 160 years. When Don Dunstan got up and changed the constitution that Aboriginals would have the right to vote, we lived under three laws — our Aboriginal laws, the Protector's laws and we had to live under the Commonwealth laws as well. How much more can the Aboriginal people take of the white man's policies, laws, destruction? We are human beings. We came into this world the same way and we will definitely go out the same way. And for all you women there, you may be white, but you have the same organs as I've got.

Ladies and gentlemen, thank you. [applause]

There was a standing ovation and a big burst of applause that seemed to go on forever and then the emcee took a call from the floor to make a resolution. After some discussion, she read out the resolution. It said:

> that we women attending the International Women's Day luncheon of 1995 deplore and condemn the unethical actions of the Federal Member for Barker in permitting the secrets of the Ngarrindjeri women to be divulged to persons unauthorised or forbidden to know them and that on behalf of all Australians who

sincerely respect the cultural beliefs and traditions of our Indigenous people, we deeply apologise to our Aboriginal sisters for the grief, shock, anger and sense of betrayal that this outrage has caused.

I could hardly believe the applause, whistling and cheering that followed this resolution. There were calls from the floor to read it again and that's what the emcee did. Then someone called for a further resolution that the Minister be called on to resign. Again there was whistling and cheering and after a vote, this second resolution was passed unanimously.

It was still no consolation when two days later McLachlan did resign, or even when Deane Fergie brought the secret envelopes back from Canberra. I was feeling really disturbed, really sick to my stomach about it all. The press was all wanting to hear from me. That's when I told them the traditional thing for revealing secrets would be a punishment.[3]

This proved to be a prophecy. McLachlan didn't get anything like the punishment I was to get. And McLachlan's actions were just the start of a big dirty tricks campaign that was going on behind the scenes. It wasn't until Margaret Simons brought out her book, *The Meeting of the Waters*, in 2003, that the full extent of that campaign became clear.

I spent all this week with Sandra Saunders, staying at her house in the city. Although we had known each other as acquaintants for years, after that day I developed a wonderful friendship with Sandy, and I don't know how I would have managed all the events that came next without her. As Director of ALRM, she knew a lot more about how the system worked and was always there to answer questions and offer advice. As Ngarrindjeri women we felt for each other. She put me up and took me round the city and helped me understand all the things that were going on. When McLachlan resigned his position I remember Sandy saying, 'We'll rue the day this happened. He's such a powerful man and he's not going to let up'. And she was right about that.

We still didn't have the envelopes back. The Liberal MP Chris Gallus said she wasn't going to return the envelopes to me, but to

Sarah Milera. They were nothing to do with Sarah. We found out that Chris Gallus was attending a meeting relating to Aboriginal issues down on Cross Road, so we decided to pay her a little visit. Sandra and I drove down there. Matt Rigney was leading the meeting and Yami Lester[4] was there. We charged in and let Chris Gallus have a tongue-lashing about giving back the envelopes. Some of the blackfellas bolted when they saw us coming, others were confused. Chris Gallus was shocked and trembling. Yami tried to calm us down and told us the meeting was important, that we shouldn't ruin it. We didn't care. I told him it was too important to us. We told Chris Gallus there was no way she was going to fucking hand those envelopes back to Sarah. That's when she agreed to give them to Sue Kee. They never had their meeting that day.

By this time things were exploding. Politicians were calling for each others' resignations, even the Prime Minister, Paul Keating, and the Leader of the Opposition, John Howard. The Attorney-General was threatening to sue Howard if the envelopes weren't returned immediately and McLachlan was threatened with jail. The Chapmans were carrying on about 'fighting for justice'! Not only that but the South Australian Museum Director, Chris Anderson, goes on the record to say the Museum is impartial, but admits that they provided information to McLachlan. To my way of thinking the Museum was starting to show that it wasn't impartial at all. Everything was happening so quick, which is just against Ngarrindjeri way. It's best to sit down and think everything through and the implications of what happens next. But there was no time. Everyone was bombing me with information and trying to boss me around and tell me what to do. I wasn't having it.

The letter from Aunty Laura

The following week a letter is read out in State Parliament from Aunty Laura Kartinyeri saying there is no women's business. Aunty Laura is one of the people who told me these things! I have a tape of Aunty Laura from 1979 when I recorded her talking about kinship for me, but she would never *let* me record anything of the women's business we talked about. It was a shocking thing the way they used that old lady. She was eighty-nine years old and very frail. As soon as I heard about this I did the correct thing (unlike the others, who just turned up) and got in touch with her granddaughter Rosemary and asked if I could go and see Aunty Laura. Rosemary said, 'Yes, Aunt Dodo, come up'. I asked her if she could be there when I saw Aunty Laura, so Rosemary and her brother Dennis agreed to be there.

Aunty Laura told me she didn't know who the people were that took the letter to her to sign. When I read the letter to her, she told me that she had been told the letter was to stop the bridge. They completely duped that dear old lady and took advantage of her failing eyesight to get her to sign a letter when she didn't know what's in it. And that poor old lady was really upset because it had been on television and that letter had been tabled in Parliament by Peter Lewis. And there he was in Parliament calling her 'Nanna Laura', like he was close with her; calling her 'Nanna' for political reasons. I was really angry at the way they used her; she finished up in hospital after that and I went over to Murray Bridge to visit her.

First dissidents

All of a sudden, on 20 May 1995, there's a smiling photo of Bertha Gollan (née Wilson) and Dulcie Wilson on the front page of *The Advertiser*. They were saying the women's business was 'bull-crap' and part of a 'conspiracy' to stop the bridge and bankrupt the development. Together with Dorrie Wilson and Bertha's two daughters, Audrey Dix and Rita Wilson, they talked all about what had occurred at the Graham's Castle meeting and at the Mouth House and said the men made up the women's business and then brought me in to back it up. Ha! Imagine me the puppet of the men!

In some ways this really didn't surprise me. Like I said, I felt that Dulcie always considered herself better than me, and that went for most other blackfellas. It stuck in my gut that they were made out to be fine upstanding Christian women. Usually photos of them in the paper were around a table having tea and scones to make them look more respectable than me, although I had all my children to my husband, was a faithful partner and a good wife and raised eight children and twenty-three foster children. Because I was angry I was made to look like a criminal, when I done nothing wrong. It is my opinion that the image of the dissident woman was invented, created by whitefellas. It seemed to me that only one or two were allowed to talk to the media, and I believe that was because if the others talked, they would be shown up as not like that.

And when Dorrie said at a meeting at Camp Coorong that Dulcie was a friend of Ian McLachlan's wife, it didn't take much to put two and two together. She said they'd been mates for years. That lot and my mob had never got on and it seemed to me that this was now being used for McLachlan's political advantage. I just couldn't believe that Dulcie didn't at least know there was women's business. Her husband Lyndsay was very knowledgeable about our culture. But she still wasn't told anything of the traditional knowledge, so to me it looked as though she must not have been considered suitable to tell, unlike Veronica who knows she wasn't told anything when she was younger because she wasn't suitable, but did learn later in life when she was.

Both Sandy and I rang Dulcie up when we first heard about her position, and we talked very reasonably to her, trying to find out what was going on. But then the media reported that I had been intimidating her into changing her stance. Same with Bertha. We got her on the phone to check the facts because there was so much misinformation going around. As soon as we did that, it was used against us. It was really hard for me to actually know who to trust and who not to, because when I spoke to them it was taken out of context every time. So I kept to a small select group of people close to me.

I also knew Dorrie was fighting with Victor over her family's control of the Lower Murray Nungas' Club. Dorrie applied for a job there and Isobel Norvill got it instead, so Dorrie wasn't happy. Dorrie was married to Isobel's brother Billy Wilson, but they had a bitter break-up a long time before all this started. After that she was against anything that the Wilsons got involved with, especially Victor, Isobel and Billy. So when they supported me, she was pissed off. Her husband came up and gave me a kiss and a hug at Murray Bridge and I just happened to look over Billy's shoulder as she was just coming out of the shop, and she stopped dead. They hadn't been together for years, but she was still very bitter. Victor, Isobel and Billy's mother was my dearly loved cousin, Aileen, who with her husband Mark was so kind to me when I first went to Point Pearce. Aileen got an MBE from the Queen for the work she done in Murray Bridge. And as far as I'm concerned Dorrie got involved on the other side in the Kumarangk business simply because she personally didn't like the Wilsons. I couldn't understand otherwise how she would have changed her position; because she was coming and talking to me when it all began.

Others had their nose put out of joint. I felt that Chirpy Campbell's sister Amelia was annoyed that the women had given me the authority to speak on their behalf and not her. But I was a *yanun maldi* [better talker]. Dorrie and Dulcie and Bertha and them were late in claiming we made up the women's business, but Chirpy didn't come on the scene until even later.

Like I say, the media talked a lot about the splits this whole business caused in the Ngarrindjeri community, but the only splits in the Ngarrindjeri community were the ones that were always there. In fact it united the community and drew support from people I never thought I'd get support from. For example, Dulcie's grand-daughter Janice Rigney stood with us in a circle, traditional way, at Camp Coorong and cried. Dulcie's daughter Joy Wilson also supported me, as well as her granddaughter Terri and brother Roger. I was equally surprised at some of those who didn't support me I felt should have. Aunty Rosie's granddaughter Peggy Cross, who had been raised by Aunty Rosie, spoke out against me.

If there was a lot of interest in the media before these women said we lied, the frenzy was just beginning. Robert Tickner accused the Liberal Party of plotting against us and I reckon he was right. It seemed to me that McLachlan wasn't going to forgive us easily for having to resign and it also seemed to me too much of a coincidence that his wife's friend Dulcie Wilson suddenly comes out against us. There was a cartoon in *The Advertiser* on 23 May 1995, that showed Keating, Tickner and John Howard in a big fight on a bridge going nowhere.

They were being watched by Aboriginal women and the caption said, 'Politicians' business'. This was more like the truth to me and sure enough, it came out the next day that Sue Lawrie was involved in getting together the 'dissident women' as they were now known.

Sue Lawrie is the granddaughter of old W.T., the headmaster at Raukkan for all those years. She was also working for the Liberal Party, and she came over from Victoria to organise meetings for those women, using her family connections. Another big coincidence to my way of thinking. Good-natured Aunty Maggie invited her to one of our meetings and we let her come, but if I she'd given us any indication of what she was there for, I would not have had her in that meeting. Poor Aunty Maggie felt bad about that later, because she really turned on us.

Meeting at Camp Coorong

The same day this news was out, 24 May, about sixty women were meeting at Camp Coorong. The only ones older than me from Raukkan were Aunty Gracie Sumner, Aunty Sheila, Auntie Marj and Aunty Laura, but because she couldn't get there, Aunty Laura got Aunty Connie [Roberts] to go down and represent her. Also Lorraine Wilson who is four or five years older than me. They weren't very available but they attended a few rallies and meetings down at Kumarangk. So they supported me, but I was prepared to take the full responsibility of what I was doing, and I told them that. Dorrie Wilson was there. I hadn't caught up yet that she was against us.

We had several meetings before I worked out what was going on, and finally the word was starting to weave. I worked out we had a spy among us because of a comment that the reporter Colin James made. I'm not a stupid woman and I knew that I did not say that in public; it would have to have come from a closed meeting, so I started to think then. When I was trying to work out who it could be, I couldn't point my finger at anybody, I couldn't. They all seemed genuine; they all seemed as if they believed and supported me, and yet there was someone that was leaking stuff out to the media. And when Dorrie told us at the meeting that Dulcie was a long-time friend of McLachlan's wife, I put one and two together and came up with millions! I stood up and put it to the meeting. I said, 'If any one of you feel that you don't believe in Ngarrindjeri culture, Ngarrindjeri tradition and what I'm saying and doing; if there are any spies in the camp who want to go and take anything else out of this meeting, I'd ask you to leave right now'. Dorrie then left the meeting.

Not long after, when we finally heard about those women speaking against us, some of the women went to talk to Dorrie. They asked her why she was saying those things. They said, 'You were sitting in the room there with Aunt Dodo a few months ago and you was taking it all in and you reckoned your own mother told you'. And she denied it!

Meantime the Pitjantjatjara women elders got in touch to give us their support and we arranged to take them down to Kumarangk. Those lovely ladies helped give us a lot of strength. Aunty Ivy Makinti Stewart (Syd's *kabbarli*), Eileen Unkari Crombie and Emily Munyungka Austin reaffirmed our women's Dreamings that the River Murray mouth is the source of all life and that a bridge would be a threat to Ngarrindjeri women's fertility.

Next thing I know, the Chapmans are suing Tickner. From what I heard they came to sue a lot of people. But this time they were apply-ing for me to hand over the envelopes that we had so much trouble getting back. I told them those envelopes would never be found because I burnt them! Well, did that cause a stir. The lawyer Andrew Collett is in court and the judge asks him if it's true that the envelopes have been burnt? I heard that next thing Andrew Collett and Chris Charles are on the phone trying to find out if that's true. They couldn't get hold of me but Sandy said she told them it wasn't true, so Andrew Collett goes back into court and tells the judge the envelopes are safe and secure and gives a personal undertaking that he will make sure they stay that way. I was furious with Andrew Collett for saying that because people might think I gave the envelopes to a man for safekeeping when I didn't.

They got Robyn Layton QC, who was acting for Legal Rights, to ring me up and talk to me. Robyn suggested we could put the envelopes in her safety box and give me the key. I was really edgy about this idea, but the pressure was being put on for this to be the solution; otherwise it would all be a big disaster. But it wouldn't have been a disaster for us, only for the lawyers. Anyway we gave in, and Sandy, Connie, Rhonda and I went round to Robyn Layton's that night and put them in the safety box. As soon as the case was finished Sandra and I went back and got them before the courts could get hold of them again in the other cases the Chapmans had coming up.

But that was the last straw. I decided that before any more damage could be done, the time had come to burn the envelopes. Sandra got a nice fire going in her combustion heater and burnt the lot — white paper and black words.

The Museum

Up until I talked out about Kumarangk, I felt my position at the Museum had been good. Then I started to feel that there was tension there. These whitefellas I had been working with started to take sides. I knew Steve Hemming supported my right to do what I was doing and Barry Craig did. But Philip Jones, Philip Clarke and several others were talking out against me. As far as they were concerned, they were 'experts' in my culture, which I still can't understand today how that could be when they are not Ngarrindjeri or women. I would have thought Philip Clarke had learned enough from me that he would never give evidence against me. And I never got anything from him in return. I felt betrayed. Then they called in other staff members, including Neva, to ask them what they knew about my work. They asked them to make a formal statement about it.

This was before there was any discussion of holding a Royal Commission into my beliefs, so whether or not they had some inside information on that, I don't know. I would have thought my employers should have supported me, but it really felt like they were out to get me. So I up and decided if they were going to talk about me amongst themselves like that, I wasn't going to stand there and take it. So I put in my resignation.

Honoured woman

Next thing I know, everything is really hectic and suddenly out of the blue I get a letter telling me I was to be awarded an Honorary Doctorate by the University of South Australia for all my work at the University and the Museum. I was stunned! This little black woman who only went to Grade 3; I was really over the moon. This was a great reward and a great honour, but I felt it was like I was two different people — a genealogist and author who was awarded by white academics on one hand, and a custodian of knowledge and protester being criticised by the white press on the other. I heard from Rosemary Burdon, who used to work in the Task Force next door to me when I was at the university, that it had been in the pipeline for quite a while, so I was grateful to know it had nothing to do with the Hindmarsh Island thing

On the day of the presentation of my award on 29 May 1995, I was invited to lunch with Dame Roma Mitchell. I'd met Dame Roma on several occasions before because she was very involved with the University when I was working there. She came into the Hughes Building a few times, and she'd always stop and say hello to me and ask what I was doing. A lovely person, and I had the honour of sitting down and having lunch with her. Then when I was putting my robes on before the ceremony she came in and wished me well, and I thought that was very nice.

The ceremony went very well and several of the Aboriginal students also graduated that day. I gave a little speech about my work and the impact on the Stolen Generations, and afterwards the Aboriginal academic with UniSA, Dr Maryanne Bin-Salik, congratulated me on it. The Chancellor presented me with my award and I was very proud to receive it in front of my sisters Doris and Connie, and my children Kandy, Dibby and Brenton, who were in the audience. Not all of them got on the invitation list because Kandy was protecting us from the media. But, after the ceremony, sure enough there was Chris Kenny wanting to interview me about Kumarangk. I told him, 'If you don't mind, this has nothing to do with Hindmarsh Island. I've earned this degree with all my work and publication of my books on Aboriginal people'. He took off when he saw big, tall Kandy with me and the look on his face. *The Advertiser* printed a lovely photo of me and my relations and the students.

> Doreen Kartinyeri has been given a happy respite from the Hindmarsh Island drama. The woman at the centre of the 'women's business' controversy yesterday celebrated receiving an honorary doctorate from the University of South Australia, for her contribution to the education of Aboriginal people.
>
> The mother of seven [sic] is considered an authority on Aboriginal genealogy, on which she has written four books. The doctorate was presented at the Faculty of Aboriginal and Islander Studies' graduation ceremony at the Adelaide Festival Theatre. It came after an extremely distressing week for the main proponent of the secret women's business, which was last week labeled a hoax by a small group of Ngarrindjeri women. (*The Adelaide Advertiser*, 30 May 1995)

Doug

We had another blow in our efforts to stop the bridge when on 6 June, Doug Milera was reported as saying we women had invented our beliefs. I think this was the biggest thing that happened to me during all this. I was coping fine until this time because I knew I never lied. Then I got a phone call from Sandra to say Doug was going to be on TV that night.

I was sick to the gut. I just could not think this was possible. Most of them in the Goolwa district knew that Doug was a reformed alcoholic. They knew he had given up the drink and was on the State Aboriginal Heritage Committee and was doing very well. And what they done? I heard someone goes and shouts Doug a beer and that starts him drinking. Apparently he had quite a few drinks that afternoon. Chris Kenny later admitted that he gave Doug $200 to put him up in a motel for the night.

Lots of people said to me that you could see it was a set up, but I didn't care about that. It should never have happened. That night when I watched Chris Kenny interviewing Doug I was really angry with Doug. I could only listen; I couldn't bear to see his face, so I closed my eyes. Later when I forced myself to watch a tape of it again

I saw in the expression on his face that he looked like he was under enormous pressure. You know when you might tell a kid to clean up their mess and that kid will do it but not because he wants to, but because he's made to? That's how I felt about Doug.

To my way of thinking that was the biggest fabricated thing, the biggest dishonesty, them white people that done that to Doug. And here I am fighting for my rights to be able to get through with my honesty, and people were using an alcoholic to get what they wanted. In the end Doug didn't live very long after that.

It wasn't long afterwards that Doug came out and told how he was set up and how what he said wasn't true, and he changed back to support the women's business, but it was too late, the biggest damage was done. The front-page banner headline the day after that event read, 'The Great Lie of Hindmarsh Island'. From then on, as far as the public was concerned I was a liar, and the witch-hunt to prove it began.

8
The Royal Witch-Hunt

The Royal Commission

On Friday, 9 June 1995 I was at the Aboriginal Community Centre in Murray Bridge attending meetings, when Dean Brown announced that a Royal Commission would be held to investigate whether our beliefs were fabricated. Later the same day Robert Tickner announced the Federal Government would conduct its own judicial inquiry. The Royal Commission was supposed to report in less than two months — by 1 September — so Dean Brown was obviously trying to get in first. How could it investigate properly all the things that had gone on in that time, especially if I wasn't going to cooperate? I didn't even know what a Royal Commission was, but I felt confident that a Federal inquiry would have to override a State one, and still held out hope that this would happen.

That was my very first reaction to that Royal Commission. I couldn't believe they could hold an investigation into our traditional religious beliefs. Nor could the churches, who were quick to condemn such an outrageous thing. Sister Janet Mead[1] was always very supportive. The first thing I did was to say to Sandra and Val and Muriel was that I would not co-operate with that Royal Commission, and they agreed with my decision and supported it. All the women who supported me also agreed — Aunty Connie, Veronica, Aunty Maggie — lots of them — and so we worked on a document.

The ALRM had its lawyers, and the Ngarrindjeri men got Steve Kenny to represent them. Claire O'Connor agreed to act for the women. Whitefellas had been in charge of me and my family all my life; they weren't going to tell me what to do now, so I wanted us not to appear in the Royal Commission.

Next thing Bertha Gollan is quoted in the media as saying she and the other dissident women's lives have been threatened. Bertha is saying someone's gone up north to the Pitjantjatjara Lands to get a kadaitcha man [sorcerer, clever person, assassin] to come down to 'sing her to death'. Funny how they believe in this, but not their own Ngarrindjeri culture. I never knew anything about threats against them. Maybe someone misunderstood the visit of the women from Coober Pedy or maybe someone did threaten that. I had plenty of Aboriginal people who told me I just had to say the word and they would do someone over. In fact I had my work cut out calming people down and stopping violent things from happening. Anyway, it worked both ways. We were getting threats too, but we didn't go running to the media about it, because we didn't have a guilty conscience.

We got support from the Aboriginal leaders in the country. The national native title conference held in Melbourne at the time called for the Royal Commission to be disbanded because they saw it as an attack on the rights of Aboriginal people. ALRM tried its hardest to stop the Royal Commission too, by challenging its validity in the Supreme Court, but without success.

On the opening day we got Claire O'Connor to ask the Commissioner Iris Stevens if we could speak to her in private, so she agreed to ask all men and white women to leave the room. When they left, Mantatjara Wilson [a Pitjantjatjara elder], who had come down from the Lands [the Anangu Pitjantjatjara Yankunytjatjara Lands] especially, presented two traditional women's items to the Commissioner — a ceremonial law stick and a painting. Iris Stevens looked horrified, but we tried our best to explain to her what women's business meant to us and to get her to feel how important it was. She said she would take this as evidence. But she never mentioned it in her final report.

After that the commission went back to proceedings and all the men and white women came back into the room. Claire O'Connor stood up and addressed the Royal Commission. She read out the statement we had prepared. It said:

> We as Ngarrindjeri women believe the women's business, the subject of the Royal Commission into Hindmarsh Island is true.
>
> We are deeply offended that a Government in this day and age has the audacity to order an inquiry into our secret, sacred, spiritual beliefs. Never before have any group of people had their spiritual beliefs scrutinised in this way.
>
> Under Aboriginal law, women cannot speak about women's business where there are men concerned.
>
> Our law for Aboriginal women prohibits us from talking about this business, not only to any men, but also to those not privileged to be given that information.
>
> It is our responsibility as custodians of this knowledge to protect it, not only from men, but also from those not entitled to this knowledge. We have a duty to keep Aboriginal law in this country.
>
> Women's business does exist, has existed since time immemorial and will continue to exist where there are Aboriginal women who are able to continue to practice their culture.
>
> … The most common thread linking all Aboriginal peoples is the way in which we record our history. Aboriginal history is recorded orally. It is passed on orally. Does that fact invalidate our history? Aboriginal law is strict and uncompromising. Despite all the efforts both past and present of Government bodies and agents to cast the law aside, stamp it out and ignore it, business exists.
>
> We do not seek to be represented at this Royal Commission. We do not recognise the authority of this Royal Commission to debate and ultimately to conclude that women's business relating to Hindmarsh Island exists. We know women's business exists and is true.
>
> We do not recognise you, Madam Commissioner, as a custodian of law in our society. We shall continue to practise our customs and law according to our customs and law as Aboriginal people have since time began and especially since the invasion.

Our only motivation for protecting our stories is our responsibility to the land and surrounding waters and to our people.

We refuse outright to recognise your commission as having any right to decide whether we fabricated anything when we know that we have not.

There is also the issue that there is to be a Federal inquiry into this matter. We are prepared to participate and co-operate fully with this inquiry, because we feel that we can be confident that this inquiry will investigate the matters sensitively and appropriately and with the respect our spiritual beliefs warrant. We believe the Federal inquiry will achieve the appropriate goals of uncovering the actual fabrications in this matter and the motives and corruption associated with those fabrications, determine who is to benefit from those fabrications and make the necessary recommendations.

The timing of Premier Brown's Royal Commission is entirely inappropriate. The Federal Court is still to determine the appeal before it and there is an appeal before the South Australian Supreme Court that has yet to be determined against the refusal yesterday to grant an injunction. What is the hurry? Whose interests are being served by the holding of this Royal Commission now?[2]

At the end of all the opening statements Iris Stevens met with the women. Andrea Simpson [junior counsel assisting the Royal Commission] and Iris Stevens were the only white women at that meeting, and no men were allowed to be there. After the meeting, I got up and walked out, with honesty, dignity and pride for my people. The others followed me. No disrespect to Christianity, but that day I felt like I was about to be crucified. I wondered if anyone had ever walked out on a Royal Commission before, but I didn't care if they had or not.

After the private viewing of the objects with Iris Stevens, a few days later Colin James was saying that a curse had been put on the Royal Commission by Mantatjara. He was saying the Commission would have to move to another building because of it, and he had been told this by Chirpy Campbell. Chirpy reckoned he was going to turn up in traditional clothes to defy the curse. At this stage Sandra was mostly keeping the papers away from me. She didn't want me to see what was being said because it made me so angry and hurt. But the sight of Chirpy turning up at the Commission in a cloak made of car-seat covers was too much! This just made a mockery of our culture, while I was trying to protect it.

It was a shock to hear that the first witness to the Royal Commission was Philip Clarke. He was apparently sitting up there accusing me of fabricating stories and bringing them down from the north. This was a young man I had taught, that I'd worked closely with, that I'd so generously shared my knowledge with and who should have respected me. I was devastated to hear that he would do that. I felt he really betrayed me and I was disgusted.

Sandy was putting me up at her house and doing her best to protect me from all that was going round about us. I wasn't involved with the Royal Commission but I was constantly dodging the media, who wouldn't leave me alone. Sandra gave me a key to her house, and if she got wind of anything happening that might cause the media to come after me, she would ring me and say, 'Go home and get out of the way'. So I'd get a taxi back to Sandra's and let myself in, lock the doors and wait. People didn't catch on that I was there with her; they thought I was still staying with my friends Margie and Ron at Croydon Park, because that's where I first stayed when all this blew up. I had to go and stay somewhere else after there was a high-speed police chase and the police caught the driver outside Margie and Ron's house. We went outside to see what was happening and there were all the media. The Channel Seven reporter said, 'Doreen, what are you doing here?' I quickly said, 'I've come to visit a friend'. But they cottoned on that I was staying there and were harassing Margie and Ron in the end. The media just never let up. They even went round to my sister Doris's house one time, because she was in the phone book as 'D. Kartinyeri'. Doris suffers from bipolar disorder and I was worried they would make her sick.

Sandra wouldn't let me read the newspapers, especially the *Adelaide Review*. Christopher Pearson was the editor of the *Adelaide Review*, and he and Chris Kenny wrote a lot of really nasty articles about me and the others. They were dead set against us right from the start, and in with the Liberal Party, and all their articles rubbished us something terrible. In my opinion they were not good journalists, but they both ended up getting promoted. Christopher Pearson went on to be Prime Minister John Howard's speech writer — which says quite a lot considering Howard's position on Aboriginal issues — and Kenny wrote a book that I think is very one-sided.

In the early days Betty Fisher first got in touch with me to tell me she also had evidence from tapes she had done with some of the old Ngarrindjeri ladies in the 1960s, including Kumi, Veronica Brodie's mother. I told her to go straight away and get them out of the State Library and put them somewhere safe and that she was never to let anyone have access to them. We talked about how she would handle it and I agreed that I didn't mind if she appeared to the Royal Commission, but under no circumstances could she show the details of those tapes. I was very grateful for Betty's co-operation with this.

Even though I never went into the Royal Commission again, just walking around town with Sandra the media would be chasing us. I remember one day we were walking along Gawler Place and all the reporters spotted us coming and they were standing there in our way and we didn't know what to do. Suddenly Sandra grabbed me and we rushed into the nearest shop. We didn't have time to see until we got inside, but it was a bridal shop! One of the reporters said, 'What are you doing in there?' Sandy said, 'We're getting married!' I had to catch my breath, so we just stayed there laughing and saying how ridiculous it was. All the people in the shop were looking at us and wondering what was going on.

In our travels around town, say of an evening we would stop in for a drink at the Crown & Sceptre or the Arab Steed or one of the other pubs, if there was a pile of *Adelaide Reviews* there, Sandy would just pick them up in big bunches and dump them in the bin outside so that other people couldn't read them. True! Everywhere we saw that free paper, Sandra would do that. I didn't do it because I was too frightened that I might get into trouble. We ended up sticking to certain pubs, because people would harass us most places we'd go.

Sandy and I spent a lot of time at her home just sitting round with the combustion fire going and *yanun* and I told her lots of stories about my life and about my children and what was happening in their life, and Sandy did the same with me. Sandy became like my sister and we shared things. I think we bonded really close that night we heard about McLachlan tabling the envelopes, and our relationship just grew stronger from there. We got closer and closer, and now I think of her and her kids as being part of my family.

Of course, our children were affected by all the publicity. They were being challenged by people and copping the flak. One of my sons ended up punching someone who said something bad about me, and so did one of my granddaughters. I remember my daughter Christabel and Sandy's son Malcolm were in the pub in Port Lincoln watching the news on TV. Christabel said, 'There's my Mum and Sandra'. At the same time Malcolm said, 'There's my Mum and Doreen'. Although they already knew each other, they didn't know who each other's mother was!

Between calls from the Ngarrindjeri people and from reporters, Sandra's phone was running hot all the time. Sandy always let Val and Muriel know when I was in town, because we are very close cousins. If a reporter rang, Sandra might say, 'Well I think she's in town, but I don't know. You could try Legal Rights'. And I'd be sitting right there. Shirley Peisley and Vi Deuschle often came round to Sandra's to see how I was getting on. So did the lawyers from Legal Rights, and Steve Kenny and Deane Fergie came round to keep us informed on what was happening in the Royal Commission.

It seemed to me like a lot of the people who spoke out against us were getting funded from one source or another. I couldn't understand why Coral, Joy and Peggy Weetra, Aunty Rosie's granddaughters, spoke out against us. It seems their grandmother did not tell them anything. Coral ran away from home as a young fifteen-year-old girl, so maybe she was thought not to be suitable to tell anything important, and nor was Joy. I can remember Aunty Rosie always trying to discipline Joy, but she would just sit about reading comics all day. On the other hand Aunty Rosie's other grannies, Laurel and Rose, gave me their support, so what does that say? How come the dissident women's numbers kept growing all the time when to me there was no good reason for that?

I got the chance to see Doug Milera again a couple of months after his interview with Chris Kenny. We called a meeting down at Murray Bridge in the Lower Murray Nungas' Club, and we decided to close the gates to all the media because they weren't doing the right thing by us. We also asked the police to keep away. Some people didn't like the idea of closing the gates, because we normally are open to everybody, but this is the sort of thing we became forced to do. We had a lot of the young boys to stand guard around the fences. One of the TV stations sent a helicopter, but people got in its way and it couldn't land. Then I heard one of the boys say, 'Aunt Dodo, Uncle Mayo's coming'. Mayo is Doug Milera. So I said, 'Open the gate for him' and I stayed outside until they drove in. The media were all trying to get shots of him and there were cameras everywhere through the fence. Doug got out of the car and I wondered what he was going to do. He walked towards us and straight up to me. He just put his arms out. I could not help it, I just had to put my arms out and we just hung on to one another. He couldn't talk. He couldn't even say sorry. He just trembled in my arms. So I got hold of his hand and I led him inside. And you could see tears coming into people's eyes. Sarah and Doug both had tears in their eyes. And I thought, 'It looks like I've got to be the strong one again'. And we all walked inside.

As usual, we stood in a big circle, all holding hands. There must have been about 120 of us in the hall. I looked round that circle and everyone had tears in their eyes. I couldn't talk; Doug couldn't talk. No-one could talk. And it must have took a good long time before Victor spoke. He spoke beautifully. He said, 'I would like to open this meeting and we welcome Doug back in with us'. I never asked him to say that, he just did it. Doug was forgiven.

When I went back to Point Pearce I found myself getting into arguments with white people in the wider community I had known for many years and who I had considered my friends. I remember running into Gwen, down at Port Victoria. She had heard me talking on radio. She said, 'Do you think it's the right thing for your people to try and stop a big development?' And I thought, she's had a lot of meetings with me in the past and she knows the way I feel about Aboriginal people. But what the hell did she know about our history and culture; how could she be a judge of what was right for us?

Even through all of this I tried to keep busy. I worked at Koonanda packing food and clothing parcels to be sent up to the Anangu Pitjantjatjara Lands. Then I got an invitation from Jennie George, who was about to become ACTU President, to attend the Women and Labour Conference at Macquarie University in Sydney. They flew me over to speak to the conference on 1 October 1995. This was right in the middle of the Royal Commission proceedings, so it was a good opportunity to have a bit of a say. I gave a speech which was unanimously supported by over 200 delegates. At the conference Sir Ronald Wilson saw me outside having a cigarette and came over to thank me. He was also very interested in my work, because he was conducting the Inquiry into the Separation of Aboriginal and Torres Strait Islander children from their families, and that Inquiry exposed the extent of the Stolen Generations when he released his report two years later.

Prominent Aboriginal people came over to Adelaide to show their support and talk for us. Marcia Langton wrote a couple of articles and addressed a meeting at Way Hall.

Then I was invited to the United States National Women's Studies Conference. It was to be held in Albuquerque in New Mexico and thousands of people from all round the world were going. Wow! But I had so much on my plate and I still didn't like the idea of flying such a long way, so I just couldn't think about going. So I asked Sandy if she would go in my place and she was happy about that. Di Bell and Sue Hawthorn from Spinifex Press had organised a session. Sandra spoke and told our story and she got a standing ovation. Apparently she came across so well that after her talk lots of different women were looking her up to talk to her.

I was also invited to Alice Springs by the Pitjantjatjara and Alice Springs women and the women from Kunypi. They told me they had been following the Kumarangk business and they wanted to know if there was anything they could do. I said I would very much like for Ngarrindjeri women to meet with them. So a big meeting was organised in Alice Springs on the way to Kunypi.

At this meeting of about forty or fifty people, I met a Frenchman who was visiting on behalf of the United Nations Human Rights Commission. There was a Frenchwoman translating for the Human Rights Commissioner, and Rosie Monk (Rosie Kunoth, who was in Fullarton Home with me) translated into Pitjantjatjara, so it was quite an interesting meeting. He had been following the Kumarangk story in the media and he said one of the best things that he's ever experienced in his whole career was being there to hear people in positions like us fighting for their rights, to keep their beliefs.

After that we hopped in the bus and made the long, long journey to Kunypi. It is right on the border of South Australia, the Northern Territory and Western Australia in a very remote area. The people were lovely; they danced for us and yarned with us and we were very respectful. The whole feeling at Kunypi made me feel good. Although I was very tired from the Hindmarsh thing and it was a very long trip, it still revived my spirit and helped me to go on.

Back in the Royal Commission they were using all sorts of tactics to try and get the contents of the envelopes revealed. Deane and Sandra were both threatened with jail. It was unbelievable, but they were just making me more and more determined they wouldn't get their hands on those envelopes. I was disgusted that they showed the video of Doug Milera's interview in the Royal Commission. Val was in the gallery and she caused a big uproar about it, but they just had no shame. So many organisations were speaking out against the Royal Commission, and there were calls to get the United Nations involved, but nothing seemed to get through.

Deane Fergie was told she was in contempt of the Royal Commission because she gave her copy of the envelopes and her notes to ALRM. I certainly had contempt for that Royal Commission. Then the Royal Commission asked for ALRM documents to be handed over to them. But Sandra wouldn't give them up. It was like a war was going on. People from the Royal Commission got a warrant to search Sandra's house. They never got what they wanted, but I was shocked at the lengths the 'authorities' were prepared to go to. The threatening and bullying was going on all over the place.

Protests were happening closer to home as well. On 11 October a huge protest was held in Victoria Square. We called it the 'Great Wurley Gig'. That was when the Cherokee women came over from America to support us and they put up a big teepee. I think they became interested in our fight after they met Ellen and Tom Trevorrow, who went to the US for a weaving conference. Ellen is a great Ngarrindjeri weaver. They were led by Aunty Agnes Baker Pilgrim, a Rogue River elder. We had lots of speakers, including the American Indians, and a really big crowd of supporters, and we walked down to Parliament House with a message of protest against the Royal Commission and presented it to Parliament.

Aunty Aggie told me that she went to a conference back in America where she met Nelson Mandela. She told me Nelson Mandela had caught up with our fight and told her he admired what I was doing and said the world needed more strong women like me. Wow! But then there was a disaster in America, and they had to go back home. Before they flew out, we wanted to say something to thank them for their support, but Aunty Aggie said, 'No need to say anything'. She held her hand to her heart and said, 'We understand', and it was very emotional. She gave a beautiful carved and inlaid medallion to Aunty Maggie before she left, and Aunty Maggie treasured that. When Aunty Maggie died she was buried with that medallion. But the protests couldn't stop the racist media reports that were all over the papers and on TV, and all the efforts that were being used to crush us.

After that we had the Long Walk to save Kumarangk. Hundreds of people gathered in Victoria Square again on 25 November, and with me and Sandra and some of the others holding our flag saying, 'Grandmother's Law' we set off. I was too unwell to walk the 85 kilometres to Goolwa, so I was driven down to meet the walkers, who arrived at Amelia Park on Saturday the 30th. They were led by Ruby Hunter, who carried a combined Aboriginal and Ngarrindjeri flag. When they arrived it was all very emotional, and a group of us, including the Mayor of Goolwa, sang Dot Shaw's song about Kumarangk, and there were speeches and tears.

Although I wasn't prepared to be bailed up on the street, I was still talking to the media in arranged interviews. Ray Martin wanted to interview me, and I got Sandra to tell them I would talk to him, provided he didn't ask questions about women's business. He agreed. Then during the interview he asked about abortions on Kumarangk. I made the mistake of saying that did happen, and then he made a big thing about how that was the Hindmarsh Island women's business. Whitefellas just have to crack a black secret! I also talked to Richard Carleton on *Sixty Minutes*. Veronica, Aunty Maggie, Dot and I took him over to Kumarangk to show him round. We got on well and had a good time and a few laughs. Then back in the studio I didn't want to do an interview, so Sandy agreed to do it. He asked her about twenty times what the women's business was, but she stuck to her line and wouldn't give anything away. He didn't use any of the footage with Sandra.

During all this that was going on, Sandy took up painting. She had never painted before, but she was painting all the lawyers and the museum and the people and feelings involved. She did some wonderful paintings and often she would stay up half the night to finish a picture. We don't know where that all came from, but it must have been a way for her to cope with all the terrible events going on around us. Those paintings came to be in big demand across the country.

The royal witch-hunt wound up at the end of November 1995, and while we waited for the outcome, we heard that Robert Tickner lost his appeal overturning his decision to ban the bridge for twenty-five years. Okay, here we go again. Another hurdle being put in front of us. So I sat down and wrote another letter to him and told him that since he would get Rosemary Crowley [Federal Minister for Family Services] to read the envelopes for him, I would cooperate with the inquiry he had set up headed by Justice Jane Mathews.

On 21 December the Royal Commission report was released. I didn't go down to hear it because I knew I would be swamped by the media, but Sandra couldn't help herself. When she told me that their conclusion was that the whole thing had been fabricated, my guts felt that sick again. The banner headlines across the nation next day read, 'LIES, LIES, LIES!' And of course that was directly aimed at me. I was in shock. We all tried to comfort one other and everyone was fussing over me, but there was nothing to help this pain. I cried enough tears to flush the River Murray.

This is three days before Christmas. I can't even remember Christmas that year. I was just devastated. I am one of the most honest people I know, and with all the lying and cheating and working away behind the scenes that was going on against me, I couldn't believe they could call me a liar when they hadn't even heard my side of the story. Tom and the men had given evidence; Veronica was the only Ngarrindjeri woman who gave evidence for our side, and there was Betty Fisher, Deane and Steve Hemming who gave evidence for us, but because the rest of us women didn't appear, Iris Stevens found we had made it all up. I couldn't see how she could reach that decision. I felt like I had left my body.

Then I thought, 'Right, now there's the Mathews Inquiry. I'll just have to get on to that'. On to the next avenue of appeal; I wasn't giving up until they were all exhausted. I just knew what I had to do for my Aunty Rosie and my Mummy and the old ladies and the young ones to come. Some people had turned against us, but those who stayed together bonded so strong we became very close loved friends, and I think that is how I could stand up to all that was thrown at me.

The Mathews Inquiry

I was happy to appear for Justice Jane Mathews because I believed she would get all the facts and she would be able to turn the verdict around when she heard what our women would tell her. Robert Tickner came to Adelaide at the start of this inquiry. He met with me, Auntie Connie, Sarah, Muriel and some of the others. He wanted to tell us that when McLachlan tabled the envelopes, he wouldn't touch them after that because he knew they had been opened. That man suffered a lot out of all this too. I was happy that it was a closed inquiry, because the media were making my life hell and this way they wouldn't have anything to feed off. I turned up and made sure I told Justice Mathews exactly enough to explain to her the sacredness of Kumarangk and how anything built between the water and the sky would ruin the fertility of Ngarrindjeri women. I told her about the Seven Sisters Dreaming story Aunty Rosie had told me and all the information I had talked about before. Justice Mathews seemed to accept this information and things seemed to be going well. I was thinking surely we must get justice this time.

I had such high hopes that we would be actually 'listened to', that it was another kick in the guts when Justice Mathews told us the Minister would not agree to appointing a woman to read her report. The Liberal Party had just got in power and the Minister was of course a man and he insisted on reading it himself. So we had no choice. We asked for our evidence to be given back and for it to be left out of the report. Without our evidence there wasn't enough to stop the bridge.

What a tragedy!

So the Federal Government went ahead and introduced the Hindmarsh Island Bridge Bill. This was to get around the Aboriginal Heritage Act, specially so they could build the bridge. Again, I had to challenge that. How could they just change the law for a development? I got Steve Kenny to fight it because he said he thought it was unconstitutional. A couple of us women went over to Canberra with Steve to hear that case, and while we were there, Steve's little daughter died. I felt so bad about that. It was just too much to bear. A lot of awful things happened during the time we were fighting for Kumarangk — someone's baby daughter got epilepsy; I heard that something happened to someone's grandson. The bad things happened to little children. Good things didn't start happening again until it was all over. And the good things were all about having children, the renewal of life.

Syd and I were still living in Port Germein, but things were not going too good in my private life and I just wanted to be on my own. I couldn't think; I couldn't sleep and I couldn't eat properly and I was starting to suffer with ulcers. There was only so much kicking my guts could take. So I went back home to live at Point Pearce in a little flat

I built on the back of Dibby and Willie's house. I didn't know what was going to happen and I was getting very tired.

I took all the paperwork for my *Narungga Nation* book so I could keep working on that from home, even if I didn't have my job any more. One day, Parry Agius, who is the Director of the Native Title Unit of the Aboriginal Legal Rights Movement, was over at Point Pearce visiting his family. He came down to see me, and when he saw the genealogies I was putting together, he thought that would be really useful for native title work, so he asked me would I like to be employed by the Native Title Unit. I jumped at the chance.

I was also working with Di Bell, who had come back from her job as a big professor in America to be the anthropologist for the Mathews inquiry. She was talking to as many Ngarrindjeri people as she could and she had people doing research in the archives.

Ngarrindjeri Anzacs

At the same time, I decided to get back to a book I had been working on about the Raukkan men who served in the First World War. This had been put on hold when I left the Museum. After all the things Aunty Rosie told me, and with my childhood memories of Anzac Day and my uncles, I really had to let the world know that Aboriginal men fought on the other side of the world for their country and that some of them never came back. A couple of years back Steve Hemming put me on to a guy from Veterans' Affairs, but I found that most of the records are restricted. So I did three trips to the War Memorial in Canberra to get what information I could, because I was determined. *Ngarrindjeri Anzacs* was published in 1996 and we launched it at Raukkan. My only regret was that Aunty Rosie wasn't there to share that day with us. But when I unveiled the plaque that I got made, I saluted them and I said, 'This is from Aunty Rose'.

I was very pleased with this little tribute because those men never got any recognition from the government when they came back, and some of them were badly wounded and needed medical treatment for the rest of their lives. I didn't receive any royalties for my genealogies because I was an employee of the Museum, but in this case I asked the

Museum for some money to donate towards the repair of the Raukkan church Anzac memorial window that was installed in 1925 and had been smashed in the last twenty years. The window was installed in memory of the men who made the supreme sacrifice. I raised $1900 for the Raukkan Council, but it makes me sad that they still haven't repaired that beautiful window. I spent some time describing all the colours of the different glass in the window to Steve, because the only pictures we have of it are in black and white.

Well that little book got a lot of interest, and not just in Australia. There was an article published about it in France and one in Japan. Wow! I was very proud.

My stomach

My stomach ulcers started to get worse and soon developed into cancer. I was not surprised. It was all about *ngangkari* [sorcery, magic, medicine]. Because I revealed about women's insides, that's where my punishment had to happen. There were two lumps and they were in two separate spots, and Dr Otto told me I would need to have part of my stomach removed as soon as possible. My family was all really upset. I had been close to death once, before I went into the Museum, when I caught pneumonia and fell into a coma. The doctors thought I might not pull out of it, but my time wasn't right and I did come out of it after six days, but I was very sick there for a while. Now I was facing it again, but this time I knew why — because I put black history on white paper.

As soon as the word got around that I had cancer, a big group of women came over to visit me at Point Pearce. They sat with me and sang and yarned. We sang Dot Shaw's song about Kumarangk called 'The Dreaming of a Ngarrindjeri Mi:mini' over and over, and it was wonderful. To hear that little song is overwhelming for me. It goes like this:

> This island is not just any island.
> It belongs to the Ngarrindjeri Mi:mini.
> It shelters her from the stormy weather.
> Kumarangk is all of life to the Ngarrindjeri Mi:mini.

Chorus:
Follow your heart, for your dreams will come true.
Every day, every breath you take,
God will bless the way.
Never give up, but keep your faith,
Believe in His holy grace,
Ngarrindjeri Mi:mini, Kumarangk is our home.

This island is not just any island,
It is covered by the living waters,
It is our birth from the red soil of Mother Earth.
Kumarangk is all of life to the Ngarrindjeri Mi:mini.

This island is not just any island,
From the River Murray to the Coorong Hummocks,
It welcomed everyone who lived in these homelands,
Kumarangk is all of life to the Ngarrindjeri Mi:mini.

Ngarrindjeri Mi:minis, Kumarangk is our home.

I also had a visit from Syd's *kabbarli* Aunty Ivy Stewart, and Martha Edwards and Yvonne Edwards from Yalata. Everyone was so upset, but it was wonderful to feel the strength of our love for one another.

I really didn't think my time was up, so I tried to stay positive about the operation. I figured if I came out of it I would be okay. But just in case, I decided to give some little things to those closest to me. I gave Sandy a little set of miniature woomeras and boomerangs that had been given to me years before and were very dear to me, and she thought they were absolutely gorgeous. I wanted to be sure people had something to remember me by.

I was booked in for surgery on 19 July 1996. I'll never forget the date, because it was the anniversary of the death of my son Terry-boy, forty-one years before. I still had a touch of the flu and the doctor wanted to postpone the operation for a few days, but I told him I had to get it done. When I was being wheeled into the operating theatre, Kandy was by my side crying. I remember looking up to the ceiling and seeing Mummy's face watching over me. I said a little prayer for everybody and talked to my little Toy-boy, 'Sorry, son, I'm not ready to join you yet. I have a bit more work for my people yet'.

The operation took seven and a half hours and was a success, even though they say they nearly lost me on the table, so I knew my ancestors were looking after me and that my punishment was over now. I didn't have to apologise to the old people any more. But because the cancers were not close together they had to remove quite a lot of my stomach and recovering was quite a long process. I was now a gutless wonder! For the first couple of months I just rested at Point Pearce. It took a while before I could sit up and I had to start eating lots of really tiny meals. I couldn't eat a normal meal any more for a very long time and I really wasn't able to do much work for about eighteen months after that operation.

Even after all this the harassment didn't stop. Chirpy Campbell kept sending me faxes. Dibby ended up sending him a polite fax to say please stop harassing her mother, but it didn't do any good. My children were only concerned about my health because they didn't want to lose me just yet, and they supported me in what I was doing. But they didn't want to turn the TV on any more because it was hurtful seeing what them fellas were doing to me, my own relations.

The one thing I did do was spend three days down at Clayton — that's just out from Milang and the island — with Di Bell. Since the Mathews inquiry wasn't going to work for us, she decided it might be a good idea to make her report into a book and I agreed. Di showed me the manuscript of what she was putting together. When she went back to America from her last trip over here, there were friends of hers had been doing research at the Institute of Aboriginal Studies in Canberra and the Mitchell Library in Sydney. And they found some very interesting documents. During the 1930s, Norman Tindale interviewed Reubin Walker and in those stories was evidence of the women's initiations. But I hadn't seen these things before, because this was new material that only came back to Australia after Norman Tindale died in 1993 and he left them to the South Australian Museum. Di Bell also showed me David Unaipon's unpublished stories from the Mitchell Library archives. And *Mainu* David wrote about the Ngarrindjeri Seven Sisters Dreaming and things about women's initiations — the very things the 'experts' in Ngarrindjeri culture said didn't exist. Amongst the new documents were volumes and volumes of Norman Tindale's interviews with Milerum, or Clarence Long. He also talks about the women's initiations, just as Albert Karloan told Ronald Berndt.

When Di Bell showed them to me I was very surprised to know that a Ngarrindjeri man had told Tindale these stories, because it's the grandmother's lore. But I reckon that those old fellas, even though they may have went against their culture and tradition to talk about these things, about the women's initiations, they must have known deep down in their heart that in the future when they're gone, somebody's going to need it. And when I read it, I tell you I could have jumped through the verandah I was so excited.

Women's meeting

Because of this I thought it was necessary to have an emergency meeting of Ngarrindjeri women. I also wanted to reassure everyone I was okay. We organised to meet down at Camp Coorong. Joanne Willmott[3] chaired the meeting and we taped it for the record. The women there included Jessie Sumner, Isobel Norvill, Hazel Wilson, Ellen Jackson, Linda Sumner, Eileen McHughes, Vicky Hartman, Selena Sumner, Dot Shaw, Belinda Rigney, Eunice Ashton, Glenys Wilson, Phyllis Sumner, Janice Walker, Raylene Rigney and Emily Rankine. I had hoped that Auntie Maggie and Veronica and Edie and them would come, but it was too short notice. I told everyone about the documents that had turned up in Di Bell's research and I said:

> Most of you know now that I've destroyed those envelopes because I didn't want the government to subpoena me to court with them. Even though I was prepared to go to jail over it, I didn't produce those envelopes to the government. And a lot of those stories that I read last Wednesday was actually in those envelopes. I feel a bit sorry now that I destroyed those envelopes, but I feel at the time when I did it, I did the right thing, because as long as I am communicating with you fellas and talking to you fellas and passing these stories on, then eventually we'll get it down to our descendants.

All these things came to me last Wednesday — first time I ever read them on paper — and I thought to myself this paper that's going through Parliament in March... we're going to have to do something and we're going to have to do it very quickly. Because if we lose this bill that's going through Parliament, Aboriginal history in Australia will be finished. Tradition, culture will be wiped out. The government is doing everything they can to stop us. They tried to change the Aboriginal Heritage Act. They couldn't do that, so now they're putting a bill through Parliament which is called the Hindmarsh Island Bridge Act 1996. And they have the power to do this. But we do have four new Ngarrindjeri people who have recorded women's business before I was even born, the initiation of the Ngarrindjeri women. I was overwhelmed because I knew deep in my heart I never lied to you fellas and I never lied to Tickner. Mr Tickner did not read my documents. I knew I never lied because I learnt the stories and I was taught by Auntie Rosie, my Mother's elder sister, and I knew that there are people from Raukkan who have said that I have lied. We do have a chance of proving now our belief in our culture, our tradition, our history and we have evidence to prove it. Now I'm going to give you fellas all the opportunity in the world to read these yourself, because it's important.

The two Philips in the Museum are saying I should have my doctorate taken away from me. Well they can take my doctorate if they want it, but they can't take away my brain and what is in my heart for my people at Raukkan.

So we have a decision to make. Do we keep on fighting the government to protect that island and stop that bridge? Do we pull together? This is our last chance, because once this bill goes through Parliament if the Liberal Party win, that'll be in Parliament and it'll take a lot to change it. Do we stand together and try and continue our fight? I say yes, but I've been sick and I'm tired all the time and I can no longer do it on my own. So I'm asking my people to help me.

We will still continue to fight honestly, with dignity and with pride for our people.[4]

That was a very moving meeting we had that day. The mood in that room, you could have heard a pin drop. One by one, the women began to have their say, talking really softly, as we all held hands.

I felt we had to go on because we couldn't let our grannies and great-grannies [grandchildren and great-grandchildren] read their history and think we were fabricators. Right round the world we needed to clear our names. We never got nothing out of this financially; the only thing we got is spiritual. We needed to prove to our relations, the dissident women, and to Chirpy that we did not lie and we believe in something that really happened for thousands and thousands of years.

Reconciliation

I was too tired to work, so I decided to put in my resignation with Native Title, effective as of 2 January 1997. I was sixty-two and past retirement age, and I had been through so much.

This freed up a bit of my time, so I was able to accept an invitation to the Australian Reconciliation Convention held in Melbourne from 26 to 28 May 1997. Aunty Maggie, Veronica, Dot Shaw, Eunice Ashton and Edie Rigney and me all went over together to hear what Howard had to say. We were walking round town looking at the shops when we happened to run into Che Cockatoo-Collins, a top-class Aboriginal footballer. He told us he was following us on television and wished us well, so that was lovely.

The big highlight of the Conference was a panel of speakers. We had former Labor Prime Minister Paul Keating and other politicians speaking about what they thought reconciliation should involve. The final speaker was our great Prime Minister, John Howard, who wanted to undermine anything good that was being built up for Aboriginal people. We held up our banner that read 'Grandmother's lore' for the media to pick up. Howard stood up and started to tell us how he wasn't going to say sorry to Aboriginal and Torres Strait Islander people for all the hurt we have suffered at white hands. He reckoned he didn't do anything wrong, it was the ancestors who did the wrong things to Aboriginal people, so he didn't need to say sorry. I could feel my blood starting to boil. I don't know what came over me —

I certainly hadn't planned it — but I just stood up and turned my back to that small-minded man, real pretty way. I just kept standing there, and as I peeked over my shoulder I could see that gradually one by one, my people stood up and followed my lead, and then lots of other Aboriginal people, until there were about a hundred of us standing with our backs to little Johnny Howard. People tell me they thought it was deadly when they saw it on TV. So it went down really well, that little decision of mine to have a silent protest. Afterwards Yvonne Goolagong [Yvonne Cawley after marriage, the champion tennis player] came up and shook my hand for doing that. We all had a good laugh when we watched it on the news that night.

Di Bell's book

Back in Adelaide, Di Bell was ready to launch her book. At least that way our story would get to the outside world. We were hopeful this book would help make things right. *Ngarrindjeri Wurruwarrin: A world that is, was and will be* was launched in 1998 to a big crowd of our supporters. After some pretty speeches and music and song from Archie Roach and Ruby Hunter, we all walked down to the Minister's office to present him with a copy. The staff was shocked to see so many of us crowding into the foyer of his office, demanding to see him. We were told he wasn't there, he was down at Parliament House. So off we went. When we got to Parliament House, he wouldn't come out to see us. But his Labor counterpart did come out and spoke to us. We gave him a copy of the book, but really nothing much came of it. I think no-one really wanted to know our side of the story by then.

Di Bell's book didn't have the effect we were hoping for. Nothing changed. So we all went back to our homes and our lives as publicly branded liars. I tried to get on with life as best I could. Eating lots of tiny little meals a day was hard work, keeping up with that, and I was doing my best to keep my mind occupied, so I picked up again with my work.

The Hindmarsh Island Bridge Bill was passed and the first pylon was sunk into that precious earth on Friday, 19 November 1999. The following Monday about two hundred of us got together to reclaim

Kumarangk for the Ngarrindjeri people. The Tal Kin Jeri dancers danced as we raised the Aboriginal flag, and then the Ngarrindjeri flag. Matt Rigney spoke and said we did not recognise the Hindmarsh Island Bridge Act and that we would be sending a petition to the Queen to ask her to pressure the government to give us back this land. He said this ceremony was necessary because Ngarrindjeri cultural and spiritual heritage had been 'raped' by the Australian legal and political systems for almost a decade.

I've never really looked at that bridge; I've only had a faint glance at it, but I can almost feel its presence before I get towards Goolwa. I've never walked or driven over it and I never will.

Federal Court case

A year or more passed before the Chapmans lodged their case for compensation against Deane Fergie and the Adelaide University, Professor Cheryl Saunders and Robert Tickner in the Federal Court. They didn't sue any Aboriginal people, because they knew we didn't have any money, and they wanted something like $20 million in damages. I couldn't help thinking how such a huge amount of money would go a long way to improving the health and living conditions of my people. And this was just one couple looking to use it for themselves. I thought if anyone should be suing, it should be me, for what they done to me in that witch-hunt.

The ALRM lawyers were giving me advice. They said that finally this was a way to present our case, that this would be different to the Royal Commission. This was the last thing. I was sick, I was exhausted, but I decided I was going to take the stand. All the other women agreed that they would also give evidence, so I was feeling really positive about it. I had no choice. If I felt negative then, I would have gone under.

So Tim Anderson acted as my lawyer and Alison Fitzgerald was to help him. Alison is married to the brother of the famous tennis player John Fitzgerald, and they come from Cummins. It was a big coincidence because I knew that family from when I was living there.

Lots of people were a great support to me and looked after me, like Margaret Wallace and her daughter Jess. Margaret's foster brother is

Harold Thomas, who designed the Aboriginal flag, so she grew up with an Aboriginal brother. Margaret also became a dear friend, and she and Jess couldn't do enough for me. Jess is a film-maker and she eventually did a lovely documentary on the Kumarangk business that went to air on SBS in 2002. We had a party that night round at Sandra's and everyone cried. Lots of women supported me and Aunty Maggie and Aunty Veronica, who were all in the front line. I would be sitting down at Sandra's place and someone would knock on the door and bring me a beautiful feed or someone would say, 'Do you want a massage?' Margaret brought me a lovely new coat to wear to court, and I pinned on it the little bird brooch Aunty Rosie gave me all those years ago. I treasure that brooch and I believed it would bring me good luck.

The night before I was to give evidence to the Federal Court the strangest thing happened. I was sitting down with Sandra and trying to prepare myself to mentally and physically cope with giving testimony and being cross-examined. We were trying to relax with a few drinks and were getting a little bit charged up. I could picture Aunty Rosie before my eyes and I needed to check with her if I was doing the right thing this time. I was so worried I started to cry and begged Aunty Rosie for guidance. All of a sudden, Sandra's body seemed to tense up and she went into a sort of trance. She said to me, 'This is your Aunty Rosie talking. Now is the time my girl. You get in there and you tell them what you are able to tell them. You straighten yourself up because you need to do this now for your people'. It was the most weirdest scene. Sandra was talking just like Aunty Rosie talked, using the same language and lilt in her voice. This went on for a while until Sandy eventually came out of it. We both stared at each other in shock, but I felt really relieved and ready to take it on after that.

I was on the stand for about ten days and Sandy made sure she never left my side for the whole of that time. I was still feeling physically weak, but Justice von Doussa was very polite. He treated me like a human being, allowed me a break every now and then, which I really appreciated. I would go downstairs for a cigarette and some fresh air with Sandy on one side and Margaret on the other like bodyguards, arms linked. After each day in court we'd go home to Sandy's house and I was absolutely exhausted. I'd take all evening to recover, and then next day we'd go in and I'd do it all over again. Sandy must have been exhausted too; she was a wonderful support.

It was all a very hard thing, but I was determined to get through it all with pride and dignity, and I think I did pretty well. I thought hard about every question I was asked and answered each one with complete honesty. Even when I was questioned by Marie Shaw, she thought she was really clever and that she was going to catch me out. But she asked some ridiculous questions and Justice von Doussa was constantly getting annoyed with her and asking her to be reasonable. I just kept my cool and answered honestly and in the end she got quite frustrated. After I had finished giving evidence, Tim Anderson said to me, 'Doreen, you were nothing short of brilliant!' I had to ask him what that meant, but I was proud and excited that's what he thought. Finally things felt like they were starting to come right for my people.

Well I gave my evidence and did the best I could, so Sandy and I just went home and waited for the judgment. The hard part of this was we couldn't catch up with Deane and Rod or Steve Hemming or Steve Kenny, because that might prejudice things. I couldn't even have a casual cup of coffee with them, otherwise that would be misinterpreted. So when the proceedings were finished we went round to see Deane on 19 August 2001. Deane had really been through the mill too. She suffered a lot during the Royal Commission and now she was being sued and she didn't think she had it in her to go on. She said she wasn't going to hear the von Doussa decision because she couldn't take another rejection, so we needed to talk her round that. We had the best time. We were eating and drinking and crying and talking. When we got back to Sandra's, Sandra stayed up all night and painted 'The von Doussa Judgment'.

We turned up the following morning to hear the judgment and that courtroom was packed. There was hardly any room to stand. The crowd was enormous, and you just couldn't fit one more person in that room if you tried. Kandy was with me to help me and protect me and he could see above the crowd because he's tall, but I couldn't see anything and I couldn't understand what was going on.

Then I heard Justice von Doussa talking. I whispered to Kandy to tell me what was happening, but he just told me to shoosh. Then all of a sudden there was an almighty roar and everyone was cheering and clapping. I didn't know what was happening, but everyone looked so happy, I thought it must be good. I couldn't get it to sink in.

> Upon the evidence before this Court I am not satisfied that the restricted women's knowledge was fabricated or that it was not part of genuine Aboriginal tradition.[5]

We had been vindicated at long last. Words can't explain how I felt.

9

Epilogue

It was ironic that the only reason we were vindicated was because the Chapmans' sued for around $20 million. Because their case failed and they didn't get any money, they actually caused justice to be done all round, to my way of thinking.

The Aboriginal Program, SBS Radio, 22 August 2001

Reporter:
It was phenomenal. I have to say in more than fifteen years as a journalist I haven't seen a day quite like it and I've certainly never seen this sort of a scene in a courtroom before. We're talking Hindmarsh Island, the ten-year saga of the bridge case about 80 kilometres south of Adelaide, known to the Aboriginal people, the traditional Ngarrindjeri custodians, as Kumarangk, and known to the whitefellas as Hindmarsh Island. It's been the scene of a very bitter battle between the construction of a bridge that the Ngarrindjeri people believe would severely interfere with their sacred Dreaming pertaining to women's business. The bridge, as our listeners would be aware, has been built due to a Royal Commission which found that the Aboriginal women's business was fabricated.

Now in astonishing scenes in the Federal Court yesterday, Justice John von Doussa found that in his opinion, the evidence that he was presented suggests that the women's business in fact was not fabricated: a huge, huge vindication for Aboriginal cultural beliefs here in, not just South Australia, but Australia. It essentially overturns the Royal Commission finding. We have some incredibly buoyant Aboriginal people here in Adelaide, including Dr Doreen Kartinyeri, who is the chief custodian of the women's business that was at the centre of this row and she's quite plainly elated.

Dr Doreen Kartinyeri:
I hope it can prove to the world that I am not a fabricator and I'm looking forward to my grandchildren and all other young Ngarrindjeri people learning their culture. I hoped it was going to be that finding because I knew I never lied. That I know myself. And I'm very, very happy about the decision.

After the Royal Commission

The headlines read, 'LIES, LIES, LIES!' I couldn't understand why they didn't now say, 'SORRY, SORRY, SORRY!' But of course they didn't. Just, 'Hindmarsh ruling against Chapmans'. Apparently Justice von Doussa was also very scathing of the Chapmans in his ruling, but I just didn't care.

The von Doussa decision was marvellous, and it went a long way towards justice at last. But how do you recover from events like these? How do you even begin to heal? It could possibly start with a public apology and we put together some wording for one of the politicians to read out in parliament. But we couldn't get a single one of them to find the courage.

The Adelaide Advertiser, Friday, 20 September 2002, page 15

Old bones found at Hindmarsh Island

Forensic scientists are to analyse bones uncovered last week close to the controversial Hindmarsh Island bridge.

The remains are believed to be those of a Ngarrindjeri woman and child who died up to 200 years ago, but this has yet to be confirmed. The bones were found during work for the Goolwa Wharf redevelopment.

> A Ngarrindjeri heritage group spokesman said that while it was unfortunate the burial site had been disturbed, the discovery vindicated the Ngarrindjeri people's opposition to the bridge construction.

When I first got the call to say they had uncovered a burial and that it was a woman and a little girl, I caught my breath. They were found only about 100 metres from the bridge. To my way of thinking it was no coincidence it should be a mother and daughter. This was the old people's way of confirming we were right.

The Kumarangk affair did affect the fertility of Ngarrindjeri women. One of the main women had a major bleeding on the night the envelopes were opened. Then she never had a period again. She didn't go through menopause. She blames McLachlan for taking away her womanhood. Another woman who had been through menopause got a period again. Then, during the Federal Court case, I was advising one of the female lawyers on what to do in the Ngarrindjeri way to help her get pregnant. She had being trying for some time without success. She bought one of Sandra's paintings about Hindmarsh Island, and after the case was over, the day she collected it, she found out she was pregnant. The old people were so right.

The discovery of the skeletons of the woman and child made the Alexandrina Council realise how racist the Kumarangk affair had been towards Aboriginal people. They felt their shame.

The Adelaide Advertiser, 9 October 2002, page 15

> A simple apology brought two cultures together amid hugs and tears yesterday. Neville Gollan had waited more than a decade for a formal apology to the Ngarrindjeri people, which was made during an historic meeting in Goolwa. Mr Gollan and Alexandrina councillor Mary Beckett embraced after the reading — by mayor Kym McHugh — of the council's expression of sorrow and apology to the Ngarrindjeri people.
>
> They were overcome with emotion by the event, which also included the signing of an agreement by both parties to collaborate on any future development involving traditional lands within the council area.

Mrs Beckett said the hugs had been happening all day. 'I just hope this leads the way for others to take the initiative.'

It came more than a month after Aboriginal skeletal remains were discovered during work on the $2.7 million Goolwa Wharf Redevelopment and a decade since the Hindmarsh Island bridge 'secret women's business' saga. 'We are shamed to acknowledge that there is still racism within our communities', the statement said. 'We accept that our words must match our actions and we pledge to you that we will work to remove racism and ignorance.'

The Kungun Ngarrindjeri Yunnan Agreement — meaning 'Listen to Ngarrindjeri people talking' — includes a $20,000 payment for monitors nominated by the Ngarrindjeri people to oversee future excavation work at the wharf precinct.

Mr McHugh said its signing was a significant step in the region's history.

We wouldn't allow the press to attend the reburial of the remains. We were so tired of all the publicity, and we wanted those old people to go back to their resting place in dignity and peace. The group was solemn as we faced the large hole that had been dug for the reburial. The coffin lay on the ground in the hole as Sandy and I stood with arms linked looking down in pain and sorrow. Somebody next to us had an Aboriginal flag, and I don't know what came over me, but something made me take that flag, and still linked to Sandra, I drew her slowly down into that hole and placed the flag over the coffin. We paid our respects to our ancestors. It was a lovely gesture and the crowd was very moved. A feeling of peace washed over me; our people were finally returning to their country.

The following May, 2003, soon after I received the Centenary Medal from John Howard, the Prime Minister who was so against us, the remains of three hundred Ngarrindjeri ancestors — some of them thousands of years old — were also returned to their country. After being collected and sent to Edinburgh University around the 1900s, they were finally brought home to rest. A big smoking ceremony was held to cleanse their spirits, but there was lots of mixed emotions. We were pleased that our people were coming home, but angry and sad that they had been taken so far from their country in the first place. So much work to do to rebury so many.

My culture, my family, my people, my life.

When I look back on my life now, my mind goes back to a time when I'm sitting down with Aunty Rosie at Hollywood, preparing the rushes for her to do her weaving. She is making some baskets this time. You have to have a nice, flat bottom. Then she starts to bring up the sides and she's showing me all the different stitches I have to use. And every one of those rushes that you thread through the others and every one that you use for the padding, you have the loose ends hanging and that's when you weave it all together. Then Aunty Rosie starts to say, 'They're like members of our family; you can't have them all the same size. You've got to make them this way and you've got to have that secure, like a tight family connection.' She starts to bring these things into it and I'm thinking, 'Now, what's making baskets and mats got to do with families and how many kids you have?'

Then she asks me, 'Is Aunty Dugidi still going, you know, over Raukkan?' 'Yeah', I say. 'Oh, that's my cousin.' 'How come she's your cousin?' So she explains the kinship. And she is explaining it as she is doing the weaving. And I am weaving all the kin relations in my mind. We are connecting up the weaving with the family kinship. It doesn't matter what she tells me; it all goes back to family. I can understand it now.

Afterword

This book is not a comprehensive account of Dr Doreen Kartinyeri's life, and particularly not of the Kumarangk affair. It is the way Doreen saw it; the way she remembers or doesn't remember it. Certain issues and events were simply not important to her and so don't feature strongly in her account, if at all. It is Doreen's personal recollection of events in her life, and some episodes may be remembered differently by others.

Doreen was meticulous about her sourcing and documentation. When we first began to record her story, it was envisaged that I would talk to as many people as possible in order to make sure the facts were 'right', particularly in relation to the Kumarangk affair. As an oral historian, I have not had the wherewithal to accomplish this task; and for Doreen, simply addressing the Kumarangk issue at all was extremely painful. Time and time again we had to stop talking about it because of her extreme distress. It is a testament to her strength that we were to some extent able to surmount these obstacles.

Doreen's story is her story. Other people in this story have theirs. That applies to all those beautiful Ngarrindjeri *mi:minis* who still survive — and I pay tribute and respect to you all. Some have passed on, but their memories endure. I will always have etched in my mind an image of that outstanding advocate of Ngarrindjeri women's knowledge, Aunty

Maggie Jacobs, proclaiming after the von Doussa judgment, 'I knew I never lied; are they going to pull that bridge down now?'

When Doreen and I began this project in the second half of 2001, we wrote and signed a contract of mutual respect and understanding that we hoped would take this journey forward comfortably for both of us. I needed to 'get it right' for this much maligned and misrepresented woman. I could not have begun to imagine how long and difficult a journey it would become. We agreed that the underlying theme would be social justice for Aboriginal and Torres Strait Islander peoples. We agreed that it would be written for her people in particular and that it had to be as close a representation as possible of her own voice. No more whitefellas interpreting, changing or twisting her words. This is, of course, easier said than done, even with the best of intentions. I have heard, recorded and transcribed Doreen's words, mixed them around and let them sit there.

While our aims were admirable, they proved impossible to achieve in their entirety. In particular, Doreen's health deteriorated over time, in the course of our work on the book. I believe it is, however, as true to our commitment as we could make it.

It was not originally planned that I should write an afterword. We decided towards the end of the process that this would be a good idea, because all these issues needed explaining. I should mention that the endnotes are mine.

Before this project, I had interviewed Doreen twice: once for a project with the Ngadjuri of the mid-north of South Australia, and once for the Bringing Them Home Oral History Project, for which Doreen was my first interviewee. On the second occasion, I travelled to the house where she and Syd were living at Port Germein. I was using new, expensive digital equipment, and during the two and a half hour car journey I envisaged messing something up and coming away with blank tape. Doreen noticed. She said, 'You look nervous, Sue'. I told her I was, and she calmed me with, 'Don't worry, you'll be fine as long as you don't interrupt me too much!' She was right.

Learning of her ill health, in February 2006, about sixty women made the journey from Raukkan and Murray Bridge to Point Pearce to pay their respects to Doreen and hold a 'thank-you' party, showing their gratitude for the work she has done in putting their genealogies together, recording Aboriginal history and fighting against the Hindmarsh Island bridge. On 21 March 2006 I also visited Point Pearce to work on the final chapters with Doreen. The previous week she had been hospitalised and close to death. Her daughter Lydia tried to keep things quiet, because she was afraid that when the news got out on the *nunga* grapevine Doreen would be inundated with people wanting to see her, which would tire her out. I promised not to tell anyone, but the grapevine works far too efficiently and car-loads of people were soon arriving.

When I arrived, Doreen had been home for about a week. Living with her son Jamie, she was also being cared for by Pat Kropinyeri, a friend who had come from Murray Bridge especially for this purpose. As I set up my notebook, Pat did the washing up and tidied the kitchen. While she went about the chores, she listened as I read the last three chapters to Doreen aloud. At one point relating to the Kumarangk affair, Pat stopped plumping the cushions to interrupt me. 'You know,' she quietly said, 'I was involved with the Hindmarsh Island thing from the beginning, and this woman gave us back our history, our culture and our identity'. I was deeply moved by this comment, and for that moment, I had a real sense of the depth of emotion and the level of respect Doreen evoked in those who looked to her to lead them in their fight for social justice.

Dodo worked with me solidly from 11.00 am till 4.00 pm that day — no mean feat for someone in her condition — and we arrived at a largely finished product.

Doreen's final genealogical work *Ngarrindjeri Nation*, that of the Ngarrindjeri people of her birthplace Raukkan, was published in September 2006. She passed away after a long battle with illness in the early hours of 3 December 2007.

This account of the life of Dr Doreen Kartinyeri is a tribute to her strength, honesty and tireless contribution to her people as a mother, a foster mother, a community leader, a genealogist and a true friend to many.

Sue Anderson
February 2008

Notes

Chapter 1

1. Cameron Raynes, 'A Little Flour and a Few Blankets': An Administrative History of Aboriginal Affairs in South Australia 1834–2000. Department for Administrative and Information Services, State Records of South Australia, 2002, p. 159.

Chapter 2

1. Dr Deane Fergie is an anthropologist. She was engaged to provide an expert anthropological report to Cheryl Saunders, who was conducting an independent report on the Kumarangk issues for Robert Tickner.
2. If the Aborigines' Protection Board felt that an Aboriginal person was 'by reason of his character and standard of intelligence and development' deserving of exemption from the provisions of the Act, they could be given either an unconditional or limited exemption, forfeiting their Aboriginality and becoming an 'honorary' white person. Raynes, A Little Flour and a Few Blankets, p. 50.
3. Police Offences Amendment Act 1953.

Chapter 3

1. Gladys Elphick was a Kaurna woman raised at Point Pearce, who was involved in forming the Aboriginal Women's Council, a legal aid service, a medical service and an Aboriginal community centre in Adelaide. For more information see www.womenaustralia.info.

2. The decision in the Federal Court case of *Mabo vs. State of Queensland* (1992) determined that at first settlement by Europeans, Australia was not *terra nullius* and that Indigenous people had rights over land. This led to the *Native Title Act 1994*, which effectively recognised Aboriginal and Torres Strait Islander law alongside Western law.
3. On 10 December 1992, Prime Minister Paul Keating spoke publicly of the injustices done to Aboriginal people and of the need for reconciliation. In December 1996, the Wik people of northern Queensland obtained a High Court ruling that native title could continue to exist on pastoral leases. In May 1997, Prime Minister John Howard's Ten Point Plan proposed to extinguish native title on these leases.
4. Indigenous Australian children affected by past government policies of removal from their families, as identified by the *National Inquiry into the Separation of Aboriginal and Torres Strait Islander children from their families* (1997), conducted by Sir Ronald Wilson, have come to be known as the 'Stolen Generations'.
5. GRG52/1/1947/2A State Records.
6. GRG52/1/1951/17 State Records.
7. Recorded interview between Marjory Tripp and Doreen Kartinyeri, 1 November 1988

Chapter 4

1. The Report of the Aborigines' Protection Board for the year ending 30 June 1947 noted, 'For several years the dux of the school has proved to be a native girl, and, having regard to the fact the native scholars represent only 16% of the roll strength, this may be regarded as something of an achievement'. GRG52/11947/72.

Chapter 6

1. Lewis O'Brien is a senior elder of the Kaurna people of the Adelaide Plains. One time Liaison Officer with the SA Education Department, he has also worked voluntarily on the welfare needs of the Aboriginal community. Uncle Lewis is invited to many functions to provide a Kaurna welcome to country.
2. Professor Paul Hughes AO (Yankunytjatjara/Narunnga) was the first Aboriginal person to achieve a professorship. A former primary teacher, Director of the University of South Australia's Aboriginal Centre, Chair of the National Aboriginal Education Committee and Superintendent of Aboriginal Education with the Department of Education, he is currently

Chair of the Executive of the Indigenous College of Education and Research.
3. Professor Fay Gale AO specialises in the social geography of Aboriginal communities. She rose to the position of Vice-Chancellor of the University of Western Australia from which she retired in 1997. She was the University's first woman Vice-Chancellor and the first woman Chair of the Australian Vice-Chancellor's Committee. Professor Gale is now an Honorary Senior Research Fellow with the Geography Department of the University of Adelaide.
4. Now the Australian Institute for Aboriginal and Torres Strait Islander Studies, or AIATSIS.
5. Fay Gale (ed.), *We are bosses ourselves: the status and role of Aboriginal women today*. Australian Institute of Aboriginal Studies, Canberra ACT, 1983.
6. Norman B. Tindale was with the South Australian Museum (which holds the biggest collection of Aboriginal cultural material in the world) for forty-nine years. In the 1920s and 1930s he conducted an annual expedition with the Board for Anthropological Research, during which he took over 6000 photographs of Aboriginal people. With the University of Adelaide in conjunction with Harvard University he undertook an eighteen-month national field trip in 1938–9. He undertook another major field trip in 1953–4. Tindale's *Aboriginal Tribes of Australia* (1974) mapped tribal boundaries across the continent and is only one of his many publications.
7. The Tjilbruke Project was a collaborative project between the Tjilbruke Trail Committee (which included Kaurna elders Georgina Williams and Lewis O'Brien), the South Australian Museum and local governments to document and celebrate the Kaurna Dreaming of Tjilbruke by the placing of plaques along the route Tjilbruke took when travelling down the Fleurieu Peninsula as he carried the body of his deceased nephew to his final resting place.
8. S.J. Hemming, Project Manager, Aboriginal Family History Project, South Australian Museum. *Rec. S. Aust. Mus.* 23(2), 1989, pp. 147–52.
9. In traditional practice, still widely retained today across Aboriginal Australia, it is forbidden to mention the name or show the photo of the deceased, who is referred to by a generic name for 'deceased person', sometimes followed by their surname. For this reason in Western Desert society the term *Kunamara* is used to replace the name.

10. Tregenza, John, 'Two Notable Portraits of South Australian Aborigines', in *Journal of the Historical Society of South Australia*, no. 12, 1984, pp. 22–31.
11. Ronald and Catherine Berndt were anthropologists working with Aboriginal communities at the same time as Norman Tindale. Their archives are embargoed for fifty years after the death of Catherine in 1994 (i.e. until 2044) and are held in the Berndt Museum of Anthropology at the University of Western Australia.
12. Marcia Langton, a well-known Aboriginal scholar, is now Professor of Anthropology at the University of Melbourne.

Chapter 7

1. Isobel Norvill is a well-respected Ngarrindjeri elder who has worked in the Aboriginal health sector for many years.
2. Betty Fisher, a white woman, was involved with the International Women's Day committee. She interviewed senior Ngarrindjeri women in the 1960s and says they told her about women's business then.
3. *The Weekend Australian*, 11–12 March 1995, p. 4.
4. Yami Lester is a senior Yankunytjatjara man from the north of South Australia. He is said to have been blinded as a young person by the bomb testing at Maralinga in the 1950s, and also spent some time in the Colebrook Home. He has written his own autobiography, *Yami: the autobiography of Yami Lester* (Institute for Aboriginal Development, Alice Springs NT, 1993) and continues to act as a leader in his community.

Chapter 8

1. Sister Janet Mead is remembered for her chart-topping version of 'Ave Maria' in the 1970s. She is a Catholic nun with the Sisters of Mercy.
2. Text from the Dr Doreen Kartinyeri Archival Collection, Native Title Unit, Aboriginal Legal Rights Movements, Adelaide.
3. Joanne Willmott is a well-known Aboriginal activist, originally from Queensland.
4. Speech transcribed from tape of the meeting by Sue Anderson.
5. *Chapmans v Luminis, Fergie, Saunders, Tickner and C'wealth*, 21 August 2001:12.

Index

ABC, 86
  Life Matters program, 144
Aboriginal and Torres Strait Islander Commission (ATSIC), 111, 151
Aboriginal Family History Unit, *see* South Australian Museum, Doreen's employment at
Aboriginal Health Agency, 116
Aboriginal Heritage Act 1988, 43–4, 45, 152, 187
Aboriginal Heritage Branch, 130–1
Aboriginal Housing Authority, 111
Aboriginal Legal Rights Movement (ALRM/Legal Rights), 153, 157–8, 161
  Chapmans' compensation case lawyers, 196, 198, 202
  Charles, Chris, 26, 169
  Doreen's statement to Professor Saunders, 67
  Layton, Robyn, 169–70
  Native Title Act meeting, 47
  Native Title Unit, 135, 188, 194
  Royal Commission and Royal Commission period, 175, 180, 183
  Woolley Tim, 1, 26, 159; at Mount House meeting, 150
  see also Fergie, Dr Deane; Saunders, Sandra
Aboriginal of the Year, 159–60
Aboriginality, proof of, 111
Aborigines' Friends Association, 9
Aborigines' Protection Board, *see* Protector of Aborigines
abortions, 155, 185
Adelaide City Baths, 55
Adelaide jail, 126
Adelaide Review, 178–9
Adelaide University, *see* University of Adelaide
Adelaide Zoo, 78
The Advertiser, 140, 165, 173
  article on Doreen's Honorary Doctorate, 172
  articles on remains found at Hindmarsh Island, 201–3
  article on Una and Pat Rigney, 73
  cartoon on 'Politicians' business', 167–8
  interviews with Doreen, 43–4, 159–60
  James, Colin, 157–8, 168, 177
  photos of Grandfather Gordon, 122
Agius, Josie, 137
Agius, Aunty Laura, 123
Agius, Parry, 188
Agius, Rhonda, 158, 170

Index

agriculture, 19–20, 98, 121
  stump picking, 7, 21–2, 33, 96
  see also shearing
alcohol, 23, 98, 120
  after Melbourne Cup win, 117
  Globe Hotel, 120–1
  Milera, Doug, 172
  smuggling into Raukkan, 82–3
  Wanganeen, Terry, 112–13
Alexandrina Council, 150, 158, 202–3
Alice Springs, 182–3
Alport, Kate, 46
ALRM, see Aboriginal Legal Rights Movement
Amelia Park, 151, 155, 184–5
Anderson, Chris, 46, 164
Anderson, Tim, 196, 198
Angas (Tripp), Marj, 59, 97, 126
Angie, Linda, 110
Angie, Rita, 111
Ankel, Valma, 131
anthropologists' classification, 20–1
Anzac Day, 122
Appleton, Lieutenant, 69
apprenticeships, 97
aquatic displays, 54–5
archives, 124, 135–8
  Poonindie records, 130–1
  see also Tindale collection
Armstrong, Amelia, 106
Armstrong, Ellen, 106
Armstrong, Joanne, 106
Ashton, Eunice, 192, 194
assimilation policies, 110, 118–19
ATSIC, 111, 151
Austin, Emily, 143, 169
Australian Institute of Aboriginal Studies, 123, 191
Australian Reconciliation Convention, 194–5

babies, see births
babies' cradles, 100
Badlie, 142
bag sewing, 98
Ballarat, 146
balls, 110, 112, 159
bank accounts, 80
Bannon, John, 139
Barmera, 93–4, 109
Baroota, 114–15, 146
Bartlett, Mr and Mrs Clarrie and family, 12, 33, 37
Barton Vale, 70
basketball (netball), 107
baskets, see weaving
Beckett, Mary, 202–3
Bell, Diane, 182, 188, 191–2, 195
Bendigo, 133
Berndt, Ron and Catherine, 137–8
Berri, 92–3, 95
Bertani, Peter, 144
Beryl (sister of Dorrie Wilson), 156, 158
Bessie, *Mutha,* 15, 75
Betts, Zola, 137
Bickmore, Bob, 93
Bickmore, Graham, 93–4
Bickmore, Wendy, 93
Bin-Salik, Dr Maryanne, 171
birds, 8, 9
births, 29, 100–1
  Doreen, 4
  Doreen's children, 101–2, 107, 109
  Doreen's mother, 103
  Doreen's siblings, 5, 23–4, 25, 79
  fertility, 169, 187, 202
  Kartinyeri, Eileen, 118
  Rankine, Janice ('Daughter'), 89–90
  see also Child Endowment; *putharis*
Block K, 22
Boandik, 5
Boer War, 140
boney bream, 10
books and articles, 125, 126
  Kartinyeri Family, 130
  Narrunga Nation, 145, 188
  Ngarrindjeri Anzacs, 121, 188–9
  Ngarrindjeri Nation, 207
  Poonindie: The Rise and Destruction of an Aboriginal Agricultural Community, 130–1

Index

Rigney Family, 124, 126
Sumner Family, 160
Tandanya Opening Day Souvenir Program Introduction, 139–140
Wanganeen Family, 125, 128, 144
We Are Bosses Ourselves, 125
Wilson Family, 143
Booth House, *see* Fullarton Girls' Home
boyfriend, first, 85
bream, 10
breast milk, 102–3
Bringing Them Home Oral History Project, 206
Brisbane, 125–6, 137, 143, 146
Bristol Archives, 131
Brock, Peggy, 130–1
Brodie, Veronica, 45, 154, 185, 194, 197
    grandmother, 24
    interview by Cheryl Saunders, 158
    mother (Aunty Kumi), 16, 179
    Royal Commission, 174, 186
    sister, 157
    when younger, 166
Brown, Dean, 43–4, 159–60, 174
Brown, Eileen, 143
Brumby, Daisy, 56
Brumby, Muriel, 56
Brumby, Rosie, 51, 52, 56, 57, 60, 73
Bryant, Laurie, 56
Buckskin, Vince, 128, 137
Bundaleer station, 106
Burdon, Rosemary, 171
burial grounds, 44, 147, 152, 155, 158–9
    bones uncovered in 2002, 201–3
    Point Pearce, 104
    West Terrace cemetery, 139, 144
Butcher, Granny Tokey, 4, 15

Cadell, 126
Camp Coorong, 146, 157
    meetings at, 166, 167, 168–9, 192–4
Campbell, Amelia, 154, 155, 167
Campbell, Chirpy, 177–8, 191
    mother, 156
    sister, 167
Campbell, June, 51, 52, 57, 60
Campbell, Stella, 156
Canberra, 21, 187
    Australian Institute of Aboriginal Studies, 123, 191
    COMA, 125
    War Memorial, 188
    see also Federal Parliament
candles, 6, 18
Cape York, 126
Carleton, Richard, 185
carpentry, 19, 20, 97, 102
cars, 107, 119
Carter, Bronwyn, 149
Carter, Brucey, 149
Carter, Cathy, 149
Carter, Aunty Fidy, 15, 16
Carter (Wilson), Glenys, 149, 154, 192
Carter, Proughton, 15
Carter, Uncle Roland, 15
Carter, Vernon, 15
Catholics, 55–6
Cawley (Goolagong), Yvonne, 195
Ceduna, 118, 141, 146
Centenary Medal, 203
Challenger, Benjamin, 125
Challenger, Melrose, 125
Challenger, Meryl, 125
Challenger, Samuel, 125
Chamberlain, Jenny, 121
Chamberlain, Kym, 121
Chamberlain, Pam, 121
Chamberlain, Syd, 120–1, 122, 160, 187
    Baroota, 114, 146–7
    family, 121, 141, 142, 146, 169, 190
    field trip with, 141–3
    job on Woodville Council, 132
    wurley making at Camp Coorong, 157
Chamberlain, Wayne, 121
Channel Seven, 178
Chapman, Tom and Wendy, 115, 147, 151, 164
    building of first marina, 155

Ngarrindjeri Council talks with, 154
see also court cases
Charles, Chris, 26, 169
Charleston, 70–7
Cheltenham, 119–20
Cherbourg, 126
Child Endowment, 20–1, 35, 53, 85, 108
  Aborigines' Protection Board use of, 36, 76
  signing over to Aborigines' Protection Board, 32
child removal, *see* Stolen Generation
childhood, 4–25, 27–42, 114
children, *see* births; foster children; illegitimate children
Christianity, *see* church and religion
Christmas Pageant, 56
church and religion, 31–2, 80–1, 174
  Catholics, 55–6
  Doreen's wedding, 95
  Fullarton Girls' Home, 53–4
  Kartinyeri, Nanna Sally, 15, 33–4
  Point Pearce, 96–7
  Poonindie, 15, 131
  Unaipon, *Mainu* David, 16
  see also Dreaming stories
church and religion, Raukkan, 4, 15–16, 18, 19, 80–1
  Anzac memorial window, 16, 189
  hand-me-down clothing sales, 9
  Nancy's funeral, 24
Church Home League, 19
cinema, *see* movies
Clark, Bert, 116, 117–18
Clarke, Philip, 46, 128, 129, 133–4, 170, 193
  field trips with, 128, 131–2, 133, 139
  Royal Commission witness, 178
classification, 20–1
Clayton, 191
clothing, 109, 197
  debutante ball wear, 112
  Fullarton Girls' Home, 41, 51, 53, 54, 58, 60; after leaving, 70, 76

Sister McKenzie's jumper, 61–3
Raukkan, 9, 17, 18–19, 24
shoes, 94
wedding dress, 95
Cockatoo-Collins, Che, 194
Colebrook Home, 29
  Doris in, 50–2, 56–7, 95; Doreen's visits, 60–1, 76–7
Collett, Andrew, 169
comb shears, 20
compensation case (von Doussa judgment), 196–201, 202, 206
conferences, 139, 143, 146
  museum anthropologists (COMA), 125–6
  native title, 175
  United States, 182
  women's, 136–7, 161–3, 182
Congregationalists, 80
Connie, *see* Kartinyeri, Connie; Roberts, Aunty Connie
Coober Pedy, 143, 146, 175
cooking, 8, 9, 10, 13, 18
  Baroota, 146–7
  taught by Aunty Rosie, 106
Coonalpyn, 77
Coorong (Kurangk), 7–9, 54
  Ngurunderi story, 133–4
  plans for road down over, 158–9
  Raukkan women going down to, 100
  streams down around, 158
  summer holidays with Syd, 121
  see also Camp Coorong
Coral (granddaughter of Aunty Rosie Kropinyeri), 180
Cornwillan, Samuel, 131
Coulthard, Faith, 56, 60
Country Women's Association, 73
court cases, 67, 160, 185
  application to hand secret envelopes over, 169–70
  challenging Royal Commission, 175
  for compensation (von Doussa judgment), 196–201, 202, 206
Cox Foyers, 70

215

Index

cradles, 100
craftwork, 13, 16–19, 20, 73
　see also feather flowers; weaving
Craig, Barry, 130, 141, 142, 170
Cravens, 60
cricketers in Crossland paintings, 131
crochet, 19
Crombie, Eileen, 143, 169
Cross, Jim, 89
Cross (Weetra), Peggy (granddaughter of Aunty Rosie Kropinyeri), 110, 121, 167, 180
Crossland paintings, Aboriginal subjects of, 131
Crowley, Rosemary, 185
Croydon Park, 178
Croydon Park School, 136
Cumeragunja mission, 132
Cummings, Bart, 117
Cummins, 121, 196

dancing, 14
　balls, 110, 112, 159
　pata winema, 86
Darwin, 143, 146
David Unaipon School, Underdale, 123
Davies, Mrs Stan, 112
Davoren Park, 121
Deacon, Maxie, 58
deaths, 29, 104–5, 108, 124, 157
　Jacobs, Aunty Maggie, 184
　Jimmy (Aunty Rosie's grandson), 91–2
　Kartinyeri, Alma, 5
　Kartinyeri, Doreen, 207
　Kartinyeri, Uncle Francie (Uncle Buddha), 92
　Kartinyeri, Nancy, 23–4, 27, 77
　Kartinyeri, Oscar (brother), 141
　Kartinyeri, Oscar (father), 120
　Kartinyeri, Terrence (Toy-boy, Terry-boy), 104–5, 190
　Kartinyeri, Thelma, 25, 27–8, 31–2, 34–5, 77
　Kenny, Steve, daughter of, 187
　Kropinyeri, Aunty Rosie, 122;
　daughters of, 99
　Lawrie, W. T., 15
　massacres, 5, 93, 147
　Sister McKenzie's letter to Mrs Dunn, 74–5
　refusal to allow Squashy to attend relative's funeral, 99
　Rigney, Aunty Eva, 18–19
　see also burial grounds
debutante balls, 112
Dennis (grandson of Aunty Laura Kartinyeri), 165
Department of Environment and Planning, 130
Department of State Aboriginal Affairs, 45, 97, 149
Deuschle, Vi, 154, 180
Devon Park, 122
Dibby, see Wanganeen, Lydia Dawn
Disher (Rigney), Rachel, 5, 79–80, 103
Disher, Richard, 5
'dissident women', 155, 165–9, 175, 180–1
　see also Wilson, Dorrie
Dix, Audrey, 165
Doctorate, Honorary, 171–2
Dodd, Steve, 56
Dodd, Uncle Seth, 11
'Dodo', 2
'dog tags', 35
domestic violence, 112–13
domestic work, 4, 5, 21, 36
　Doreen, 71–9, 85, 86, 91
Doogue, Geraldine, 144
Doris, see Kartinyeri, Doris Eileen
Draper, Neale, 148
'The Dreaming of Ngarrindjeri Mi:mini' (Dot Shaw's song), 185, 189–90
Dreaming stories, 84, 169
　Ngurunderi, 133–4
　Seven Sisters, 158, 187, 191–2
ducks, 9
Dugidi, Aunty (cousin to Rosie Kropinyeri), 16, 204
Dunn family, 70–7, 112

Dunstan, Don and Dunstan era, 46, 111, 112, 162
Dunstan, Gretel, 111

Earl, Mr, 99, 104
Eddie, Pappa, 122–3
Eden Hills, see Colebrook Home
Edinburgh University, 147, 203
Edith (cousin of Doreen), 64
education, see schools and schooling
Edwards, Aunty Martha, 146, 190
Edwards, Yvonne, 190
electricity, 6, 91, 96
Elphick, Aunty Gladdie, 46–7, 123
Elva (cousin of Doreen), 95
employment, 19–20, 35, 36
    Chamberlain, Syd, 121, 132, 146
    Kartinyeri, Archie, 20
    Kartinyeri, Klynton, 111
    Kartinyeri, Oscar (brother), 33, 95, 118
    Kartinyeri, Oscar (father), 19, 25, 77, 85
    at koala farm near Zoo, 78–9
    at Poltalloch, 4, 5
    Wanganeen, Daryl (Snacka), 117
    Wanganeen, Terry, 95, 98, 119
    see also pay; trades
employment, Doreen
    Aboriginal Heritage Branch, Department of Environment and Planning, 130–1
    with Dunn and Motteram families, 71–9
    Maitland Hotel, 91
    Native Title Unit, ALRM, 135, 188, 194
    Riverland, 93
    with Swalling family, 85–6
    see also genealogies; South Australian Museum, Doreen's employment at
envelopes, see secret envelopes
Escort House, 35
exemptions, 35–6, 82, 83, 90
    abolition, 118

family trees, see genealogies
family violence, 112–13
Fatt, Lillian, 143
feather flowers, 16, 17, 85, 125
    making with Aunty Rosie, 91, 99–100
Federal Court, see court cases
Federal Parliament, tabling of secret envelopes in, 1–2, 26–7, 160–3, 186
    affect on Ngarrindjeri women's fertility, 202
    Weekend Australian interview after, 66–8
fences and fencing wire, 10, 22
Fergie, Dr Deane, 153–4
    Chapmans' compensation case against, 196–9
    report for Professor Cheryl Saunders, 67
    Royal Commission, 180, 183
    secret envelopes, 27, 159, 183
field trips, 128, 131–3, 141–4
'Finding my People' project, 123–5
fire, 112
First World War, 5, 40–1, 122, 140, 188–9
    Raukkan church window commemorating, 16, 189
Fisher, Betty, 161, 179
Fisheries Act 1917, 10
fishing, 9–11, 99
Fitzgerald, Alison, 196
Flinders University, 146
food, 9–11, 18
    sheep meat, 19–20
    see also cooking; rations; wild food
football, 27–8, 89, 98, 107–8, 137
foster children, 3, 86, 88, 108, 135–6
    when Doreen had blue with Terry, 113
    after Doreen left Terry, 119–20
foster children raised by Thelma Kartinyeri, see Rigney, Elsie; Rigney, Lila; Rigney, Thelma
Fourmile, Henrietta, 137

Index

France, 189
Freda, *Kami* (stepmother of Syd Chamberlain), 142
Friends of Goolwa meeting, 154
fruit, 11, 12, 55, 93
   mantharis (wild tomatoes), 11, 18, 155
   sheoak apples, 7
Fudge, Aunty Olga, 123
'full-bloods', 10, 20–1
Fullarton Girls' Home, 24, 40–2, 48–65, 68–9, 75
   Dunns' opinions about, 72, 73
funerals, *see* deaths

Gale, Fay, 123, 125, 126–7, 128, 137
Gale, Milton, 127
Gallus, Chris, 26, 27, 68, 163–4
Garnett, Keith, 144
Garnett, Peter, 144
Garnett, Spencer, 144
genealogies, 2–5, 91, 100, 105–6, 122–45
   first attempt at putting on paper, 112
   Honorary Doctorate for, 171–2
   incident causing Doreen's interest to blossom, 84
   see also books and articles
George, Jennie, 182
Gertie and Knocky, 8–9
Glenelg, 79
Globe Hotel, 120–1
Goldsmith, Aunty Gertie, 93
Goldsmith, Pearl, 94
Goldsmith, Peter, 94
Goldsmith, Aunty Sheila, 45, 115, 157, 168
Gollan, Beattie, 4
Gollan (Wilson), Bertha, 6, 165, 166, 167, 175
Gollan, Cissy, 15
Gollan, Neville, 202
Goodhand, Bill, 12
Goodwin, Captain, 41, 63
Goodwood Orphanage, 55–6
Goolagong, Yvonne, 195
Goolwa, 15, 115, 148–51, 153–7

Graham's Castle meeting, 153, 154–7, 165
Long Walk to save Kumarangk, 184–5
Ngurunderi story, 134–5
tourists on old steamer from, 16–17
Wharf redevelopment, 201–3
see also Hindmarsh Island
Graham, Aunty Doris, 110, 140
Graham, Aunty Sarah, 96, 109
Graham's Castle meeting, 153, 154–7, 165
grandfathers, *see* Kartinyeri, *Mainu* Archie; Rigney, Grandfather Ben
grape picking, 93
'Great Wurley Gig', 184
group therapy, 116
guest lectures, 146
   International Women's Day Committee luncheon, 161–3
Gunning, Don, 107
Gwen (Port Victoria), 181–2

hair, 8, 14, 41
Hale, Mathew, 130–1
'half-castes', 20–1
Hammond, Ruby, 116
Hanchant, Deanne, 46
handicrafts, 13, 16–19, 20, 73
   see also feather flowers; weaving
Harris, Granny Glanville, 24
Hart, Connie, 131–2
Hartman, Vicky, 192
Hawthorn, Sue, 182
Head, Winston, 134
health, 12, 23, 69
   Kartinyeri, Doreen, 25, 187–8, 189–91, 206–7; fruit picking injuries, 12, 55
   Kartinyeri, Doris, 178
   Kartinyeri, *Mainu* Archie, 22
   Kartinyeri, Mattie, 109
   Kartinyeri, Oscar (father), 32, 110, 119, 120
   Kartinyeri, Ron, 35
   Kartinyeri, Nanna Sally, 12, 79, 94; depression, 31, 32–3, 92
   Kropinyeri, Aunty Rosie, 90, 121

Wanganeen, Klynton (Kandy), 119
Wanganeen, Terry, 113
see also deaths
Hemming, Steve, 128, 130, 143, 170, 188, 189
   article in *Records of the South Australian Museum*, 129
   Doreen's advice about Ngurunderi exhibition, 134
   Doreen's letter to Tickner, 45–6, 151–2
   field trips with, 131–2, 133, 139
   films produced by, 133, 157
   meeting with Port Adelaide mob, 137
   Royal Commission, 186
Hepper, Captain, 41, 53
high school, 73, 129
Highways Department, 119
Hillcrest Psychiatric Hospital, 113, 116–18
Hindmarsh Island (Kumarangk), 43–7, 87–8, 114–15, 147–87, 195–203, 207
   anthropological reports, 147–8
   Aunty Rosie's story about looking for *mantharis*, 18, 155
   corroboree and sing-song after Sturt Re-enactment, 86
   'The Dreaming of Ngarrindjeri Mi:mini' (song), 189–90
   evidence turned up in Di Bell's research, 191–4
   Mathews inquiry, 185, 186–7, 188, 191
   media reports on what island represents, 150, 157–8
   Royal Commission, 170, 174–8, 179, 180, 183–4; report, 185–6
   salt pans, 11
   see also Chapman, Tom and Wendy; secret envelopes
Hindmarsh Island Bridge Bill, 187, 193, 195–6
Hollywood, 90–1
   see also Kropinyeri, Aunty Rosie
honey, 11

Honorary Doctorate, 171–2
horse racing, 117
   TAB, 138
hotels, 120–1, 179
house fire, 112
Howard, John, 164, 167–8, 203
   Australian Reconciliation Convention, 194–5
   speech writer, 179
Huggins, Jackie, 125–6
Hughes, Paul, 123
Humphries, Keith (Woppy), 38, 39, 82–3
Hunter, Ruby, 184, 195
hunting, 9–11, 147
Hutchings, Dr Suzi, 128
Hyde, Sister, 60

illegitimate children, 132
   Tindale's mark for, 137
initiation, 84
   women, 91, 157, 159, 191–2
Institute of Aboriginal Studies, 123, 191
International Women's Day conference, 136–7, 161–3

Jackson, Charmaine, 108
Jackson, Ellen, 192
Jackson, Meredith, 108
Jackson, Nelson, 108
Jackson (Rankine), Sarah, 13, 33, 37
   children, 14, 88, 90, 108
Jackson, Stuart, 108
Jackson, Warren, 108
Jacobs, Jane, 123–4, 130
Jacobs, Aunty Maggie, 161, 174, 185, 194, 197
   interview by Cheryl Saunders, 158
   invitation to Sue Lawrie, 168
   knowledge, 115, 153–4, 156–7
   medallion given by Aunty Aggie Pilgrim, 184
   proclamation after von Doussa judgment, 205–6
jail, 99
   visits to, 126

Index

James, Colin, 157–8, 168, 177
Jamie, *see* Wanganeen, Ronald Douglas
Janice (granddaughter of Aunty Rosie Kropinyeri), 110
Japan, 189
'Jedda', 63
Jimmy (grandson of Aunty Rosie), 91–2
John (Hindmarsh Island puntman), 158
Jones, Lieutenant, 41, 65, 68
Jones, Phillip, 128–9, 170, 193
Joy (granddaughter of Aunty Rosie Kropinyeri), 91, 110, 180
Julie (childhood friend), 22, 157

Kalgoorlie, 99
Kandwillan, Samuel, 131
Kandy, *see* Wanganeen, Klynton Bruce
Kapunda, 119
Karloan, Albert, 138
Karpany, Bill, 4
Karpany, Donny, 121
Karpany, Aunty Ivy, 4, 102, 109
Karpany, May, 121
Karpany, Aunty Sarah, 4
Karpany, Uncle Ted, 4
Karpany, Val, *see* Power, Val
Karpany (van der Byl), Muriel, 154, 174, 180, 186
Kartinyeri, *Mainu* Archie, 5, 25, 33–5, 89, 106
  bleeding hand, 22
  description of Doreen, 14
  Doreen's wedding, 95, 96
  stories told by, 8, 17; meaning of name Kartinyeri, 3
  trades practised, 20
Kartinyeri, Connie, 5, 6, 25, 37, 94, 171
  complexion and looks, 21, 50
  Doreen's wedding, 95, 96
  incident with Sister Pearl McKenzie, 23–4
  person named after, 8

photograph, 77
reaction to Thelma's death, 34
sewing machine lent to, 112
temperament, 91
Kartinyeri, Aunty Connie, 8, 79, 81
Kartinyeri, Doris Alma, 5
Kartinyeri, Doris Eileen, 56–7, 95, 171, 178
  acknowledgement of family, 76–7
  birth, 25
  complexion and looks, 21, 50
  Doreen told location of, 50; by Sister McKenzie, 51–2
  Doreen's first visit, 59–60
  reason for Doreen agreeing to go to Fullarton, 38, 39, 42, 48–9
  removal, 28–33, 108
  temperament, 91
Kartinyeri, Aunty Dorrie, 37, 83
Kartinyeri, Eileen, 118
Kartinyeri (Milera), Ellen, 95, 110–11, 118
Kartinyeri, Uncle Francie (Uncle Buddha), 92
Kartinyeri, Laura, 105
Kartinyeri, Aunty Laura, 8, 140
  Camp Coorong meeting representative, 168
  children, 38, 109
  knowledge, 46, 91, 152, 154, 156; *puthari* (midwife), 88, 89–90, 101, 105
  letter saying there is no women's business, 164–5
  police visits to, 10
  relationship to Daisy Rankine, 154
Kartinyeri, Uncle Matthew, 120
Kartinyeri, Mattie, 81, 105, 109
Kartinyeri, Mavis, 38, 82
Kartinyeri (Wanganeen), May, 94, 96, 103–4, 105
Kartinyeri, Nancy, 5, 23–4, 27, 77
Kartinyeri, Oscar (brother), 5, 23, 25, 39, 86, 132
  'an Aboriginal under the influence', 98
  daughter, 118

Index

with Don Dunstan, 111
Doreen's wedding, 95
grave, 104, 141
pinching apricots with, 12
rabbit hunting, 10
reason for Doreen's nickname, 2
story about showing 'means of support', 31
stump-picking, 33
after Thelma's death, 27–8, 31–2, 34
visit to Doris in Colebrook Home, 77
Kartinyeri, Oscar (father), 2–3, 4–5, 18, 25, 84
brother lost in First World War, 40, 41
cousins, 93
Doreen's dream of, 114
Doreen's removal, 37, 39
Doris' removal, 28–33
employment, 19, 25, 77, 85
forbidding Doreen to see Jack Sumner, 85
health, 32, 110, 119, 120
knocked out by Squashy, 99
Nancy's death, 23
when Nanna Sally got pleurisy, 12
opinion of white people, 32, 77
sisters, see Rankine, Aunty Martha; Roberts, Aunty Connie
skin colour ('classification'), 20, 21
Thelma's death, 27–8, 32
visits to Doreen in Fullarton, 50–1, 64
Kartinyeri, Aunty Phyllis, 29, 35, 37, 38–9
Kartinyeri, Rachel, 120
Kartinyeri, Uncle Rangi, 38
Kartinyeri, Uncle Roly, 8, 9
Kartinyeri, Ron (Squashy), 5, 25, 37, 94, 132
arrest, 99
Doreen's wedding, 95, 96
photograph of, 77
reaction to Thelma's death, 34–5
return from Western Australia, 120
visits to Aunty Connie at Three Miles, 81–2
Kartinyeri, Nanna Sally, 5, 84
cooking *thukeris* (boney bream), 10
Doreen's removal, 36–9, 48
Doreen's return for school holidays, 60
Doreen's return to care for, 79, 85, 89, 92
Doreen's wedding, 95, 96
Doris' removal, 29, 31, 32, 50
health, 12, 79, 94; depression, 31, 32–3, 92
knowledge, 66, 152, 156
languages, 13
mother, 79
Nancy's death, 24
religion, 15, 33–4
siblings, 13, 79, 89, 106
sons, 92; killed in First World War, 41, 122
Thelma's death, 25, 28, 31
tidying up after, 75
Ware family and, 143
warning against answering white people's questions, 8
W.T. Lawrie's death, 15
Kartinyeri, Thelma, 2–3, 4–5, 16, 18–19, 23–5
birth, 103
brothers, 40, 91, 122, 158
death, 25, 27–8, 31–2, 34–5, 77
Doreen's photos and memorabilia, 77, 112
first cousin, 85
sisters, 8; see also Kropinyeri, Aunty Rosie
skin colour ('classification'), 20, 21
stopping bleeding tribal way, 12
uncle, see Rigney, Grandfather Gordon
Kartinyeri, Theo, 78
Kartinyeri, Wilfie, 81
Kartinyeri Family genealogies, 130
Kate, Aunty (sister of Joycie Rigney), 69
Kaurna people, 140

Keating, Paul, 164, 167–8, 194
Kee, Sue, 1, 26, 27, 164
Kenny, Chris, 171, 172, 178–9
Kenny, Steve, 175, 180, 187
Kent Town Boys' Home, 29, 56, 57–8
kindergarten, Point Pearce, 111
Kings Park, 74, 75, 77–9
knitting, 19, 61, 73
Knocky and Gertie, 8–9
koala farm, 78–9
Koolmatrie, Aunty Marj, 132, 154, 157, 168
Koonanda, 182
Koonibba, 141, 142–3
Kropinyeri (Sandel), Doris, 138–40
Kropinyeri, Kim, 91
Kropinyeri, Uncle Nat, 25, 89, 90, 99, 106
Kropinyeri, Pat, 207
Kropinyeri, Aunty Rosie, 25, 89, 90–1, 99–101, 105–7
  bird brooch given to Doreen, 197
  cousin (Aunty Dugidi), 16, 204
  daughters, 99
  death, 122
  exemption, 36, 90
  grandchildren, 91–2, 99, 110, 121, 180–1
  grave, 104
  health, 90, 121
  photographs returned to Doreen after fire, 112
  siblings, 91, 106, 122
Kropinyeri, Aunty Rosie, knowledge and stories told to Doreen by, 66, 91, 99–101, 110, 140–1, 156
  belief about deaths related to childbirth, 29
  collecting *mantharis* on Kumarangk (Hindmarsh Island), 18, 155
  cooking, 106
  dressing up for tourists, 17
  genealogy, 5, 105–6, 122, 188, 204
  Steve Hemming told about, 46
  letter informing Tickner about, 152
  Seven Sisters, 158
  snakes and breast milk, 102–3
  talking through Sandra Saunders, 197
  told to Justice Mathews, 187
  warning about telling whitefellas about culture, 2
Kropinyeri, Stella, 99
Kropinyeri, William, 140
Kropinyeri, Winnie, 99
Kumarangk, *see* Hindmarsh Island
kumari, meaning of, 155
Kumi, Aunty (mother of Veronica Brodie), 16, 179
Kundjawara, 44
Kunoth, Lilly, 63
Kunoth, Rosie, 63, 183
Kunypi, 182–3
Kurangk, *see* Coorong

Lainie (Point Pearce), 110
Lake Alexandrina, 10, 18, 19, 103
  see also Raukkan
Lake Bonney, 93–4
Lake Condah and Lake Ebenezer people, 133
land clearing (stump picking), 7, 21–2, 33, 96
land rights, 143
Langton, Marcia, 143, 182
languages, 13, 57, 69
Laura, Aunty, *see* Kartinyeri, Aunty Laura
Laurel (granddaughter of Aunty Rosie Kropinyeri), 180–1
Lawrie, Wilfred Theodore ('W. T.') and family, 13–15, 23, 31, 134–5, 168
Layton, Robyn, 169–70
legislation, 10, 162
  Aboriginal heritage, 43–4, 45, 152, 187
  exemptions, 35–6, 83, 90; abolition, 118
  Hindmarsh Island Bridge Bill, 187, 193, 195–6
  native title, 47
Lester, Yami, 164
Lewis, Peter, 165

Liberal Party, 167–8, 179, 187
  Brown, Dean, 43–4, 159–60, 174
  Gallus, Chris, 26, 27, 68, 163–4
  see also Howard, John; McLachlan, Ian
Life Matters program, 144
London Archives, 131
Long, Clarence (Milerum), 8, 138, 192
Long, Clarrie, 84
Long, Henry, 78
Long Walk to save Kumarangk, 184–5
Lorna, Aunty, 16
Lovegrove, Uncle Frank, 28
Lovegrove, Vivien, 132
Lovers' Lane, 84–5
Lower Murray, 146
Lower Murray Nungas' Club, 149, 166
  meeting in, 181
Lucas, Anne, 149
Lucas, Rod, 148

Mabo, Eddie, 47
McCarthy, Wally, 56
McHugh, Kym, 202, 203
McHughes, Eileen, 192
McHughes, Ricken, 81
Mack, Grannie Pinkie, 86, 114
McKenzie, Sister Pearl, 52, 59–60, 74–5, 81–2
  after Connie's birth, 23–4
  Doreen's removal, 37–40, 49; from Fullarton Girls' Home, 69–70, 71–2
  Doris' removal, 29–30, 51–2
  jumper incident, 61–3
McLachlan, Ian, 1–2, 26–7, 68, 160–4, 167, 186
  affect of opening envelopes on Ngarrindjeri women's fertility, 202
  wife, 166
McNamara, Ally, 117
Macquarie University, 182
Maggie, Aunty, *see* Jacobs, Aunty Maggie

Mail, 11, 13, 82–3
  blankets brought in by, 19
  Doreen's warning if Sister McKenzie's on board, 38, 39
  Squashy's arrest, 99
Mainu, see Kartinyeri, *Mainu* Archie
Maitland, 104, 107, 119
  Methodist church, 95
Maitland Hospital, 101, 102, 113, 121–2
Maitland Hotel, 91
Malpurini, 44, 115
Mandela, Nelson, 184
mantharis, 11, 18, 155
Marangoon, 82
Mareeba Hospital, 25
Margie (Croydon Park), 178
Mark's Point, 114, 115
marriage, 94, 95–6
  Mrs Dunn's sister, 75
  Kropinyeri, William, 140
  Rigney, Grandfather Gordon, 138
  Wanganeen, Garnett, 144
Marshall, Rocky, 153, 154
Martha, Aunty, *see* Rankine, Aunty Martha
Martin, Ray, 185
Maternity Allowance, 21
  see also Child Endowment
Mathews, Justice Jane, inquiry by, 185, 186–7, 188, 191
mats, *see* weaving
Matthew (maternal uncle of Aunty Doris Sandel), 140
Mead, Sister Janet, 174
The Meeting of the Waters, 163
Melbourne, 55, 146
  Australian Reconciliation Convention, 194–5
  field trips to, 131–2, 139, 143
  national native title conference, 175
Melbourne Cup, 117
Meldrum, Dr, 103, 104
Meningie, 101
  police from, 23, 32, 82–3
midwives, *see putharis*

Index

Mildura, 92
Milera, Doug, 149, 150, 151, 181
   television interview, 172–3, 183
Milera (Kartinyeri), Ellen, 95,
   110–11, 118
Milera, Sarah, 149, 154, 181
   at Amelia Park protest, 151
   Gallus' intention to return
   envelopes to, 27, 164
   interview by Cheryl Saunders, 158
   letter to Tickner, 150
   meeting with David Rathman in
   State Aboriginal Affairs, 45, 149
   meeting with Tickner, 186
Milerum, 8, 138, 192
milk, 19
Milky Way, 134
Mills, Mrs, 69
Milson, Betty, 64–5
Milson, Shirley, 64–5
Mitchell, Dame Roma, 171
Mitchell Library, 191
Mobilong jail, 126
money, 95, 98
   donation towards repair of
   Raukkan church Anzac memorial
   window, 189
   in Doreen's Point McLeay bank
   account, 80
   funding for Aborigines' Protection
   Board, 36, 78
   funding for Doreen's genealogical
   work, 123
   funding for Fullarton Girls'
   Home, 53
   funding for this book, 111
   fundraising at Point Pearce, 110
   'insufficient means of support', 31
   selling handicrafts to tourists,
   16–17
   won at Melbourne Cup, 117
   see also Child Endowment; pay
Monk (Kunoth), Rosie, 63, 183
Moriarty, John, 56
Mortlock Library, 131
Mother's Day, 80
Motteram, Mr and Mrs Walter, 74,
   75, 77–9

Mount Barker, 84
Mount Barker Boys' Home, 29, 56
Mount Lofty, 84
Mouth House meeting, 149–50, 165
movies, 14, 40, 73–4
   'Jedda', 63
Mundoo Island, 152, 158
Murphy, Joan, 129
Murray Bridge, 105, 118, 146, 154,
   166–7, 174
   Lower Murray Nungas' Club, 149,
   166; meeting in, 181
   Mobilong jail, 126
   Red Cross, 18
   see also Three Miles
Murray Bridge Hospital, 25, 28, 165
Mutjuli, 5
Mypolonga, 5

NAIDOC ball, 159
Nanna, see Kartinyeri, Nanna Sally
Nannultera, 131
Narrung, 13, 14, 80, 99
Narrunga Nation, 145, 188
native title, 47, 87–8
   national conference, 175
Native Title Unit, 135, 188, 194
Natoon, Gwen (Aunty Sudi), 94
Nelson (cousin of Doreen), 50
netball, 107
New South Wales, see Sydney
Newchurch, Elaine, 110
Newchurch, Harry, 108
Newchurch, Stella and Ron, 105
Ngarrindjeri Action Group, 151
Ngarrindjeri Anzacs, 122, 188–9
Ngarrindjeri Council, 154
Ngarrindjeri Heritage Committee,
   148, 154
Ngarrindjeri language, 13
Ngarrindjeri Nation, 207
*Ngarrindjeri Wurruwarrin: A world
   that is, was and will be*, 195
Ngarrindjerri Pulgi, 150
Ngurunderi, 133–4
Northern Territory, 143, 146, 182–3
Norvill, Isobel, 154, 158, 166,
   167, 192

Index

O'Brien, Lewis, 122–3
O'Brien, Pauline, 122–3
O'Connor, Claire, 175, 176
O'Donoghue, Amy, 56
O'Donoghue, Eileen, 56
O'Donoghue, Lois (Lowitja), 56, 76, 116
Otto, Dr, 189

Pam (Point Pearce deb), 112
Parkside Primary, 49
Parliament, 44–5, 164–5, 184, 195
see also Federal Parliament
Parry, Jean, 140
pay, 36, 78–9, 97, 98
  Doreen's, 76, 85, 95; at Museum, 132
Payneham, 15
Pearson, Christopher, 178–9
Peisley, Shirley, 154, 180
Penhall, W. R., 30, 74, 77
  Doreen's meeting with, 69–70
  Doris' removal, 30, 32
  letter from State Savings Bank from, 80
People's Stores, 59
Perkins, Charlie, 56
Perna Adjunda Rudkee, 140
Pilgrim, Aunty Agnes Baker, 184
The Pines, 149
Point McLeay, see Raukkan
Point Pearce, 94–113, 118–19, 120, 181–2, 187–91, 206–7
  field trip to, 133
  holidays over to, 25, 89, 90–2
  Karpany, Ivy and Bill, 4
Point Pearce Council, 107
  letter to, 98–9
Point Pearce School Welfare Club, 110–11
Point Pearce Women's Centre, 111
police, 23, 32, 35, 104, 124
  Amelia Park protest meeting, 151
  fencing incidents, 10, 22
  finding Daryl at the show, 109
  proving 'means of support' to, 31
  searching for alcohol, 82–3
  Squashy's arrests, 99

Poltalloch, 4, 5, 80
Poonindie, 13, 15, 79, 130–1
Poonindie: The Rise and Destruction of an Aboriginal Agricultural Community, 131
Pooraka, 119
Port Adelaide, 137
Port Augusta, 99, 118, 141, 146
Port Germein, 160, 187, 206
Port Lincoln, 118, 141, 144, 146, 180
Port Pirie, 118
Port Victoria, 91, 98–9
  Davies, Mrs Stan, 112
  Gwen down at, 181–2
  police from, 104
  pub hold up, 119–20
Power, Sandra, 104–5
Power, Val, 154, 174, 180, 183
  trip to Darwin, 143
Pretty, Graham, 127–8, 130
prisoners, 99
  visits to, 126
Protector of Aborigines and protection system, 12–13, 28–42, 48–65, 68–85, 104, 110
  exemptions, 35–6, 82, 83, 90; abolition, 118
  permissions required, 3, 12, 50, 64, 76, 77, 95
  Point Pearce superintendent, 97
  records, 124, 135, 137
  Ron (Squashy) sent to Port Augusta, 99
  white tourism, 16–17
  see also McKenzie, Sister Pearl; Penhall, W. R.; Raukkan superintendents; Stolen Generation
psychiatric hospital, 113, 116–18
Pubelie, Bobby, 86, 108
publications, see books and articles
putharis (midwives), 4, 29, 88, 89–90, 100–1
  at Doreen's confinements, 102, 107, 109

qualifications, see schools and schooling

Index

'quarter-castes', 20–1
Queen Elizabeth Hospital, 120
Queen Victoria Hospital, 109
Queensland, 137, 143, 146, 157
   COMA conference, Brisbane, 126

rabbit skins, 10
racism, 13, 73–4, 75, 87–8
   in hospitals, 101–2, 118
Rankine, Aunty Beryl, 107, 109
Rankine, Daisy, 154, 158
Rankine, Dennis, 50
Rankine, Dick, 88, 89, 108
Rankine, Eddie, 88, 89, 108
Rankine, Ellen (Topsy), 13, 37, 89
   children, 50, 88, 89–90
Rankine, Emily, 192
Rankine, Flo, 22, 23, 33, 37, 39
   move into Doreen's home to help, 35
   removal, 50
Rankine, Aunty Fofon, 16, 17
Rankine, Francis, 50
Rankine, Heather, 86, 108
Rankine, Uncle Hendle, 13
Rankine, Henry, 154
Rankine, James, 5
Rankine, Janice ('Daughter'), 89–90, 108
Rankine, Jean, 128, 154
Rankine, Jimmy (Coco), 39, 78
Rankine, Leila, 157
Rankine, Aunty Martha, 4, 5, 13, 16, 35
   advice to Doreen about leaving Raukkan, 92
   Doreen's removal, 36, 37, 39
   Doris' removal, 28, 29, 32
   at Nancy's funeral, 24
   superintendents' letters written about, 124
Rankine, Mary, 37
Rankine, Paddy, 83
Rankine, Uncle Reggie, 5, 36
Rankine, Ronald, 86, 108
Rankine, Sarah, *see* Jackson, Sarah
Rankine, Wayne, 88, 89, 108

rape, 44, 158
   abortions after, 155
Rathman, David, 45, 149
rations, 7, 19, 35, 124
   Doreen's grandparents, 85, 95
Raukkan (Point McLeay), 3–25, 27–39, 74–5, 110
   archives relating to, 124, 132
   bank agency, 80
   church Anzac memorial window, 16, 189
   holidays at, 3, 76–7, 78, 94; from Fullarton, 59–60, 61–2
   mass grave of people from, 147
   Ngurunderi story, 133–4
   people at Hindmarsh Bridge meetings from, 154, 168
   return to care for Nanna Kartinyeri, 79–86, 88–92
   rushes for weaving, 18, 101
   Sandel (Kropinyeri), Doris, 138–40
   Squashy's arrest, 99
   Woods children, 55–6
Raukkan Council, 189
Raukkan Hospital, 23, 25
Raukkan store, 9, 12
Raukkan superintendents, 11, 12, 39
   job vacancy notices, 36
   land clearing, 7, 22
   letters about Martha Rankine, 124
   notified when Aboriginal girls in Fullarton got into trouble, 64
   Swalling, Ross, 85–6
reading, 52–3, 73, 78
Reconciliation Convention, 194–5
Records of the South Australian Museum, 129
Red Cross, 18
Reid, Mr, 24
Reid, Mrs, 18
religion, *see* church and religion
Renmark, 5
repatriation of ancestral remains, 46, 203
retirement, 194
Rigney, Belinda, 192
Rigney, Grandfather Ben, 5, 19, 103

looking for *mantharis* on Kumarangk (Hindmarsh Island), 18, 155
Rigney, Cyril, 122
Rigney, Edie, 22, 57, 79, 194
Rigney, Elsie, 18–19, 75, 78
  Berri, 92–3
  Fullarton Girls' Home, 24, 42, 48, 64; reason for Doreen agreeing to go to, 38, 39
Rigney, Aunty Eva, 18–19
Rigney, Grandfather Gordon, 22, 25, 27–8, 122
  marriages, 138
Rigney, Hester, 22, 23
Rigney, Janice, 167
Rigney, Aunty Joycie, 69
Rigney, Lester, 88
Rigney, Lila, 18–19, 24, 38, 92
Rigney, Matt, 151, 164, 196
Rigney, Pat, 39, 51, 61, 73
Rigney, Percy, 21
Rigney (Kartinyeri), Phyllis, 29, 35, 37, 38–9
Rigney, Grandmother Rachel, 5, 79–80, 103
Rigney, Raylene, 192
Rigney, Rosie, *see* Kropinyeri, Aunty Rosie
Rigney, Rufus, 122
Rigney, Spencer, 84
Rigney, Ted, 81
Rigney, Thelma, *see* Kartinyeri, Thelma
Rigney, Thelma (foster child), 18, 24, 38
Rigney, Una, 39, 42, 73
Rigney Family genealogies, 125, 126
Riverland, 5, 92–4, 95, 109, 146
Roach, Archie, 195
Roberts, Aunty Connie, 45, 153, 170, 174
  Camp Coorong meeting, 168
  interview by Cheryl Saunders, 158
  meeting with Tickner, 186
Robinson, Bill, 29, 30, 99
Rodney, King James, 140

Roger (brother of Dulcie Wilson), 167
Ron (Croydon Park), 178
  see also Kartinyeri, Ron; Wanganeen, Ronald Douglas
Rosemary (granddaughter of Aunty Laura Kartinyeri), 165, 180
Rosie, Aunty, *see* Kropinyeri, Aunty Rosie
Rosie (granddaughter of Aunty Rosie Kropinyeri), 110
Royal Commission, 170, 174–8, 179, 180, 183–4
  report, 185–6
Rudkee, Perna Adjunda, 140
Rumblelow, Bruce, 89
rushes, 103
  cooking with, 9
  for weaving, 99, 101, 132, 204; picking, 18
Ruth, Aunty, 37

St Francis Boys' Home, 56
Salvation Army, 80–1, 109
  see also Fullarton Girls' Home
Sandel, Doris, and family, 138–40
Sandra, *see* Saunders, Sandra
Sarah, *see* Jackson, Sarah; Milera, Sarah
Saunders, Professor Cheryl, 67, 153, 158, 160
  Chapmans' compensation case against, 196–9
Saunders, Malcolm, 180
Saunders, Sandra, 154, 160, 172, 179–80
  Chapmans' compensation case, 197–8
  gift of miniature woomeras and boomerangs to, 190
  Long Walk to save Kumarangk, 184
  paintings, 185, 202
  reburial of remains found during Goolwa Wharf redevelopment, 203
  Royal Commission and, 174, 177, 178, 183–4, 185–6

Index

secret envelopes, 1–2, 26–7, 160–1, 163–4, 169–70; affect on relationship with, 180; Royal Commission action to get, 183–4
telephone calls to dissident women, 166
television interviews and interviewers, 185
United States National Women's Studies Conference, 182
Savings Bank of South Australia, 80
SBS, 200
  documentary on Kunarangk business, 197
schools and schooling, 13–15, 17, 23, 31
  Doreen's children, 129–30, 136
  Fullarton, 49, 52–3, 63–4, 73
  Point Pearce kindergarten, 111
  Ron (Squashy) after Thelma's death, 34–5
  trade qualifications, 97
secondary education, 73, 129
secret envelopes, 1–2, 26–7, 160–4, 185, 186
  affect on Ngarrindjeri women's fertility, 202
  Chapman's application to hand over, 169–70
  contents sealed in, 159, 192
  return to Doreen, 27, 163–4
  Royal Commission tactics to get, 183–4
  Weekend Australian interview after disclosure, 66–8
Semaphore Boys' Home, 56
Seven Sisters Dreaming story, 158, 187, 191–2
sewing, 13, 18–19, 109, 112
  bags, 98
Shaw, Dot, 125, 185, 192, 194
  song by, 185, 189–90
Shaw, Marie, 198
shearing, 19, 95, 97, 98, 121
  comb shears, 20
  Point Pearce men going to Raukkan, 101
sheep, 19–20
sheoak apples, 7
shoes, 94
shovels, 11
Simons, Margaret, 163
Simpson, Andrea, 177
singing, 14, 16, 59, 114
  in Hillcrest, 116
  Kartinyeri, Mattie, 109
  Kartinyeri, Oscar, 111
  Natoon, Gwen (Aunty Sudy), 94
  song by Dot Shaw, 185, 189–90
  Sturt Re-enactment, 86
Sixty Minutes program, 185
skin colour, 17, 20–1, 55–6, 111, 149
Slaughter's packing shed, 93
Snacka, *see* Wanganeen, Daryl James
snakes, 102–3
South Australian Aboriginal of the Year, 159–60
South Australian Museum, 8, 125
  disclosure of information to McLachlan, 164
  displays and exhibitions, 134, 139
  money for Raukkan church Anzac memorial window, 189
  report on bones found when building Swanport bridge, 147
  see also Clarke, Philip; Hemming, Steve; Tindale collection
South Australian Museum, Doreen's employment at, 128–30, 131–44, 146, 153–4
  during bridge issue, 45–6, 160, 170
  COMA conference, Brisbane, 125–6
  meetings with people wanting to know about Ngarrindjeri culture, 47
  visits from Marj Angas (Tripp), 126
  see also books and articles
South Australian Parliament, 44–5, 164–5, 184, 195
South Australian State Heritage Committee, 148, 172
Spinifex Press, 182

sports, 73
    Crossland paintings of Poonindie cricketers, 131
    football, 27–8, 89, 98, 107–8, 137
    Melbourne Cup, 117
    swimming, 54–5
    Yorke Valley Association, 107–8
Squashy, see Kartinyeri, Ron
St Francis Boys' Home, 56
Stanton, Dr John, 138
State Heritage Committee, 148, 172
State Library, 179
State Records, 124, 131
Stevens, Commissioner Iris, 175–7, 186
Stewart, Aunty Ivy, 143, 146, 169, 190
Stirling, Edward, 147
Stolen Generation (child removal), 36, 94, 135–8, 171
    Doreen's removal, 36–42, 48
    Doris' removal, 28–33
    Wilson, Sir Ronald, 182
    Woods children, Raukkan, 55–6
    see also Colebrook Home; Fullarton Girls' Home; McKenzie, Sister Pearl
stump picking (land clearing), 7, 21–2, 33, 96
Sturt Re-enactment, 85–6
Sudy, Aunty, 94
Sumner, Benjamin, wives of, 44
Sumner (Rigney), Eva, 18–19
Sumner, Fred, 84
Sumner, Aunty Gracie, 45, 168
Sumner, Isabella (Mutjuli), 5
Sumner, Jack, 84–5
Sumner, Jessie, 192
Sumner, Linda, 192
Sumner, Phyllis, 192
Sumner, Selena, 192
Sumner family genealogies, 160
Sussex Street, 69–70
Sutton, Peter, 128, 130, 143
Swalling, Mr and Mrs Ross, 85–6
Swanport bridge, 147
swans, 9

swimming, 17, 54–5, 81–2
Syd, see Chamberlain, Syd
Sydney, 143, 144, 146
    Mitchell Library, 191
    Women and Labour Conference, 182

Tailem Bend, 6, 16, 27–8, 154
    bank branch, 80
    cinema, 73–4
    doctor from, 12
    police from, 99
    Three Miles, 8–9, 81–2
Tal Kin Jeri dancers, 196
Tamberlin, Johnny, 58
Tandanya, 139–40
Taplin, George, 140
Taylor, Alex, 108
Taylor, Dianne, 108
Taylor, Grant, 86
Taylor, Irene, 108
Taylor, Yvonne, 108
Taylor (Wanganeen), Kathleen, 96
    death, 108
Teringie, 22
Terri (granddaughter of Dulcie Wilson), 167
thalgis, 11
Think Big, 117
Thomas, Harold, 197
Thornber, Mrs, 18
Three Miles, 8–9, 81–2
    see also Kartinyeri, Aunty Laura
thukeris, 10
Tickner, Robert, 67–8, 167–8
    banning of bridge building, 43–4, 67, 153; for 25 years, 160, 185
    court cases with Chapmans, 67, 160, 169–70, 185; for compensation, 196–9
    judicial (Mathews) inquiry, 174, 185, 186–7, 188, 191
    Kee, Sue, 1, 26, 27, 164
    letters to, 150; from Doreen, 45–6, 47, 151–3, 185
Tindale, Norman, 126, 127–8
    informants, 138, 191, 192

Index

mark used for illegitimacy, 137
permissions given by, 128, 130, 143
Raukkan visit, 132
secretary, 129
Tindale collection, 127–8, 130, 133, 135, 136
field trips with, 132, 141–4
release of material for all States, 143
Tindale's writing, 129
Tongerie, George, 56, 118
Tongerie, Maude, 118
tonsils, 23
tools, 20
Top Row, 6, 24
Totalizator Agency Board (TAB), 138
Toy-boy (Terry-boy), 102–5, 190
trades, 19–20, 36
land clearing (stump picking), 7, 21–2, 33, 96
qualifications, 97
see also domestic work; shearing
Traeger, Elaine, 119–20, 136
trams, 75
Travis, Cheryl, 108
Tregenza, John, 131
Trevorrow, Ellen, 184
Trevorrow, George, 149
Trevorrow, Shirley, 149
Trevorrow, Tom, 114–15, 149, 184, 186
Tripp (Angas), Marj, 59, 97, 126
Tumsie (niece of Terry Wanganeen), 117
Turner, Dr, 23

Ucko, Dr Peter, 123
Unaipon, *Mainu* David, 16, 20, 81, 191–2
Underdale, 123
Unger, Patty, 50, 57
United Nations Human Rights Commission, 183
United States, 184
National Women's Studies Conference, 182
University of Adelaide, 123–8, 146, 153
Chapmans' compensation case against, 196–9
see also Fergie, Dr Deane
University of South Australia, 123, 146
Goolwa centre, 150
Honorary Doctorate, 171–2
Unley pool, 55

van der Byl, Muriel, 154, 174, 180, 186
Varcoe, Granny Ada, 79
Varcoe (Kartinyeri), Connie, 8, 79, 81
Varcoe, *Pike* Dennis, 13
Varcoe, Gerry*, 79
Varcoe, Holly, 89
Varcoe, *Pike* Jerry, 13
Varcoe, Sally (Sarah), see Kartinyeri, Nanna Sally
Varcoe, Uncle Wilf, 89, 106
Veronica, see Brodie, Veronica
Victoria, 138–9, 146, 168
field trip to Bendigo, 133
see also Melbourne
Victoria Park Race Course, 117
Victoria Square protests, 184
von Doussa, Justice, 197–201, 206

waddies, 10, 20
wages, see pay
Walker, Janice, 192
Walker, Kaurno, 31
Walker, Reubin, 191
Walker, Robert, 84
Wallace, Jess, 196–7
Wallace, Margaret, 196–7
Wallaroo Hospital, 102, 107, 109
Wanda (childhood friend), 22
Wanganeen, Bob (father-in-law), 21, 96, 107
brother, 144
Wanganeen, Brenton Clark (Dooley), 97, 109, 120, 171
Wanganeen, Christabel Violet, 109, 136, 180
Wanganeen, Clifford, 108, 119

Index

Wanganeen, Daryl James (Snacka), 107, 109, 117
  after Doreen left Terry, 119
Wanganeen, Edward (Tiny), 104, 108
Wanganeen, Everett, 96
Wanganeen, Garnett Spencer, 144
Wanganeen, Joycey, 21
Wanganeen (Taylor), Kathleen, 96, 108
Wanganeen, Klynton Bruce (Kandy), 107, 109, 171, 190, 198–9
  after Doreen left Terry, 119
  ATSIC Commissioner, 111
  health, 119
  trade certificate, 97
Wanganeen, Lorna, 96
Wanganeen, Lydia Dawn (Dibby), 121, 171, 188, 191, 207
  birth, 102, 109
  debutante ball, 112
Wanganeen, May, 94, 96, 103–4, 105
Wanganeen, Opie, 21
Wanganeen, Raymond, 96
Wanganeen, Ricky Keith, 109, 136
Wanganeen, Robin Grant, 102, 109, 129
  run over by Doreen, 119
Wanganeen, Ronald Douglas (Jamie), 107, 112, 207
  after Doreen left Terry, 119
  pregnant with, 105
  trade certificate, 97
Wanganeen, Stella, 104
Wanganeen, Terrence Oswald (Toy-boy, Terry-boy), 102–5, 190
Wanganeen, Terry, 91, 94–8, 99, 107, 110
  blue with, 112–13, 118
  chair for Aunty Rosie, 102
  cousins, 94, 95, 107, 108, 110, 144
  end of marriage, 119
  father, *see* Wanganeen, Bob
  mother's half-sister, 123
  niece, 117
  siblings, 94, 96, 104, 108, 113
  Toy-boy's death, 104
Wanganeen, Trevor, 108, 119
Wanganeen, Wendy, 108, 113, 119
Wanganeen Family genealogies, 125, 128, 144
War Memorial, 30, 51–2, 122
  Canberra, 188
Wards of State, *see* Stolen Generation
Ware family, 130–1, 143
  Nanny Kartinyeri's mother, 79
Warrell, Dr Lindy, 147
Warrior, Keith, 107–8
Wassa, Louisa, 29
water rats, 10
Watson, Matron, 40, 49, 55, 62, 72
  expulsion by, 65
  at prayers, 54
Way Hall, 182
We Are Bosses Ourselves article, 125
weaving, 5, 17–18, 85
  with Aunty Rosie, 91, 99–100, 101, 204
  Hart, Connie, 132
  Trevorrow, Ellen, 184
Webster, Aunty Emmo, 154
weddings, *see* marriage
Weekend Australian interview, 66–8
Weetra, Ellen, 107
Weetra, Keith, 108
Weetra, Kenny, 108, 113, 119
Weetra (Cross), Peggy (granddaughter of Aunty Rosie Kropinyeri), 110, 121, 167, 180
Weetra, Robert, 121
Weetra, Trevor, 108, 113, 119
Weetra, Aunty Viney, 110
Weise, Barbara, 44–5, 149
welding, 97
Welfare, 120, 135–6
Wellington punt, 147
West Terrace cemetery, 139, 144
Western Australia, 99, 120, 144
Whyalla, 141, 142, 146
Wigby, Dr, 79
wild food, 7, 8, 9–11
  mantharis (wild tomatoes), 11, 18, 155
Williams, Georgina, 128

Williams, Mary, 140
Williams, Aunty Muriel, 25
Willis, Peter, 123
Willmott, Joanne, 192
Wilson, Adeline, 29
Wilson, Aileen, 91, 92, 95, 105, 167
Wilson (Gollan), Bertha, 6, 165, 166, 167, 175
Wilson, Billy, 149, 166–7
Wilson, Cliffie, 121
Wilson, Dan, 114
Wilson, Dorrie, 156, 165, 166–7
  Camp Coorong meetings, 149, 166, 168–9
  Isobel Norvill and, 158, 166
  letter to Tickner, 150
Wilson, Dulcie, 150, 154, 165–6, 167
  Doreen's relationship with, 149
  family, 81, 132, 167
Wilson, Glenys, 149, 154, 192
Wilson, Hazel, 192
Wilson, Aunty Hilda, 110, 140
Wilson, Joy, 167
Wilson, Lorraine, 168
Wilson, Uncle Lyndsay, 132, 154, 157, 166
  map drawn by, 139
Wilson, Mantatjara, 175, 177
Wilson, Mark, 91, 95, 105, 114
Wilson, Auntie May, 45
Wilson, Minnie, 29
Wilson, Neva, 130, 134, 137, 170
  field trips, 141, 142, 143
  Life Matters' interview, 144
Wilson, Nicodemus, 131
Wilson, Nyumsi, 102

Wilson, Pansy, 51, 55, 78, 154
Wilson, Pearl, 51, 74–5
Wilson, Rebecca, 114
Wilson, Rita, 165
Wilson, Sir Ronald, 182
Wilson, Ruby, 23, 39, 42, 48–9
  escapade to Kent Town Boys Home, 57–8
Wilson, Shirley, 42, 48
Wilson, Victor, 115, 148–9, 154, 181
  fight with Dorrie Wilson, 149, 166
Wilson, Viola, 39, 48
Wilson Family genealogies, 143
Wingfield, 119
Wingfield, Eileen, 143
Women and Labour Conference, 182
Woods children, 55–6
Woodside Library, 73
Woodville, 25
Woodville Council, 132
wool, 19
  see also shearing
Woolley, Tim, 1, 26, 159
  at Mount House meeting, 150
workshops, 125, 141, 146
World War I, *see* First World War
Wundersitz, Joy, 123–4, 125, 127, 130
wurlies, 7, 134, 157

Yalata, 141–2, 146, 190
Yalkarie, 22, 33
Yorke Valley Association sports, 107–8

Zoo, 78